WHAT HAPPENS IN
HAMLET

WHAT HAPPENS IN
HAMLET

BY

J. DOVER WILSON

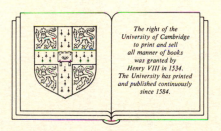

The right of the
University of Cambridge
to print and sell
all manner of books
was granted by
Henry VIII in 1534.
The University has printed
and published continuously
since 1584.

CAMBRIDGE UNIVERSITY PRESS

CAMBRIDGE

LONDON   NEW YORK   NEW ROCHELLE
MELBOURNE   SYDNEY

Published by the Press Syndicate of the University of Cambridge
The Pitt Building, Trumpington Street, Cambridge CB2 1RP
32 East 57th Street, New York, NY 10022, USA
10 Stamford Road, Oakleigh, Melbourne 3166, Australia

ISBN: 0 521 06835 5 hard covers
ISBN: 0 521 09109 8 paperback

First published 1935
Second edition 1937
Reprinted 1940
Third edition 1951
Reprinted 1956
First paperback edition 1959
Reprinted 11 times, 1960–1984
Reprinted 1986

Printed in Great Britain at the
University Press, Cambridge

CONTENTS

PREFACE TO THE THIRD EDITION

Since the second edition of this essay was added in 1937 to the ever-flowing, ever-increasing, stream of books and articles about the play, the two most memorable in my view to appear are *On Hamlet*, 1948, by Don Salvador de Madariaga and *Hamlet and Oedipus*, 1949, by Dr Ernest Jones, both exceedingly readable and attractive volumes. The stimulus I derived from the first was indeed so powerful that I was driven to re-think the play scene by scene and to re-affirm the traditional conception of the Prince's character in the form of a review which by the courtesy of Professor Sisson is reprinted with one slight alteration as Appendix F below. The other, an expansion of Dr Jones's famous article in *Essays in Applied Psychoanalysis*, 1923, is no less brilliant. Yet though I read it to the last page with the willing suspension of disbelief that the charm and persuasiveness of his style must impose on any but an obdurate reader, the objection expressed in my Introduction to *Hamlet* 1934 remained unshaken: viz. that to abstract one figure from an elaborate dramatic composition and study it as a case in the psycho-analytical clinic is to attempt something at once wrong in method and futile in aim. And when he gathered (p. 43) from these pages that I believed "personality" in *Hamlet* to be "consistent" I realized that my chapter VI had been written in vain, as far as he was concerned, and that we must go our several ways each convinced he is being misunderstood by the other.

The text of the first edition once again remains unaltered apart from the new appendix just spoken of, the correction of one or two misprints observed since 1937 and the rewording of a brief passage on pp. 111–12 which second thoughts have led me to modify.

J. D. W.

July 1950

PREFACE TO THE SECOND EDITION

Since the appearance of this book in the autumn of 1935, Dr Harley Granville-Barker, to give him the description we are proud of in Edinburgh, has published his long and eagerly awaited *Preface to Hamlet* (Sidgwick and Jackson, 1937)—a major event in the history of Shakespearian criticism, with which every wise reader of what follows will make himself acquainted if he has not already done so. Of his subtle sympathy and imaginative skill in interpretation it would be impertinence in me to speak.[1] But, though his references to these pages have been uniformly kind and generous, I shall, I suppose, be expected to say something on the three main points upon which we differ, viz. Osric's part in the fencing-match, the dramatic setting of the dumb-show, and Hamlet's entry in the Fishmonger scene. His views about the first may perhaps have been modified since he wrote by Mr A. H. J. Knight's discovery[2] that, according to the seventeenth-century stage-tradition preserved in *Der bestrafte Brudermord*, Osric was represented as an accomplice in the plot against Hamlet, as I contend he should be. The other two matters are more serious, since they turn upon what is effective, or even possible, in the theatre, a sphere in which Dr Granville-Barker moves by sovereign right as actor, dramatist and one of the greatest producers alive, while I am

---

[1] To take stock of all the fresh light he has thrown upon the play would require the re-writing of this book. I have, however, drawn attention to a few points of contact in the Notes at the end of the volume.

[2] *Vide The Modern Language Review*, July 1936, pp. 385–91.

only an academic scribe on the wrong side of the curtain. But I knew his opinion before I went to press, and deliberately took my life in my hand when I dared to set up my judgment against his. The odds are desperate; but I have found unexpected allies in the theatre itself, as will presently appear, while it was encouraging to learn from Mr Esme Percy that on one of the two technical points contested by Dr Granville-Barker I had the support of no less a person than the late Mr William Poel, who was giving Hamlet the earlier entry in act 2 scene 2 in a production as long ago as 1914.[1]

By others also the book has been more kindly received than I expected or deserved. All I hoped was that it would provoke discussion, and this it has certainly succeeded in doing. My first antagonist, Dr W. W. Greg, replied to it in a delightful and characteristic essay entitled "What happens in *Hamlet*?"[2] in which generosity and scepticism were judiciously mingled. It drew from Mr J. P. Malleson a series of interesting letters in *The Times Literary Supplement*,[3] challenging my views on the succession in Denmark, a challenge which I fenced with at the time and hope to take up more seriously at a later date. It prompted a number of articles[4] in learned journals, like *The Modern Language Review* and *The Review of English Studies*, dealing—some critically and others in confirmation—with points I had raised. It was even, I am informed, publicly butchered on December 29, 1936, to make an American holiday, at the annual conference of the Modern Language Association, the

[1] *Vide* Mr Percy's letter in *The Times* of July 16, 1937.
[2] *The Modern Language Review*, April 1936.
[3] *Vide* p. 321 (note on p. 38) *infra* for the dates.
[4] References to most of these will be found in the Notes.

Shakespeare section of which was invited to discuss a paper announced as

Wings over Elsinore;
or What Does NOT Happen in "Hamlet".

Most welcome of all to the author, it has found readers among actors and producers, amateur and professional, and its ideas have been utilized by more than one company in public performances, sometimes even—could tribute be more delicate?—when its spokesmen were openly deriding the book beyond the theatre walls.

Of these performances the most notable were those given by Mr Michael MacOwan at the Westminster Theatre in July last. Having produced Dr Granville-Barker's *Waste* a year ago, he decided, with fine impartiality and a courage I cannot too much admire, to try out the notions set forth in this book. Accordingly, he put on *Hamlet*, with Mr Christopher Oldham as the Prince of Denmark, for a limited number of nights. It ran for a fortnight; was well attended, considering the time of year; and gave rise to an entertaining silly-season correspondence in the columns of *The Times*. Unhappily for myself, I was accidentally prevented from seeing anything of it except the first half of the dress-rehearsal.[1] But even had I been present at every performance, my opinion of the experiment would, of course, be valueless to anyone but myself. I was kept posted, however, with news of the play by Mr Harold Child, who saw it twice and took a prominent part in the public debate with which the untiring producer

---

[1] After which I was—not poisoned by Lucianus for sacrilege, as Mr Michael Innes, author of *Hamlet, Revenge*, might perhaps surmise, but—obliged to leave England for the continent.

crowned his endeavours. As will be seen from the open letter that follows this preface, Mr Child has now been good enough to place his impressions on record. He is not, he says, the ideal witness. That, I suppose, would be an intelligent person who, ignorant not only of this ephemeral commentary but even of Shakespeare's *Hamlet* itself, yet found nothing in the Westminster production either forced or bewildering. Sixty-seven years after the Education Act of 1870, it would be difficult to discover anyone in this country who could witness *Hamlet* without previous knowledge of the play. But, in such a case, where ignorance is unobtainable, the best alternative is as much knowledge of the theatre, modern and Elizabethan, as much critical acumen and as much playgoing experience as may be found in one individual. Believing as I do that there are very few Englishmen who possess these qualities in fuller measure than Mr Child, I count myself exceedingly fortunate in having secured a verdict from him.

My book was written, however, not to prove a case or to win support for its suggestions, but to raise issues which will, I hope, after further discussion and experiment in the theatre, lead to the clearer understanding of Shakespeare's purposes and the better playing of *Hamlet*. If it does that, it will have fulfilled its aim, even if every notion within its covers prove to be unworkable on the stage. For it is with the stage that the final decision rests.

> There the action lies
> In his true nature,

provided it be directed by a practical and practising producer, possessing a competent knowledge of Elizabethan stage-conditions and of the character of Elizabethan play-books. Without such knowledge, the man of the theatre, however accomplished be his production of modern plays, is a blind guide so far as Shakespeare is concerned. Scarcely less dangerous, on questions of stage-technique, is the judgment of the man of the study who lacks direct theatrical experience, however learned a scholar he may be. To show my readers the kind of danger that threatens them from this quarter, in other words from this book, let me conclude by quoting a critic who is at once man of the theatre and man of the study, Mr Allardyce Nicoll, Professor of the History of Drama and Dramatic Criticism, and Chairman of the Department of Drama, at the University of Yale. The criticism in question, which may be read at length in the current number of *The Year's Work in English Studies*, is chiefly concerned with the two points of stage-technique on which, as already stated, I find myself, greatly daring, in opposition to Dr Granville-Barker. In regard to my suggested setting for the dumb-show, Mr Nicoll writes:

On paper, Wilson's defence of this interpretation is convincing; but *Hamlet* is not a mere collection of words set in lines upon paper sheets—it is a play, and as a play must be construed. So considered, it is evident that no spectator ignorant of the *Hamlet* theme could possibly follow so tortuous a dramatic procedure.

His objection to an earlier entrance for Hamlet in the Fish-monger scene is similar:

Again the paper argument is convincing, but its manipulation on the stage leaves us confident that, had Shakespeare so intended it, he would have made his purpose clearer in actual words. Much may be allusive and suggestive in these plays, but rarely does Shakespeare fail to provide clues to the interpretation of such scenes as those described.

And he takes his stand upon the results of an actual stage-experiment, that of the Marlowe Society's production at Cambridge in the summer of 1936:

Were proof needed of the impossibility of this interpretation, the performance of the play by the Marlowe Society would provide it. There the Wilson procedure was followed; but, even to those familiar with *What Happens in 'Hamlet'* the points could not adequately be conveyed by actors to audience.

What is to be said in reply to this crushing pronouncement? Nothing by me. For, though I was present at that Cambridge performance, and could a tale unfold, my evidence is justly nonsuited. And so I leave the case in Mr Child's hands. But, gentle reader, you have been warned!

It only remains to add that, with the exception of a few trivial corrections, the text of this edition stands as it was in 1935. I have, however, added several pages of notes at the end of the volume, inserting asterisks in the text, which should guide the reader to them. Many of these notes relate to contributions from my critics or to help received from Dr Greg and Dr Granville-Barker; others to suggestive books, like Professor Trench's *Hamlet, a new commentary* and a French edition of the play by R. Travers, which appeared before mine but of which I was ignorant in 1935. I should like to say, too, that since then I have re-read Professor A. J. A. Waldock's brilliant little essay, and am now inclined to believe that this study owes more to it than I at first realised.

J. D. W.

September, 1937

A LETTER BY MR HAROLD CHILD ON SOME RECENT PRODUCTIONS OF *HAMLET*

Dear Dover Wilson,

When the third edition of your New Shakespeare *Hamlet* is called for, the stage-history must include two or three productions which have given opportunities of seeing in action some or all of the suggestions which you make in *What Happens in "Hamlet"*. The performance at the Sloane School, Chelsea, in March 1933, before the publication of that book, has been already mentioned in the stage-history. To my regret, I did not see the Marlowe Society's production at Cambridge in August 1936; but this summer I have seen the production at the Westminster Theatre, and also Mr Iden Payne's production at the Memorial Theatre, Stratford-on-Avon, which closely resembles your notion of the action in several very important matters although it was stated by Mr Donald Wolfit (see *The Times* of September 4, 1937) to owe these particulars to some other (unnamed) source. Mr Michael MacOwan's production at the Westminster Theatre was, as you know, an avowed attempt to give your well-proportioned thoughts their act. In answer to your request, I will try to set down my impressions of how your ideas worked out in practice. But I ought to say first that I do not consider myself a very good judge, because *I knew what to look for*. Your Ideal Spectator for this purpose would be a very thorough and intelligent Shakespearian who knew *Hamlet* well but (to his shame) had not read *What Happens in "Hamlet"*—if anyone could be said to know *Hamlet* well without having read your book.

On one or two topics the Westminster Theatre production left no doubt. The play gains greatly in substance and in coherence by making clear your points about incest, about usurpation, and about the several attitudes to the Ghost—especially if Hamlet takes so much care as Mr Christopher Oldham did, in the course of a performance of exceptional intelligence and beauty, to show that when Hamlet asks "Shall I couple hell?" he knows what he is saying and means it. In both productions, also, the sour Protestant doctor is a grimly dramatic figure, besides helping to explain Laertes's outburst and so leading up to Hamlet's. And in both versions the rapier-and-dagger fight (at the Westminster Theatre a really terrifying affair) was perfectly easy to follow and raised no difficulties. At Stratford in particular it was made clear that Osric (though the character was cut down almost to nothing) was in the plot.

Certain points depend more, I fancy, upon the individual actors than upon the producer; though it is obvious that the actors have a better chance in a complete version of the play, as at the Westminster Theatre, than in an abbreviated version. It is in Hamlet's hands, for the most part, to make it clear—or not to make it clear—that his antic disposition is put on, indeed, and used for particular ends, but that Hamlet is also, up to a point, mad. The actor, in effect, can express in performance all that your readers will find on pp. 91–93 of this book. The Westminster Hamlet showed less "emotional instability" than the Stratford Hamlet (Mr Donald Wolfit), being altogether quieter; but the mental state of his Hamlet was perhaps somewhat plainer to read. The long duel between Hamlet and Claudius, again, is a matter, as it seemed to me, for the actors; but the performances left me in no doubt that the course of it can be exhibited clearly to an audience that has not been primed before the curtain goes up.

Now for the two matters that have roused the most public interest. First, Hamlet's entrance in 2. 2. At Stratford Hamlet was able to enter up stage at "Within the centre", and, on overhearing the King and Polonius, to pass out of sight behind the thrones and to appear again farther down stage at "We will try it". The Westminster Theatre production was on a bare stage, so that Hamlet had nowhere to hide. But in both versions I found your idea convincing. It gave certainty and point to Hamlet's attack on Polonius, and prepared clearly for a dangerous mood that in the Nunnery Scene would not spare any slip that Ophelia might make. In fact, it seemed to give just the sort of "clue to the interpretation" of subsequent scenes which Allardyce Nicoll looks for in his very shrewd English Association criticism of *What Happens in "Hamlet"*.[1]

Of the Play Scene it is not possible to be so sure, because the issue is not so simple. At the Westminster Theatre Horatio was placed at the O.P. corner of the Players' (slightly raised) stage; Hamlet and Ophelia were farther down stage on the same side; the King, the Queen and Polonius on the prompt side and rather farther up stage than Hamlet. From his place at the apex of this triangle Horatio could be plainly seen keeping his close watch on the King. At Stratford Horatio was on the same side as Hamlet, but a little farther down stage.

The first essential is that the King, the Queen and Polonius

---

[1] *Supra*, pp. xi–xii.

should make it clear beyond doubt that during the Dumb Show they are talking about Hamlet, and that it is Hamlet's latest and most daring exhibition of "idleness" which distracts their attention from a show in which they are not in any case much interested, being only present in order to please (or to watch) Hamlet. At the Westminster Theatre (this, I suspect, was rather a matter of the actor than of the producer) Polonius looked too much as if he were purposely blocking the King's view of the Dumb Show. When it was over, he went to his place at the prompt-side corner of the Players' stage, opposite Horatio's. At Stratford, Hamlet was so upset by the Dumb Show that in the course of it he sprang up, rushed across the stage and prevented the King from seeing the poisoning by thrusting the book of the play under his nose—a piece of business which certainly owes nothing to you.

Both productions—the Stratford rather more forcibly than the Westminster Theatre—made it plain that Hamlet was surprised and infuriated at the Dumb Show. At the Westminster Theatre, Horatio came down at "miching mallecho" to lay a restraining hand on Hamlet's shoulder, and Hamlet went a step or two up stage to meet him and spoke directly to him the line: "The players cannot keep counsel; they'll tell all." At Stratford, Hamlet, before rushing across to the King, showed his feelings very effectively by turning round towards Horatio (down stage) with a face of fury and dismay. In both performances my companion and I (both of us, I must once more remark, knowing what to look for) found it perfectly easy to watch Hamlet and Ophelia, Horatio, and the King-Queen-Polonius group, while still giving the Dumb Show all the attention that it needs. In both productions lines which hitherto had had no precise meaning sprang to life and dramatic purpose; and in both productions the kaleidoscopic lights of the Dumb Show and Prologue business seemed to make the poison-mousetrap-murder-nephew dialogue blaze like lightning. My own failure was to keep an eye on the courtiers. Mr MacOwan sat them on the floor with their backs to us, and facing the Players' stage. Mr Iden Payne's were grouped in the more usual manner on either side. Perhaps the newer grouping brings them more directly into the picture, and so does all that is really necessary by reminding the spectator that they, with their own notions and feelings, are part of that manifold and complex whole.

That, then, was my personal experience: that there is nothing in your interpretation of the play which the stage cannot express, and which audiences of average intelligence cannot take in; and it leaves no word nor act in the play without its definite meaning and use in the story.

Yours ever,

HAROLD CHILD

September, 1937

PREFACE TO THE FIRST EDITION

On the appearance of this, the last of three studies of *Hamlet* completed since August 1, 1933, I desire to express publicly my very grateful thanks to the Trustees of the Leverhulme Research Fellowships and to the Delegacy of King's College, University of London, for the year's liberty and peace which made that completion possible.

It would be tedious to catalogue here the innumerable books on *Hamlet* to which I, like most other students of the play, stand indebted. Two, however, must be named. I belong to the generation which, having lived for thirty years with Dr Bradley's *Shakespearean Tragedy*, find it difficult to look at *Hamlet* except through his eyes. It is the fashion in younger circles, I am told, to decry it; and it is, I suppose, inevitable that, with our growing appreciation of Shakespeare's craft on its theatrical side, Dr Bradley's general attitude towards the plays should become a little outmoded. I have myself made bold to criticise him here and there; for if one had nothing new to say, why write upon *Hamlet* at all? But many of the new views have been caught from critical outposts which he first established; and the farther I went in my exploration, the more careful I was to scrutinise every clue he had left behind on his. Above all, I am persuaded that on the side of character his patient insight has never before been equalled and is never likely to be surpassed.

The other book, an edition of *Hamlet* (Houghton Mifflin Company, 1929) with an elaborate commentary by Professor

J. Q. Adams of the Folger Shakespeare Library, Washington, came to my hands too late for me to make more than casual use of it. Very different in outlook from Dr Bradley, and sometimes voicing opinions from which I find myself in almost violent disagreement, Professor Adams is equipped with the full panoply of modern Elizabethan scholarship, anticipates me at several points, and has undoubtedly given us the most original commentary on *Hamlet* of our time, which when it comes to be better known in England is likely to provoke much discussion.

A few brief passages in the following book have already appeared in the Notes and Introduction to my edition of *Hamlet* ("The New Shakespeare") and in the monograph entitled *The Manuscript of Shakespeare's Hamlet* which preceded it. Quotations from and references to *Hamlet* are taken from my edition.

As its title implies, this study is mainly concerned with matters of plot and dramatic technique. It makes no pretence to furnish an aesthetic interpretation of the play as a whole, though I hope it may do something to ease the path of future interpreters, whether in the study or on the stage.

I am indebted to Mrs Murrie for help with the proofs and the General Index.

J. D. W.

June, 1935

I

THE ROAD TO ELSINORE

—But what in faith make you from Wittenberg?
—A truant disposition, good my lord.

I

THE ROAD TO ELSINORE

being an epistle dedicatory to

WALTER WILSON GREG

My dear Greg,

You will not agree with this book; I am not at all sure you will like it; but it is yours, whether you like it or not. And I dedicate it to you, without asking your permission, as a trifling retaliation for the spell you put upon me (without asking my permission) eighteen years ago, a spell which changed the whole tenor of my existence, and still dominates it in part. You may have guessed something of this, but you cannot know it all; and as the story of how you forced yourself into my life will explain to others the origin and purpose of this book, you must bear with the telling of it.

It begins some time in the November of 1917. The exact date escapes me, but the occasion retains the sharp outlines and fresh colours of an intensely felt experience. All unconscious of impending fate, I was at the time an inspector of the Board of Education stationed in Leeds, and one of those few fortunate but unhappy men of military age whom a government department even in the fourth year of hostilities had not yet "released" for war service. My chiefs, however, arranged for me to carry on, or attempt to carry on, two men's jobs in educational administration, and permitted me also, as a kind of salve for a sick conscience, to undertake inspection duty for the Ministry of Munitions. There were no week-ends in such a life, and no time off, except that spent in getting from place to place by rail. Yet there was little—too little—to occupy the mind; for the problems I had to cope with were largely those of routine and reporting. I read, of course, in the train, except when it was too packed for one to turn over the leaves of a book; but I found it difficult to concentrate upon anything unconnected with the War. And though Bridges's *Spirit of Man*, Hardy's *Dynasts* and Tolstoy's *War and Peace*, together with fitful and unsuccessful attempts to learn Russian, kept the mind alive for weeks at a time, the hours of travel were mostly occupied in reading the newspapers and in poring over those endless vermicular diagrams in *Land and Water*—you will recall them no doubt only too well—by means of which Belloc deceived himself and us into believing that we were following what was happening on the various fronts. In short, though I did not know it, my spiritual condition was critical, not to say dangerous, a condition in which a man becomes converted, falls in love, or gives way to a mania for wild speculation. In a sense all three destinies awaited me.

After the usual week's knocking about Lancashire or the West Riding I reached home one Saturday evening to find an urgent telephone message awaiting me from Alan Barlow, my chief at the Ministry of Munitions, instructing me to proceed by the first train to Sunderland, where some trouble had arisen with local trade-union officials. It was too late to catch the only remaining express of the day, but there was a slow train in about an hour's time; so I swallowed a meal, thrust into my bag the correspondence that had silted up during my absence, and set off back to the station, resigned to a long journey lasting until after midnight. Stopping trains, you will remember, had one advantage in those days; they were emptier than quick ones: and I actually found a compartment to myself. With four hours in front of me and room to spread my papers I ought no doubt to have written official minutes. But I was tired, and turned instead to look through my private letters.

Among them was a square envelope containing the latest issue of *The Modern Language Review*, that for October 1917. You were one of the Advisory Board which founded that excellent periodical. But other readers may be unhappily ignorant of it. I had, therefore, better quote its sub-title, "A quarterly journal devoted to the study of medieval and modern literature and philology", which should be enough to explain its scope; and I may add that at this time it was the only learned review in England to deal with English language and literature, and that this department of it was then under the able editorship of Moore Smith of Sheffield University. A sober kind of publication to fill a man with a sort of insanity for many weeks! But this was no ordinary number, for it opened with an article by you that might have thrown any mind off its balance, an article ominously entitled "Hamlet's Hallucination", in which you launched an attack upon the orthodox interpretation of the play, that for sheer audacity, close-knit reasoning and specious paralogism must be unique in the history of Shakespearian criticism.

Whether you actually believed in your own theory I have never been able to discover. But it was first-rate sport; and you certainly put a brazen face upon it. Evidently what started you off was a remarkable point in connection with the dumb-show in the play scene, which earlier critics seem to have almost completely ignored. How comes it, you asked, that Claudius, who brings the Gonzago play to a sudden end "upon the talk of the poisoning", sits totally unmoved through the same scene when enacted in dumb-show a few minutes earlier? And you went on to point out that if the King's insensibility to the dumb-show is strange, there are circumstances scarcely less strange about the actors' play itself. Hamlet's adaptation extends to the insertion of "a speech of some dozen or sixteen lines". How was it that the players had in their repertory a drama which was in effect "a minutely applicable representation of the affairs of the Danish court and of the alleged murder of the late king"? To assume that they had such a play was, surely, to make "impossible demands upon the credulity of the audience". The conclusions which you drew from these anomalies were startling and at first blush overwhelming. Forgive me if I briefly summarise them for the sake of others:

(1) The King does not blench at the dumb-show for the simple reason that he does not recognise his own crime either in that or in the Gonzago play itself, which is a mere verbal repetition of it.

(2) The information which the Ghost gives to Hamlet is, therefore, an incorrect version of what took place.

(3) Consequently the Ghost's speech must be interpreted as nothing but a figment of Hamlet's overwrought brain.

(4) And finally, the essential feature of the story (the poisoning through the ears of the victim) could only have

taken root in Hamlet's mind through a subconscious memory of the very play which he afterwards employed "to catch the conscience of the king".

This bald summary does serious wrong to your brilliant exposition. A dozen "buts" rise at once to the lips. You had foreseen them all, or nearly all, and had a reply to each, always suggestive and generally on the face of it convincing. Why had Shakespeare, deliberately it seems, deceived us in this way for three centuries? You declared that Shakespeare is not likely to have himself believed in ghosts, that the Ghost in *Hamlet* is the only specimen in the plays for whose objective reality there is even plausible evidence, and that in this case Shakespeare allowed for a double interpretation— the groundlings should have the ghost they had paid for, while the "judicious", who sat on the stage or in the "lords' room", should have the subtle additional entertainment of knowing that the Ghost was really a hallucination. Or again, why did Claudius break up the gathering in the play scene, if not because his conscience had been caught? You came forward with a highly interesting exposition of the whole scene, worked out in great detail, to show that it was Hamlet's insufferable conduct and not the play at all which left the King so "marvellous distempered", and could point to the attitude of the whole court after the scene is over as evidence of this. Once more, if Hamlet was under the spell of his own imagination during his interview with the Ghost, what of its previous appearances, what of Marcellus, Barnardo and Horatio the doughty sceptic? You attempted to discredit the Ghost by putting all the persons who saw it through a sort of cross-examination, with the object of proving their credulity or unreliability. This was, I think, the weakest part of your case. Yet even here Hamlet's own indisputable and recurring doubts about the Ghost, doubts which have been strangely minimised by the critics and of which even you might have made more than you did, furnished what seemed strong corroborative evidence.

I must have read the article half a dozen times before reaching Sunderland, and from the first realised that I had been born to answer it. What the answer should be was far less clear. At that time I knew no more about *Hamlet* than the average reader. But your theory raged "like the hectic in my blood", and my first anxiety was lest some one should slip in and cross swords before I could have at you. I forgot *Land and Water*, the Ministry of Munitions, the War itself. All Europe and America would, I felt, shortly be reading the October number of *The Modern Language Review*, and I must stake out a claim without delay. Accordingly, on my way to the hotel, I dropped into a pillar-box a postcard to the editor bearing the following words:

Greg's article devilish ingenious, but damnably wrong. Will you accept a rejoinder?

You will see from this that I was in a state of some considerable excitement.

In due course a favourable reply came from Sheffield. But long before that I was at work. I wrote in trains, on draughty railway stations, at the back of class-rooms, and in the august but sordid local offices of the Ministry of Munitions. I could not stop writing, and I wrote in a ferment, which I look back upon as a highly pleasurable experience. Official duties were not I hope neglected; but at last I had something to occupy the mind, a pastime for the train, an escape from the overwhelming war-time issues in which I had no partnership and which I could do nothing either to solve or to alleviate.

Moreover, I soon discovered that to reply to you was only the beginning of things. Your article raised problems which had never before been faced by critics of *Hamlet*, and these in turn led on to other problems of which you seemed unconscious. My attempt to demonstrate that your theories would not hold water was published in *The Modern Language Review* for April 1918.[1] But when I began to frame theories of my own to account for the apparent inconsistencies which you were the first writer to lay bare, I found myself pursuing such strange and unexpected paths that it was impossible to explore them fully in that rejoinder. I followed it up therefore, with four articles printed in *The Athenaeum*, during the summer and autumn of the same year, under the general title of "The Play-scene in *Hamlet* restored", portions of which expanded, pruned and rewritten have been incorporated in the present book.[2] This elaborate essay did not, however, touch upon the Ghost itself or Hamlet's doubts concerning it; and I began to take a course of reading in Elizabethan spiritualism in the hope of finding new light in that quarter. The results were set forth in a paper read before the Shakespeare Association, I think in 1919, and published some ten years

[1] To this you replied in October 1919, but before reading the *Athenaeum* articles.

[2] I am indebted to the editor of *The New Statesman and Nation* for his kind permission to make use of these articles.

later, with a few alterations and additions, as an introduction to a reprint of one of the best known ghost-books of the period, Ludwig Lavater's *Of Ghostes and Spirites walking by Nyght* (1572), edited by Miss Yardley and myself for the same association. Of this paper also I shall make use in the following pages.[1] Yet the further I went in my investigations, the more the country seemed to open out. I became aware that the problems of the dumb-show and of the Ghost were by no means the only puzzles in *Hamlet*; there were dozens of others. And I came to see that the scientific thing to do was to attack all the problems at one and the same time, seeing that the solutions must hang together, if *Hamlet* was an artistic unity at all. I was already gathering materials for this comprehensive attack in 1919, when the whole enterprise had to be laid aside, and eventually postponed for an indefinite period, in deference to more urgent claims upon my scanty leisure. For in June of that year I was asked by the Syndics of the Cambridge University Press to undertake an edition of the complete works of Shakespeare in collaboration with Sir Arthur Quiller-Couch.

This digression—for so I envisaged it at first, little thinking how far afield it would take me[2]—was deliberately accepted as an aid to the elucidation of *Hamlet*. Here was an opportunity of learning something about Shakespeare; and the more I could learn the better equipped I might hope to be for tackling *Hamlet* when the time came. On the other hand,

[1] I owe thanks likewise to the Council of the Shakespeare Association for permission to avail myself of this.

[2] The miscalculation was not as insane as it might now appear, since the original proposals of the Syndics contemplated the appearance of six or seven volumes a year!

the new undertaking was itself a development from previous work upon *Hamlet*. Side by side with the dramatic studies just referred to, I had been carrying on investigations into the text of the play; for it soon became obvious that the textual criticism of *Hamlet* was as unsatisfactory as the aesthetic, and that until the textual foundations were properly laid, there could be no security for dramatic interpretation. Here too I was favoured by fortune. For just as your article on "Hamlet's Hallucination" set my feet on the road to Elsinore, so epoch-making books by A. W. Pollard, Edward Maunde Thompson and Percy Simpson on the bibliography, handwriting and punctuation of Shakespearian texts had appeared during the years immediately preceding the publication of that article; while you yourself began at once to check and supplement those bibliographical findings by criticisms and studies of your own. Thus I found new instruments of the utmost value to my hand when I began to work at the text of Shakespeare. I tried them first upon the "bad" quarto of *Hamlet* which some pirate procured for the printer in 1603, and A. W. Pollard after criticising and helping to rewrite my efforts in draft accepted a couple of articles, now long out of date, for *The Library* in 1918. This in turn, you may remember, led to a joint attack by Pollard and myself upon the problem of pirated Shakespearian quartos in general, and during 1919 we published a series of short articles in the *Literary Supplement* of *The Times*. I am proud to think that these articles, once more in turn, prompted you to undertake a far more solid and exhaustive enquiry into the nature of bad quartos in *Alcazar and Orlando*, 1923. It was they too which happened to catch the eye of A. R. Waller of the

Cambridge University Press, then on the look out for a textual editor for the projected edition of Shakespeare.

Since the summer of 1919 what Waller dubbed "The New Shakespeare" has occupied most week-ends and almost every other moment that could be spared from a busy professional life devoted to labours remote from Shakespeare. And as the magnitude of this parergon, so lightly undertaken, revealed itself and it became clear that not more than two plays could be produced even in the best of years, I often wondered whether the present book, begun in 1917, would ever get finished. Let me gratefully acknowledge in passing that you were yourself, unconsciously and most wholesomely, the chief cause of the delay; not only through the new facts and pertinent considerations which books and articles of yours kept bringing to my notice almost, as it seemed, every month, but also through your generosity in reading the proofs of my edition from its inception and in constantly checking my theories and forcing me to develop them by your pregnant observations. Those "notes on the copy", for example, of whose length and speculative character some readers complain, would never have reached their present proportions but for the stimulus of your criticism. And as you, publicly and from the presidential chair of the Bibliographical Society itself, have likened my imaginative flights to the careerings of a not too captive balloon in a high wind,[1] I may be allowed to remind you that, if the *ballons d'essai* and the gas they contain were of my manufacture, you were yourself largely responsible for the wind.

So the digression threatened to last for the rest of my life.

[1] "The Present Position of Bibliography" (*The Library*, XI, 253).

But I refused to despair, and kept my hand in with intermittent work upon the text of *Hamlet*, as occasion offered; publishing an essay on "Misprints and Spellings in the Second Quarto" in 1924, and editing the text of the same "good" quarto for an édition de luxe of *Hamlet* printed by Count Harry Kessler at the Cranach Press in 1930. And then fortune, which had befriended me from the first, suddenly crowned her favours with a double bounty. which made it possible for me to realise my dreams. As Sandars Reader in Bibliography in the University of Cambridge for 1932, I had an opportunity for the first time of getting to serious grips with the textual problems of *Hamlet*, and as a Leverhulme Fellow for 1933–4 I found myself, almost unbelievably, at liberty to give myself up to Shakespeare without interruption for twelve consecutive months. I could finish my book, and finish it in the way I now knew it ought to be finished, namely as the third volume in a *Hamlet* trilogy.

I reach Elsinore, then, more than seventeen years after my agitated journey to Sunderland. But I have been travelling, mostly in company with you and A. W. Pollard, all the time, and had I arrived earlier I might have missed much through ignorance of the Shakespearian language and through eyes unsharpened for "necessary points" by visits to other Shakespearian capitals. Furthermore, my experience as a general editor has taught me two things, obvious enough, though hardly ever regarded by Shakespearian critics: that it is idle to embark upon dramatic interpretation of a play until one is sure what the characters are talking about, and that it is equally idle to attempt to explain the dialogue until one is sure what Shakespeare intended to write. In other words, before I could write this book I had to qualify myself by settling the text of *Hamlet* and by wrestling with the meaning of every word and sentence. That meant editing it. But *Hamlet* is no ordinary play and can be edited in no ordinary fashion. To tackle the textual problems alone has required two volumes, while text and commentary have occupied space equal to almost twice that of an average play in "The New Shakespeare". Thanks to the Leverhulme Trustees these two preliminary studies have, however, been accomplished and are now in the hands of the public. It is possible to read what follows without reference to them, but it would have been quite impossible to write it. Indeed, it is a significant fact that, apart from Dr Johnson and Edward Dowden, none of the great Shakespearian critics have been editors. This has not greatly mattered in plays the purport of which is clear and undisputed, as it is with most. But in *Hamlet*, where all is in doubt, editor, commentator and dramatic critic must go to work as a committee of one. Dowden, indeed, came near to bringing it off; he might have done, had he been young enough to be fathered by Pollard and brothered by you.

It is certain, at any rate, that, ever since Coleridge first caught sight of his own face in the mirror that Shakespeare held up to nature, critics of *Hamlet* have gone astray largely through neglecting to concentrate upon the words of the text and the details of the action which are the first concern of an editor; and never more so than in our day. For after a hundred and fifty years of criticism spent in constructing a series of metaphysical, psychological and (in the fulness of time) psycho-analytical systems out of the imaginary ingredients of Hamlet's soul, a violent reaction has very naturally set in. You and I had hardly finished our passage of arms over the meaning of the dumb-show and the objectivity of the Ghost, when a fresh group of critics entered the lists. For some reason or other, the War acted as a stimulus to the study of *Hamlet*. J. M. Robertson's *The Problem of Hamlet*, E. E. Stoll's *Hamlet, an historical and comparative Study* and L. L. Schücking's *Die Charakter-probleme bei Shakespeare* all appeared in 1919 a twelve-month or more after your article in *The Modern Language Review*, while they in their turn provoked the notable essay on "Hamlet and his problems" by T. S. Eliot.[1]

As you know, the main conclusion of these writers was that the play, full of gorgeous poetry and profound flashes of insight, is dramatically a thing of shreds and patches, that Shakespeare was, as usual, adapting an old play for his company, in the way of business, that the crudity of the original plot and characters made it impossible for him to carry through his revision without leaving loose ends and inconsistencies in many places, and that in particular the mystery of Hamlet's character may be simply explained as a failure to fuse completely the old material with the new.[2] This was a very different standpoint from that of the older, psychological, school; and yet it seems to me objectionable for exactly the same reason, viz. that it puts the cart before the horse. The "historical" critics have done good service by

[1] *Vide* below, Appendix D.
[2] "The ultimate fact is that Shakespeare *could not* make a psychologically or otherwise consistent play out of a plot which retained a strictly barbaric action while the hero was transformed into a supersubtle Elizabethan" (Robertson, p. 74).

insisting that *Hamlet* is full of obscurities which have never been rightly explained; but when they go on to explain them as "relics of an old play" or as due to the stubbornness of Shakespeare's material, without stopping to enquire whether what seems obscure may not conceal some "necessary point of the play" which they have failed to grasp, they sin against a primary canon of criticism. For I hope you agree that, in studying a Shakespearian drama, we must first understand, or do our best to understand, exactly what Shakespeare's dramatic purposes are, before we even begin to explore how the play came to be constructed. The historical critics have troubled to wrestle with the text even less than the psychological critics.

In the following enquiry I shall take a different road from theirs, the road you first showed me. I shall dare to assume that Shakespeare knew his own business as a dramatist better than his critics of either school. I shall draw attention to a large number of difficulties, of which many have hitherto passed unnoticed and most have never been explained, and I shall seek a *dramatic* reason for them all. Some will refuse to yield to aesthetic treatment, and will accordingly have to be relegated to the sphere of textual criticism. But such problems, it will be found, though interesting from the historical point of view, are neither numerous nor important; aesthetically they are negligible, since, though they may perhaps puzzle the student examining the play under a microscope in his study, they disappear entirely from view when the play is acted on the stage: in other words they cannot be labelled as dramatic defects. But the difficulties I shall be mainly concerned with are dramatic problems, which have arisen through forgetfulness of Shakespeare's purposes; forgetfulness due to textual corruption, to our ignorance of Elizabethan stage-effects, to the break in the theatrical tradition at the Puritan Revolution, and above all to the change in social customs and in the ordinary man's assumptions about the universe and politics which three centuries have brought with them. In brief, I shall try to show that parts of the plot have fallen into disuse through "bestial oblivion". Fortunately, there is nothing, I think, lost beyond recovery, nothing that care cannot restore to its pristine beauty and its original function.

The foregoing remarks, as your keen eye will have detected, carry with them a second principle less acceptable to you perhaps than the first. Shakespeare was a dramatic genius for all time who very well knew what he was about, but his mind was of a particular period. *Hamlet* and the audience for which it was written belong to the beginning of the seventeenth century, and to a given moment of its author's development; and these considerations must be allowed due weight. The fallacy, for example, which, I contend, vitiates your own interpretation of *Hamlet*, for all its ingenuity and logical coherence, is the tacit postulate that Shakespeare could no more believe in ghosts than a dramatist of the twentieth century, that his universe and the universe of the judicious spectators whom he specially had in mind was that of a modern sceptic, of even such a man as yourself.* Hoodwinked by this anachronism, your eyes were blind to the bearing of Elizabethan spiritualism upon Hamlet's doubts, and so, I think, you missed the key to the problem. You attributed not too much intelligence but too much scientific modernity to the original audience. Members of the historical school go to the other extreme. They are fond of referring to the Elizabethans as barbarous and to their drama as crude. In manners and morals Shakespeare's patrons were doubtless uncivilised by our standards, while I do not need to tell the General Editor of the Malone Society that there were very many crude plays in that age, though not more I fancy than in ours; certainly not more if we include, as we should in such a comparison, the cinema. But there is no necessary connection between morals and art; and so far from Englishmen in the seventeenth century being less sensitive to dramatic influences than we are, everything seems to show that they were far more so. What chance, for instance, would an unknown poet-dramatist stand, arriving in our London with plays as lovely and subtle as *Romeo and Juliet* and *Love's Labour's Lost*? The recent fate of Sean O'Casey's *Within the Gates* suggests an answer. Or again, how is it that the most distinguished critics of the last century and a half have overlooked, as I shall show, things in *Hamlet* which must have been perfectly obvious to a mere groundling in the Globe theatre?

Not that Shakespeare wrote *Hamlet* for the groundlings, as you rightly insist, and as is clear enough from that illuminating discussion at the opening of the play scene in which Hamlet speaks scornfully of "the unskilful" and appeals directly to the "censure" of "the judicious", which must "o'erweigh a whole theatre of others". I do not claim, then, that Shakespeare intended the more delicate portions of his detail to be obvious to the entire audience. Those on the floor of the house had enough and to spare of the food they came for, and their menu is well summed up by honest Horatio in his tale

> Of carnal, bloody, and unnatural acts,
> Of accidental judgements, casual slaughters,
> Of deaths put on by cunning and forced cause.

Hamlet is the greatest of popular dramas, and has held the stage for three centuries just because of that. Yet it is also full of "necessary points" for which "barren spectators" had no use but which its creator was most anxious that clowning and overacting should not be permitted to obscure for the judicious. There is, for instance, Hamlet's quibbling, much of it, with double or triple point, beyond the comprehension of even the nimblest-witted among the groundlings.[1] Its existence proves that Shakespeare could count upon a section of the audience at the Globe, nobles, inns-of-court men and the like, capable in swiftness of apprehension and sustained attention of almost any subtlety he cared to put them to, and moreover armed like Hamlet himself with their "tables" to set down matters which they could not at once understand or wished especially to remember. The quibbles did not worry the prentice-boys, because they, like many modern editors, took them as the nonsensical utterances of a madman; but the longer the judicious pondered them the more they found, though it is doubtful whether anyone even in Shakespeare's day ever got to the bottom of everything Hamlet

---

[1] *Vide* Introduction to my edition of *Hamlet*, pp. xli–xliii, and notes on 1.2.65 ("A little more than kin" etc.), 1.2.67 ("too much in the 'son'"), 2.2.383 ("I know a hawk from a handsaw"), 3.2.92 ("I eat the air promise-crammed" etc.), 3.2.127 ("Let the devil wear black" etc.), 3.2.337 ("by these pickers and stealers"), 4.2.26 ("The body is with the king" etc.), 4.2.27–9 ("a thing…Of nothing"), etc.

says. And so too with other matters and with the play as a whole. *Hamlet* is a dramatic essay in mystery; that is to say it is so constructed that the more it is examined the more there is to discover. The character of the Prince is, of course, the central mystery: Shakespeare expressly dared his critics from the first to "pluck out the heart of" that. But there are points, many points, in the plot also to which the majority of even the original audience probably gave little heed or which they entirely passed over. The main outline is clear enough and sufficed both for them and for their successors down to our own day. But within this framework, binding it together and filling it out with delightful dramatic filigree, lies a whole network of finer effects, which it is the purpose of this book to recover.

The process of recovery has been a thrilling adventure from which I have derived keen pleasure for many years; and I have endeavoured to set out the results in such a way that readers may share to some degree the excitement of the chase. For a chase it has been; and as one clue led on to another, the scent grew stronger and the huntsman more confident that he was on the right trail, until in the end he had run to earth—Shakespeare's own *Hamlet*, as he believes it to be! To the sleuth important clues are often provided by the most trivial or insignificant details. And so it was here. I started off with the clue you gave me, a little puzzle about a point of the play so apparently negligible that it is usually omitted in modern performances: the dumb-show in the play scene. You taught me that there was something odd about this dumb-show, something that needed explanation, and an explanation moreover which could not possibly have

anything to do with the character of the Prince of Denmark!
I began asking my own questions about it, and these questions
soon begot other questions concerning obscurities in the
dialogue connected with it. The upshot of all this was my
first, and in some ways my most delightful, find, a comic
under-plot in the play scene with the First Player as the hero,
or villain, of the piece.

Encouraged by this success, I took to scrutinising the play
scene still more closely, and was not long in discovering that
it teemed with problems which could only be solved on the
hypothesis that we had lost important lines of the plot running back into the second act. Gathering the clues together,
I found that they threw light on each other and upon the
play as a whole; and concluded this second stage of my
investigation by realising that theories about Hamlet did not
begin with Goethe and Coleridge, but with Claudius and
Polonius. I next turned to your old friend the Ghost, and
attacked the group of problems belonging to it after making
a preliminary study of sixteenth-century demonology, with
results which appeared to me no less surprising and delightful. Finally, there were the difficulties concerning Hamlet
himself, which fall into two classes: those arising from his
relations with Ophelia, and those surrounding the mystery
of his character. From the outset, I decided that the latter
must be left until all the rest had been cleared up. But
Ophelia set a puzzle which long baffled me. Indeed, it was
only about two years ago, when I began to go over the play
word by word and make editorial notes upon it, that the key
came to my hands and I perceived the root of the trouble was
nothing abstruse or deeply psychological but a simple case of

textual corruption; and, once that was solved, I was not long in penetrating what I believe to be the secret of Hamlet's character, with the help of a passage from *The Testament of Beauty*.

All seemed in train for completion and publication, when suddenly fortune presented me with new diversions. First I found myself confronted by a fresh antagonist, in his way more formidable than yourself. Granville-Barker was announced to be also writing a book on *Hamlet*, a "preface" which, as prefaces to *Hamlet* will, had developed into a whole volume. We began exchanging notes, and during the twelve-month 1933–4 hardly a week went by without a letter passing between Paris and Purley. He has, with his usual generosity, read through the ensuing pages in draft, garnishing the typescript with numerous pencil-comments, with which I must one day rejoice your private eye. They grow thickest and most ribald, you will be pleased to discover, in the chapter on the play scene. Indeed, we have fought backwards and forwards over almost every line of that scene as violently as ever Hamlet and Laertes passed at foils. The bout was played to the sound not of drums and trumpets but of laughter, and though the swords were unbated and quarter was neither asked nor given, there was nothing "incensed", still less "venomed", about our "points". And now, having finished my own book, I count the days till I may have the privilege of seeing his. Not that I look for any continuance of our duel, for there is no ground of rivalry between us, disagree as we may. All I, a journeyman editor, hope to accomplish is the elucidation of some hitherto unconsidered elements in the plot of *Hamlet*; while he, dramatist and man of the theatre, will give us the masterly interpretation of the poetic drama as a whole which his earlier prefaces have taught us to expect; though he is good enough to write and commands me here to set down that "he has been encouraged—even, despite our differences, helped—by this and my other three volumes to venture upon a closer analysis of the play's action than he has applied to any play yet, a more elaborate 'discovery' of its craft and art".

Others, submitting to a beggar's importunity, have also read my typescript, and you can guess how much I have learnt from criticisms and suggestions by A. W. Pollard and Harold Child. But the final stroke of fortune came as a chance sequel to a lecture delivered last November before the Cambridge University English Club, in which I tried out the argument of Chapter VI. My kind hosts for the evening were old friends, Stanley Bennett and his wife, Joan Bennett, whose charming and helpful study of *Four Metaphysical Poets* you like the rest of us will have been reading. And when I tell you that George Rylands of King's, producer of the notable Marlowe Society *Hamlet* of 1932, was also of the company, you will not be surprised to hear that after the lecture discussion went on far into the night. In the end, there was nothing for it but a second visit. Accordingly, a copy of the peripatetic typescript having found its way to Cambridge and passed from hand to hand, another symposium was celebrated at the Bennetts' house, during which all sorts of matters were raised and thrashed out in talk. I got much discipline and encouragement out of those hours, which rounded off the happy enterprise of seventeen years in the gayest possible manner. The play scene, as ever, was the centre of interest. Granville-Barker, Pollard, the Bennetts and Rylands have all launched their various attacks upon that citadel of my position. And though I have not yielded an inch of vital ground, I was compelled to reshape certain paragraphs in a way which will, I hope, make the chapter acceptable to four at least of them. Moreover, I now feel I know the worst that can be brought against it—until I hear you speak!

Such in outline is the abstract and brief chronicle of the adventures of a truant disposition, since I emerged marvellous distempered in mind from a North-eastern railway carriage on the Sunderland platform sometime after midnight in the month of November 1917. It would be neither convenient nor appropriate to arrange the book in the order in which its contents came to me. Nevertheless, I hope, as I have said, that the fun of the thing has not altogether evaporated. And if the reader would catch something of the initial—and final—excitement, let him plunge straight into Chapter v and begin asking himself the question with which you first sent me mad. Did Claudius see the dumb-show? and if not, why not? It is just because I think the posing of that problem a turning-point in the history of Shakespearian criticism that I have written this book. And whether I have found the right answer or not, the search has afforded me untold entertainment and refreshment of spirit for which I am and shall ever remain

Yours gratefully,

JOHN DOVER WILSON

PURLEY 1935

II

THE TRAGIC BURDEN

The time is out of joint, O curséd spite,
That ever I was born to set it right!

THE TRAGIC BURDEN

The state of Denmark

The first act of *Hamlet* unfolds the situation in which the Prince of Denmark finds himself at the beginning of his tragedy, and the nature of the task which that situation lays upon him. But the drama of which he is the hero was written by an Elizabethan for Elizabethans. If therefore we of the twentieth century desire to enter fully into that situation we must ask ourselves how it would present itself to English minds at the end of the sixteenth. Further, in our endeavour to see the play in its contemporary perspective, we must be careful not to overlook those tacit understandings between Shakespeare and his audience which, just because they were tacit, because that is to say they were part of the atmosphere of the time, are most likely to escape us. By remembering that Shakespeare was "of an age", we shall not diminish his stature. On the contrary, we shall discover that the light of contemporary thought and opinion reveals much unsuspected by traditional criticism. A hundred years hence, when mankind emerging from the communistic or corporative era that seems to lie immediately before us finds itself heading for some at present unimaginable social structure, readers or spectators of Edwardian plays like *Major Barbara* and *The Voysey Inheritance* will unconsciously miss a great deal through inability to understand, or even to realise their failure to understand, the economic facts which Bernard Shaw and Granville-Barker assumed but never spoke of because they knew their audience would assume them likewise. We are in much the same position as regards the political implications of *Hamlet*.

What kind of constitution and state, for example, would a sixteenth-century dramatist and his public imagine as an appropriate setting for this Danish tragedy? The events of the story take place at a court; the principal characters are members of a royal house; we are told of Norwegian and Polack wars; the presence of young Fortinbras is felt long before he actually makes his appearance; there is a going and coming of ambassadors; at one point a popular insurrection threatens to break out; and the last problem that agitates the mind of the dying Hamlet is the question of the succession to the throne. Shakespeare has etched this background in strokes masterly but few, for he would not detract from the main human interest. What was his model? With what thoughts did the spectators for whom he wrote piece out the hints he gave them? These are far more pertinent questions than whether Hamlet was eighteen or thirty years of age, over which the commentators have wrangled. For while the problem of Hamlet's age is probably a textual one, and in any event possesses no theatrical importance, since Hamlet is the age his impersonator makes him, that of the constitution of the state of Denmark is vital to our conception of the drama as a whole.

Nothing is more certain than that Shakespeare has England chiefly in mind in other plays. The scene may be Rome, Venice, Messina, Vienna, Athens, Verona, or what not, and the game of make-believe may be kept alive by a splash of local colour here and there, but the characters, their habits, their outlook, and even generally their costumes are "mere English":

> My hounds are bred out of the Spartan kind:
> So flewed, so sanded; and their heads are hung
> With ears that sweep away the morning dew—
> Crook-kneed, and dewlapped like Thessalian bulls;
> Slow in pursuit; but matched in mouth like bells,
> Each under each. A cry more tuneable
> Was never hollaed to, nor cheered with horn,
> In Crete, in Sparta, nor in Thessaly.

Here the Grecian colour is laid on thick, yet can we doubt that the hounds are English and not Spartan, or that the figure who uttered the lines on Shakespeare's stage was conceived as an Elizabethan nobleman and may even have worn breeches and long boots appropriate to the chase? Why should *Hamlet* be an exception to all this? The references to "ambitious Norway" or "the sledded Polacks on the ice" do not deceive us. Shakespeare no doubt took what he fancied from the old play over which he worked, and glanced now and again into Saxo or Belleforest; but to make him out a deep student of Danish history and customs is absurd. Hamlet is an English prince, the court of Elsinore is modelled upon the English court, and the Danish constitution that of England under the Virgin Queen.

Take the second scene. By following the stage-directions of the First Folio text editors have overlooked the fact that it is intended to represent a meeting of the Privy Council. *Enter Claudius, King of Denmarke, Gertrud the Queene,*

Councillors, Polonius, and his Sonne Laertes, Hamlet, Cum Alijs
is the opening direction according to the Second Quarto,
which is almost certainly printed direct from Shakespeare's
autograph manuscript.[1] Here the presence of councillors is
unquestionable. Moreover, the business which is transacted
stamps the character of the assembly. Questions of foreign
policy are discussed; ambassadors are given their commission;
Hamlet is solemnly announced as next in order of succession:
all this could only be done by "The King in Council". The
tone, too, of Claudius's speech is that of a monarch address-
ing his advisers, not of one at a court gala. In particular the
lines

> nor have we herein barred
> Your better wisdoms, which have freely gone
> With this affair along—for all, our thanks,

are a graceful recognition that he owes his crown to the
support of the Council; while later ones—

> Now for ourself, and for this time of meeting,
> Thus much the business is,—

speak the very language of a chairman of committee.
Christian IV, the reigning King of Denmark in Shakespeare's
day, no doubt held council meetings; but are we to suppose
that an English dramatist and his audience under Queen
Elizabeth troubled their heads about Danish usage? Is it not
far more natural to assume that they translated the business
into English terms and looked upon it as a meeting of
the Privy Council such as Queen Elizabeth constantly attended?

---

[1] *Vide The Manuscript of Shakespeare's Hamlet*, 1, 34. The Second Quarto
prints "Gertrad" and "Counsaile: as" for "Councillors".

A trivial point, it may be said; yet it is one that raises considerations of far-reaching importance. For if Shakespeare and his audience thought of the constitution of Denmark in English terms, then *Hamlet was the rightful heir to the throne and Claudius a usurper*. It is extraordinary how blind modern commentators have been to this fact and to all that it involves. Yet it is implicit throughout the play and even twice explicit. Hamlet describes his uncle as a usurper and refers to his own blighted hopes of the succession on two occasions:

> A murderer and a villain,
> A slave that is not twentieth part the tithe
> Of your precedent lord, a vice of kings,
> A cutpurse of the empire and the rule,
> That from a shelf the precious diadem stole
> And put it in his pocket.

These words, spoken to the Queen just before the apparition in the bedroom, are surely sufficiently plain. Equally so— apart from the word "election", to which I shall return—is another outburst, in the ear of Horatio this time, against the triple criminal who

> hath killed my king, and whored my mother,
> Popped in between th'election and my hopes.

It will be objected that these references occur very late in the play, and that had Shakespeare attached importance to the fact of usurpation he would have made it obvious at the beginning. The argument really cuts the other way. That Hamlet regarded the accession of Claudius as a grievance is proved by his words; and his expression of them so late in the play proves that Shakespeare did not think it necessary to make it plainer, that he knew his audience would assume the situation from the outset. The point was, indeed, so clear that it needed no stressing. The throne was the centre of Elizabethan political life in a way it has long ceased to be in ours, and the question of succession, as Laertes puts it, affected "the sanity and health of the whole state". How, then, would the second scene of *Hamlet* strike an audience with this political outlook? A royal couple enter with councillors, including Polonius the chief minister and his son Laertes, all clad in festive costume, followed by a weary dejected figure in black—the Prince of Denmark. The King speaks glibly but in rather embarrassed fashion of his marriage to the Queen close on the heels of his brother's death. There is something amiss here; brothers do not succeed brothers, unless there is a failure in the direct line of succession. There follows a long speech from the throne about the embassy to Norway, matter of secondary interest, which gives the audience ample time to ponder the one discordant note of the assembly and what it means. And, the mission dispatched, they are still kept in suspense. For Claudius next turns, not to the Prince, but to the other young man, Laertes the son of his chief councillor, turns and positively coos over him, caressing him with his name four times in nine lines.[1] Such graciousness expresses a weighty sense of obligation to the house of Polonius. It serves too to mark the distinction with what follows. For, when at last the royal voice addresses Hamlet, its tone changes. It begins with a "but" and with some sharpness; it presently upbraids him for "obstinate condolement"; and it then ends in terms of affection, as with

[1] I owe the point to my friend and collaborator Mr Harold Child.

a display of magnanimity it proclaims him "most immediate to our throne". The speech is a clever one, combining a show of authority with a bid for acquiescence in the accomplished fact; but it only confirms the impression already received. And when the usurper ironically nominates the man he has supplanted as his heir, we can almost hear the spectators murmuring "Why, what a king is this!" The King's face, as he tries his arts first upon Laertes then upon his "son", is recalled later in Hamlet's cry "One may smile and smile, and be a villain".

As for Hamlet himself, his sardonic air and his brief but bitter replies to his mother and uncle signify a consciousness of grievous wrong.

> But now my cousin Hamlet, and my son,

begins Claudius; and Hamlet comments in an audible aside:

> A little more than kin, and less than kind.

The alliteration will fix the words in the memory of those who hear them, and later they will perceive in the quibble "less than kind" a sinister point not immediately apparent. But the surface meaning is clear enough. It refers to Hamlet's disappointed hopes of the succession, as is proved by what follows; for when the King continues:

> How is it that the clouds still hang on you?

he gets the only reply that Hamlet vouchsafes him throughout the scene:

> Not so, my lord, I am too much in the "son".

It is another quibble, but this time direct, defiant and (to

Elizabethan ears) unambiguous. I say to Elizabethan ears, because unfortunately until recently the point has been missed by modern readers. Hamlet was known, by comparison with similar quibbles in *King Lear*[1] and other books of the period, to be alluding to the now obsolete proverbial expression "Out of heaven's blessing to the warm sun"; but it was only discovered four years ago that the true interpretation of this expression was "From an exalted, or honourable, state or occupation to a low or ignoble one", an interpretation, to quote the words of the discoverer himself, which "seems to favour the belief that one cause, among others, of Hamlet's bitterness was his exclusion from the throne".[2] Hamlet, I have said, takes no further notice of Claudius; and receives in ominous silence the declaration of his rights as heir, together with the pressing request to forgo Wittenberg and to remain

> Here in the cheer and comfort of our eye,
> Our chiefest courtier, cousin, and our son.

It is only when his mother joins "her prayers" to those of her consort that Hamlet briefly consents. The King makes what capital he can out of it. He styles it "a loving and a fair reply", and again "this gentle and unforced accord". But the contrast between his diplomatic smiles and Hamlet's deliberate rudeness is rendered only more glaring thereby. Hamlet makes no reference to the succession in the first soliloquy. He has suffered a more overwhelming wrong in the degrading incestuous marriage of his mother, a wrong which quite overshadows the other in his thoughts. But by

[1] *King Lear*, 2.2.168–9. Cf. *Hamlet*, 2.2.184 and below, pp. 105–106.
[2] P. L. Carver in *The Modern Language Review*, xxv, 478–81.

this time the spectators have grasped the fact of usurpation, and it was necessary for them to know the worse that remains behind. The unexpected revelation of this worse, just when they were looking for something else, is a master stroke, the first of many. Dr Johnson praised *Hamlet* for its "excellent variety"; its quality of surprise is equally noteworthy.

The usurpation is one of the main factors in the plot of *Hamlet*, and it is vital that we moderns should not lose sight of it. Hamlet, as we have seen, is not unmindful of it; still more important, Claudius is not unmindful either. In short, Hamlet's ambitious designs, or what his uncle takes so to be, form, not of course the most important, but a leading element in the relations between the two men throughout the play. During the first half Claudius is constantly trying to probe them; they explain much in the conversations between Hamlet and the two spies Rosencrantz and Guildenstern; they clarify the whole puzzling situation after the play scene; and they add surprising force and meaning to one of the most dramatic moments of the play scene itself. In a word, suppress the usurpation-motive and we miss half the meaning of what happens in acts 2 and 3. As an aid to the operation of the plot it is second only in importance to a true understanding of the Ghost. And this in itself is strong evidence in its favour.

It is instructive to glance at the history of the matter in Shakespearian criticism. Dr Johnson and most other eighteenth-century commentators, living before the days of modern democracy and constitutional monarchy, shared the Elizabethan standpoint and always spoke of Hamlet as robbed of his rightful inheritance.[1] I shall here, I am aware, be told that Johnson was ignorant that Denmark was an elective monarchy in Shakespeare's day, that Hamlet's own words testify to the fact in the second reference quoted above, and that therefore Hamlet, though perhaps disappointed, had no legal grievance against Claudius. Steevens was the first to make this constitutional discovery, and Blackstone corroborated it with all the weight of his legal authority,[2] since which time Hamlet's claims have gone by default. The objection is an excellent example of the dangers of the "historical" method, that is of explaining situations in Shakespeare by reference to his hypothetical sources: hypothetical, because there is no question of an elective monarchy in either Saxo or Belleforest, who tell us that Amleth's father and uncle were governors or earls of Jutland appointed by the King of Denmark. Possibly it was Kyd who enlarged the scene to include the whole kingdom, and possibly he made a point of the elective character of the Danish monarchy in his lost *Hamlet*. If the *Brudermord* owes anything to him, the following words of Hamlet spoken to Horatio just before

[1] Discussing Shakespeare's fidelity to nature in his *Preface*, Johnson writes for example: "His adherence to general nature has exposed him to the censure of criticks, who form their judgements upon narrower principles. Dennis and Rymer think his Romans not sufficiently Roman; and Voltaire censures his kings as not completely royal. Dennis is offended, that Menenius, a senator of Rome, should play the buffoon; and Voltaire, perhaps, thinks decency violated when the *Danish Usurper* is represented as a drunkard. But Shakespeare always makes nature predominate over accident.... He was inclined to show *an usurper and a murderer*, not only odious, but despicable; he therefore added drunkenness to his other qualities, knowing that kings love wine like other men, and that wine exerts its natural power upon kings." Cf. my notes, *Hamlet* 3.2.345; 3.3.56.

[2] *Vide* Boswell-Malone's *Hamlet* (1821), note 1.2.109.

the appearance of the Ghost in what corresponds with act 1, scene 4, of Shakespeare's version, perhaps gives us a hint of how the point was made:

Alas, Horatio! I know not why it is that since my father's death I am all the time so sick at heart, while my royal mother has so soon forgotten him, and this king still sooner, for while I was in Germany he had himself quickly crowned king in Denmark; but with a show of right he has made over to me the crown of Norway, and appealed to the election of the states.[1]

But if this in any way represents the old play, it affords cold comfort to the followers of Blackstone, since the words "with a show of right" indicate that Hamlet regarded the act as usurpation; while that the matter is referred to at all proves that he was suffering from a sense of injustice.

In any case, had Shakespeare himself intended to make use of this constitutional idea, we can be certain not only that he would have said more about it, but that he must have said it much earlier in the play. He could assume the audience would realise the usurpation without any emphasis on his part, because such realisation merely meant interpreting the Danish constitution in English terms. But it is absurd to suppose that he wished his spectators to imagine quite a different constitution from that familiar to themselves, when he makes no reference to it until the very last scene. It is plain to me that, in using the word "election" (borrowed conceivably from Kyd's play) in act 5, scene 2, he was quite unconscious that it denoted any procedure different from that which determined the succession in England. After all, was not the throne of Elizabeth and James an "elective" one?

[1] *Vide* Furness, *Variorum Hamlet*, II, 124.

The latter monarch, like Claudius, owed his crown to the deliberate choice of the Council, while the Council saw to it that he had the "dying voice" of Elizabeth,[1] as Fortinbras has that of Hamlet. The claims of Fortinbras and Horatio's comment upon them are indeed especially significant in this connection. Hamlet says:

> But I do prophesy th'election lights
> On Fortinbras, he has my dying voice.

And, when Fortinbras himself enters to find all the members of the royal house dead before him, he declares:

> For me, with sorrow I embrace my fortune.
> I have some rights of memory in this kingdom,
> Which now to claim my vantage doth invite me.

To which Horatio replies:

> Of that I shall have also cause to speak,
> And from his mouth whose voice will draw on more.

The three passages are a perfect illustration of the English constitutional theory of the age. Claudius being dead, Hamlet while still living is *de facto* king. His dying voice, therefore, goes some way to secure the rights of his successor. He declares for Fortinbras because, as Fortinbras himself implies, he is the next heir.* Nevertheless, though Fortinbras claims the throne by right, the form of election will be gone through, or in other words the sanction of the Council will be required; and here, as Horatio adds, Hamlet's dying voice will prove of weight. The case of James I is an exact parallel.

In the same way, upon the death of his father the "rights"

---

[1] *Vide* E. P. Cheyney, *A History of England from the defeat of the Armada to the death of Elizabeth*, II, 575.

in the kingdom had belonged to Hamlet, though his father, being murdered, could not support those rights with his dying voice. Before Hamlet, however, was able to "claim" them, the murderer had "popped in" and, by marrying the Queen and squaring Polonius and the Council, secured the "election". Claudius's description of Gertrude (1.2.9.) as "imperial jointress" is important in this connection, since the phrase signifies, not joint-monarch as some editors explain, but a widow who retains the jointure or life interest in the crown, and so points to the legal argument or quibble by means of which Hamlet was supplanted.

We can rest assured that few if any spectators and readers of *Hamlet* at the beginning of the seventeenth century gave even a passing thought to the constitutional practices of Denmark. And, if after the accession of James and his Danish consort, the audience came to include a sprinkling of courtiers more knowing than the rest, what then? The election in Denmark, as even Blackstone admitted, was in practice limited to members of the blood royal; in other words, on the death of King Hamlet the choice lay between his son and his brother. In the eyes of such spectators, therefore, Hamlet's disappointment would seem just as keen and his ambitious designs just as natural, as if the succession was legally according to the principle of primogeniture. However it be looked at, the elective throne in Shakespeare's Denmark is a mirage.*

Hamlet is a tragedy, the tragedy of a genius caught fast in the toils of circumstance and unable to fling free. Shakespeare unfolds to us the full horror of Hamlet's situation gradually, adding one load after another to the burden he has to bear until we feel that he must sink beneath it. The apparition in the first scene forewarns us of "some strange eruption" that threatens the state of Denmark. The opening of the second scene shows us the Prince robbed of his inheritance by his uncle and mourning a beloved father whom his mother has already forgotten. Here is matter for pathos, though scarcely for tragic issues. But Hamlet now steps forward and tells us what is in his heart, what overshadows his disinheritance so completely that he does not mention it. His mother is a criminal, has been guilty of a sin which blots out the stars for him, makes life a bestial thing, and even infects his very blood. She has committed incest. Modern readers, living in an age when marriage laws are the subject of free discussion and with a deceased wife's sister act upon the statute-book, can hardly be expected to enter fully into Hamlet's feelings on this matter. Yet no one who reads the first soliloquy in the Second Quarto text, with its illuminating dramatic punctuation, can doubt for one moment that Shakespeare wished here to make full dramatic capital out of Gertrude's infringement of ecclesiastical law, and expected his audience to look upon it with as much abhorrence as the Athenians felt for what we should consider the more venial, because unwitting, crime of the Œdipus of Sophocles.*

The soliloquy has often been so lightly regarded that,

familiar as it is, I must quote it here in full, modernising the spelling, rectifying one or two misprints,[1] but reproducing the original pointing.

> O that this too too sullied flesh would melt,
> 130 Thaw and resolve itself into a dew,
> Or that the Everlasting had not fixed
> His canon 'gainst self-slaughter, O God, God,
> How weary, stale, flat, and unprofitable
> Seem to me all the uses of this world!
> Fie on't, ah fie, 'tis an unweeded garden
> That grows to seed, things rank and gross in nature
> Possess it merely, that it should come to this,
> But two months dead, nay not so much, not two,
> So excellent a king, that was to this
> 140 Hyperion to a satyr, so loving to my mother,
> That he might not beteem the winds of heaven
> Visit her face too roughly, heaven and earth
> Must I remember, why she would hang on him
> As if increase of appetite had grown
> By what it fed on, and yet within a month,
> Let me not think on't; frailty thy name is woman,
> A little month or ere those shoes were old
> With which she followed my poor father's body
> Like Niobe all tears, why she, even she,
> 150 O God, a beast that wants discourse of reason
> Would have mourned longer, married with my uncle,
> My father's brother, but no more like my father
> Than I to Hercules, within a month,
> Ere yet the salt of most unrighteous tears
> Had left the flushing in her gallèd eyes

[1] I.e. "sullied" for "sallied" (129), the addition of commas after "merely" (137) and "woman" (146), "to this" for "thus" (137), the addition of "even she" (149) and the omission of commas at the ends of ll. 136, 154. Cf. *The Manuscript of Shakespeare's Hamlet* for justification of these corrections.

> She married, O most wicked speed; to post
> With such dexterity to incestuous sheets,
> It is not, nor it cannot come to good,
> But break my heart, for I must hold my tongue.

Familiar words, as I say; but with Shakespeare's punctuation, never before printed in a modern text, and with the restoration of the opening line, surely a new soliloquy and a fresh revelation of Shakespeare's invention! The traditional version, derived from the First Folio, is heavily punctuated, and contains no less than ten notes of exclamation, while semi-colons, colons, dashes and full-stops abound. It is an elaborate piece of theatrical declamation. The light pointing of the Second Quarto, with its single exclamation, and its couple of semi-colons, gives us a meditation, spoken swift as thought, but with two striking pauses. And these pauses, these two semi-colons, are the clue to the speaker's mood. Hamlet is thinking aloud. He speaks as in a dream. But the dream is a nightmare, the full meaning of which we do not realise until the last three lines. His mind turns and turns upon itself in its effort to escape giving birth to the "monster in his thought too hideous to be shown"; and at the exclamation "Let me not think on't" he seems for a moment to batten it down beneath the hatches of consciousness. But the writhings begin again, and the stream of images continues to flow as uninterruptedly as before, until there comes the second pause—this time in the middle of a sentence—and the dreadful thought is born at last with sibilants hissing like a brood of snakes:

> to post
> With such dexterity to incestuous sheets.

After this the speaker has strength for nothing more than two tremulous lines; the soliloquy ends with a sob; and when Horatio enters immediately after, his friend's eyes are so full of tears that he does not at first recognise him.

Moreover, "sullied flesh" which, subject to a slight emendation, the Second Quarto reads for the "solid flesh" of the Folio, and is the first phrase that falls from Hamlet's lips when he is alone, strikes the keynote of what follows, not only in the soliloquy, but in everything he says for the rest of the play. "Sullied—melt—thaw—dew"; the image behind these words is not difficult to guess. Hamlet is thinking of snow begrimed with soot and dirt in time of thaw, and is wishing that his "sullied flesh" might melt as snow does. For his blood is tainted, his very flesh corrupted, by what his mother has done, since he is bone of her bone and flesh of her flesh. The restored epithet anticipates "incestuous sheets" at the end of the soliloquy, and so binds the whole soliloquy together. It does more; it gives expression, for the first time, to one of the leading themes of the play. Why are Hamlet's "imaginations...as foul as Vulcan's stithy"? Why does that "couch for luxury" so perpetually haunt his thoughts? What does he mean when he warns Ophelia that "virtue cannot so innoculate our old stock but we shall relish of it", or again, "I could accuse me of such things that it were better my mother had not borne me"? "Sullied flesh" is the clue to these and other passages; it is partly also the clue to his strange conduct towards Ophelia and his equally strange language about her to Polonius. Hamlet felt himself involved in his mother's lust; he was conscious of sharing her nature in all its rankness and grossness; the stock from which he sprang was rotten.

This incest-business is so important that it is scarcely possible to make too much of it. Shakespeare places it in the very forefront of the play, he devotes a whole soliloquy to it, he shows us Hamlet's mind filled with the fumes of its poison, writhing in anguish, longing for death as an escape. I am anxious at this stage not to prejudge the question of Hamlet's "character"; but in dealing with it the critics have certainly neglected to give full weight to the opening soliloquy.[1] It is the first occasion on which Hamlet takes us into his confidence, and its position makes it, as it were, a window through which we view the rest of the drama. Mr T. S. Eliot, for example, has surely overlooked the fact of incest or he could hardly have declared the play "an artistic failure" on the ground that Hamlet is dominated "by an emotion... which is in excess of the facts as they appear".[2] Nor have other critics been fair to Hamlet himself. Goethe's condescending sentimentalism in particular moves one almost to anger. The datum of the tragedy is not "a great deed imposed upon a soul unequal to the performance of it", but a great and noble spirit subjected to a moral shock so overwhelming that it shatters all zest for life and all belief in it.* And as yet he has not begun to feel the full weight of the "yoke of inauspicious stars"; for the Ghost still awaits him on the battlements.

The interview with his father's spirit doubles the load upon Hamlet's shoulders. He learns two new facts about his father, his mother and his uncle, both more terrible than anything he has known hitherto—and he is given a commission of extra-

[1] Bradley (*op. cit.* pp. 117–20) however sees its importance, even though he does not completely grasp its meaning.
[2] *Vide* Appendix D: "Mr T. S. Eliot's theory of Hamlet".

ordinary difficulty and delicacy. He learns that Claudius has murdered his father, done him to death in a fashion horrible to think of, sent him suddenly into the next world "in the blossoms of his sin" with no time even to make his peace with Heaven. Claudius had seemed to Hamlet a satyr before this, now he knows him as something more deadly, a smiling, creeping, serpent—very venomous. He learns too that his mother, who would hang upon her first husband, "as if increase of appetite had grown by what it fed on", was even then, in his life-time, unfaithful to him, would steal from her "celestial bed" to "prey on garbage".[1] He had known she was a criminal, guilty of the filthy sin of incest; but this new revelation shows her as rotten through and through.

The task

Shakespeare asks every spectator, every reader, to *sympathise* with his hero, to feel with him, to place himself in his shoes, to understand his situation, and to attempt, in imagination, a solution. That is, in part, the meaning of tragic drama, for without complete συμπάθεια full κάθαρσις is impossible. Let us students of *Hamlet*, therefore, think ourselves into the position of this hero, whom Shakespeare surely loved above all other creatures of his brain, and feel for a moment the weight of fivefold sorrow and horror he is called upon to bear. Is not the cross intolerable? Would it not crush us to death?

> The whips and scorns of time,
> Th'oppressor's wrong, the proud man's contumely,
> The pangs of disprized love, the law's delay,

[1] The adultery has been denied by some critics, *vide* Appendix A.

> The insolence of office, and the spurns
> That patient merit of th'unworthy takes—

these are "fardels", mere everyday baggage, which it is the common lot of human kind to carry. But the burden under which Hamlet totters would annihilate us; for he is a great tragic figure, and tragedy is bestowed upon the sons of men that they may forget their little griefs in the contemplation of one which would be insufferable to themselves. To be blind to this grief, or to make light of it, is to wrong both him and Shakespeare.

Upon the bowed figure of the Prince, beaten to his knees and scarcely able to stagger to his feet, the Ghost lays one more load—the task. The broken heart is called upon to beat with even pulse, the "distracted globe" to arrive at quick decisions, the half-paralysed sinews to nerve themselves to action. Let us look at this task, and what it means.

At their private conference together the Ghost speaks some eighty lines to Hamlet, and of these a dozen at most are concerned with the commission he has come to give his son:

> If thou didst ever thy dear father love,
> Revenge his foul and most unnatural murder,—

that is the gist of it. Revenge, but how? On this point the Ghost gives no help at all:

> But howsomever thou pursues this act,

is all he says. Yet, at the same time, he attaches certain conditions, which so far from simplifying the problem, make it more complicated:

> If thou hast nature in thee bear it not,
> Let not the royal bed of Denmark be

A couch for luxury and damnéd incest.
But howsomever thou pursues this act,
Taint not thy mind, nor let thy soul contrive
Against thy mother aught—leave her to heaven,
And to those thorns that in her bosom lodge
To prick and sting her.

First there is to be an end to "luxury and damned incest". That royal couch! The thought of it, as we have just seen, had begun to "taint" Hamlet's mind before he sees the Ghost, and that it continues to do so to the end of the play is partly due to the fact that he might at any moment stop the "luxury" by a single thrust with his right arm. Thus the second injunction comes too late. Hamlet's mind is already tainted; and that in turn is partly the reason why he cannot act. "Taint not thy mind" is an ominous command.

The third condition presents practical difficulties, which would I think be obvious to Elizabethan courtiers and statesmen, who thought in dynastic terms, though easily overlooked by moderns living in a different political atmosphere. Hamlet was to avenge his father without in any way injuring the woman who shared the murderer's crown and his incestuous bed. The salvation of his Queen by the rescuing of her from the seductions of her paramour is as strong a motive with the Ghost as the vengeance itself, which is after all the only means of rehabilitating the family honour. This loyalty to Gertrude, revealed, we shall find, in the bedroom scene as a loving tenderness which blinds him to the real weakness of her character,[1] is a touching trait in the spirit of King Hamlet; but it does not make his son's task any

[1] *Vide* p. 251.

the easier. How can he, Gertrude's son, kill Claudius without contriving against her? Some critics have imagined that Hamlet's object was to bring his uncle to public conviction or exposure before proceeding to an execution which all the world would then recognise as just. Werder, the champion of this view, argues it at great length and with much force;[1] but Dr Bradley has little difficulty in showing that, specious as it seems, it lacks any basis in the text, that Hamlet's anxiety is not to convince others of Claudius's guilt but himself, and that he "never once talks, or shows a sign of thinking, of the plan of bringing the King to public justice; he always talks of using his 'sword' or his 'arm'".[2] He might have added that such an open exposure would inevitably bring about exactly the situation which the Ghost had commanded Hamlet to avoid. Life would have been impossible to Gertrude under such circumstances. It was common knowledge that she had married Claudius in indecent haste, and contrary to the canons of the Church, after her first husband's death; so much so that Hamlet does not hesitate to tax her openly on the first head in the play scene. Let it also become common knowledge that Claudius had murdered his brother, and she would inevitably be regarded as his accomplice. The facts were, indeed, so black against her, that Hamlet himself suspects her complicity, and his suspicions even lead him to entertain thoughts of exacting vengeance upon her as well as her consort.[3]

The Ghost does not enlighten Hamlet on the question of the Queen's complicity. Perhaps Shakespeare meant us to

[1] *Vide* Furness, *Variorum Hamlet*, II, 354–71.
[2] Bradley, *op. cit.* pp. 96–7. [3] *Vide* pp. 243–45.

suppose that the idea was too horrible for the dead King to contemplate. Anyhow, he was apparently so far from suspecting her himself that he wished to shield her from any knowledge of the murder. For, as will later appear, I hold that one reason for his presence in the Queen's bedroom is to prevent Hamlet taxing her with the crime and so revealing it to her.[1] And if the Ghost was anxious to spare her the shame and horror of this knowledge, still more would both father and son shrink from exposing her to public execration; for their own sakes as well as hers. When Claudius is dead and she is dead, at the end of the play, and when the court have already gathered so much that they must be given more, Hamlet is at liberty to bid Horatio tell his story and to think of his own "wounded name". There is then nothing else left to save. But while she is still alive, a queen and his mother, his honour, even

> The sanity and health of the whole state

of Denmark is involved with hers.

Thus any public exposure of Claudius was entirely out of the question, and Hamlet would avoid it quite apart from the desire to shield his mother. The awful secret was a family affair, in which the whole honour of the House of Hamlet was involved. It must at all costs be kept from the world. Before he knows what the Ghost's message will be, directly he hears that a ghost is at large, Hamlet insists upon secrecy;[2] and in the cellarage scene, as we shall see, he exacts it from the other witnesses under seal of the most terrifying oaths imaginable. Later he takes one person into his confidence,

[1] *Vide* pp. 251–52 below.   [2] 1.2.246–50.

his bosom friend, a man he can entirely trust; but he tells no other soul. Such careful concealment was not prompted by prudery or a sense of propriety. It was the attitude of a gentleman and a statesman. No decent man, even in the age of Sigmund Freud, likes to see his mother's reputation dragged through the mud in the public street. But in those days, when the whole social structure seemed to depend upon the dignity and integrity of the royal house and of the noble families surrounding and supporting it, when Majesty could be likened to

> a massy wheel
> Fixed on the summit of the highest mount,
> To whose huge spokes ten thousand lesser things
> Are mortised and adjoined, which when it falls,
> Each small annexment, petty consequence,
> Attends the boist'rous ruin,

to preserve the crown as far as possible from public scandal was an elementary principle of policy, a patriotic obligation. No one in Shakespeare's audience who had ever thought about the affairs of state would need to have so obvious a point explained to him. Hamlet's predicament would be understood by all.*

Even yet, however, we have not measured the full difficulty of that predicament. To all the other burdens which fate had piled upon the hero a last and crowning one was added, the burden of doubt. At the end of the first act Hamlet, together with Shakespeare's audience, is left in uncertainty about the "honesty" of the Ghost. The matter, which has been almost entirely overlooked hitherto and involves an enquiry into the nature of Elizabethan spiritualism, is so relevant to the plot that it demands a chapter to itself. Before turning to it, however, a still further point must be noted. At the end of the first act, the back upon which the tragic load rests begins to show signs of breaking. Not because, in Goethe's words, "a beautiful, pure, noble and most moral nature, without the strength of nerve which makes a hero, sinks beneath a burden which it can neither bear nor throw off". Nor yet because, as Coleridge diagnosed, he is endowed with "a great, an almost enormous, intellectual activity, and a proportionate aversion to real action consequent upon it". But simply because of the sheer weight of the load. So great is Hamlet's moral stature, so tough is his nerve, that the back does *not* break. But he is crippled, and the arm which should perform the Ghost's command is paralysed. Thus he continues to support the burden, but is unable to discharge it. That, in a sentence, is "the tragical history of Hamlet, Prince of Denmark".

III

GHOST OR DEVIL?

If his occulted guilt
Do not itself unkennel in one speech,
It is a damnéd ghost that we have seen.

III

GHOST OR DEVIL?

Modern difficulties

Hamlet is Shakespeare's most realistic, most modern, tragedy; the play of all others in which we seem to come closest to the spirit and life of his time, and he closest to the spirit and life of ours. It is therefore remarkable, and perhaps not without a personal significance, that he should have made the supernatural element more prominent here than in any other of his dramas. The first act is a little play in itself, and the Ghost is the hero of it; 550 out of 850 lines are concerned with him. Moreover, he is a very real spirit. Caesar at Philippi may be a student's dream; Banquo at the feast may be a false creation proceeding from Macbeth's heat-oppressed brain; but there can be no doubt, if Dr Greg will forgive me,[1] about the objectivity of the spectre of King Hamlet. He is a character in the play in the fullest sense of the term. He retains a human heart, for all his stateliness, and there is more than a touch of pathos about his majestical figure. I do not claim that Shakespeare "believed in ghosts"; we do not know what Shakespeare believed, though it seems by no means improbable that he regarded ghosts as at least a sublunary possibility. Certainly as a poet he believed in *this* ghost, and determined that his audience should believe in it likewise. The Ghost is the linchpin of *Hamlet*; remove it and the play falls to pieces.

[1] *Vide* above, pp. 5–7.

All this makes a difficulty for the modern reader, since he is not apt to take ghosts seriously. Yet, if he wishes to appreciate Shakespeare's greatest drama to the full, he must not merely attain that willing suspension of disbelief which Coleridge demanded of every reader of poetry; he must if possible share the standpoint of the Elizabethan spectator and watch with his eyes. For Shakespeare spent much thought upon this unique creature of his imagination; he made it an epitome of the ghost-lore of his age. The majesty of buried Denmark is an English spirit, English of the late sixteenth and early seventeenth centuries, and the story of *Hamlet* turns upon this fact. Thus, unless we can see it as the Elizabethans did, we shall inevitably miss, not only many beautiful touches, but, more important still, matters which concern the plot of the play, to which the Ghost is intimately related, seeing that he is the instrument which sets it in motion.

A few questions will show the kind of problems that arise for the modern playgoer or reader, unacquainted with Elizabethan ideas about the spirit world.

(i) Where does the Ghost come from: Heaven, Hell or Purgatory? and if from the last, why does Hamlet constantly associate it in his speech with Hell, and even suggest at one point that it may be a devil?

(ii) How comes it that Hamlet, after talking with the spirit of his father, refers in a later scene to the next world as

> The undiscovered country, from whose bourn
> No traveller returns?

(iii) What is really happening in the cellarage scene?

(iv) Why does Hamlet find it necessary to test the truth of

the Ghost's story by having the Gonzago interlude played before his uncle?

(v) Why does the Ghost appear in the bedroom scene? and why can Gertrude neither hear nor see him?

Here are five questions upon leading points of the play, and one might suggest a score more on matters of detail, none of which can be answered on the accepted interpretation of *Hamlet*, such as we have for example in Dr Bradley's *Shakespearean Tragedy* published in 1904. It is true that T. A. Spalding had found the reply to some of them in his too much neglected *Elizabethan Demonology* which appeared as long ago as 1880. It is true also that since 1904 a good deal has been printed about Elizabethan spiritualism which has a direct bearing upon the Ghost in *Hamlet*. Indeed, the most comprehensive treatment of the subject so far is to be found in two articles by F. W. Moorman contributed to *The Modern Language Review* a year later than the publication of Dr Bradley's book, while in 1915 Professor C. E. Whitmore's survey of *The Supernatural in Tragedy* contained a useful chapter on the ghosts in sixteenth- and seventeenth-century dramas. Yet these and kindred studies had made so little impression upon the world of scholarship by 1917 that Dr Greg began the essay on "Hamlet's Hallucination" spoken of above [1] with these words: "Somebody has doubtless written a comprehensive study of the supernatural in Shakespeare, but I must confess that I do not know the work." Moreover, the "historical" school of Shakespearian critics, most of whose work has been done since the War, as I have already said, [2] make considerable play with the ghost scenes, as

[1] *Vide* pp. 4 sqq. [2] *Vide* p. 14.

examples of old dramatic material undigested by Shakespeare, apparently unconscious of the fact that the "inconsistencies" they allege may be explained in the light of Elizabethan spiritualism.[1] Thus a proper understanding of the Ghost is no mere side-issue or antiquarian interest: what is involved is nothing less than Shakespeare's reputation as a dramatist.

Shakespeare's realism

Shakespeare's Ghost was a revolutionary innovation in the history of dramatic literature, as Moorman shows in the earlier of his two articles, which furnishes an admirable chronicle of the dramatic ghost from Æschylus to Marston.[2] The stock apparition of the Elizabethan theatre was a classical puppet, borrowed from Seneca, a kind of Jack-in-the-box, popping up from Tartarus at appropriate moments, the nature and appearance of which is best described in the following lines from the Induction to *A Warning for Fair Women* (*c.* 1599):

> Then, too, a filthy whining ghost,
> Lapt in some foul sheet or a leather pilch,
> Comes screaming like a pig half sticked,
> And cries, "Vindicta! Revenge, Revenge!"
> With that a little resin flasheth forth,
> Like smoke out of a tobacco pipe or a boy's squib.

Its function was commonly that of prologue, and as such it

[1] *Vide* Introduction to my edition of *Hamlet*, pp. lii–liii.
[2] *Hamlet* is supposed to be indebted to Marston's *Antonio's Revenge*. There are many links between the two plays though the priority of Marston's has not to my thinking been proved; but the Ghost of King Hamlet certainly owes nothing to that of Andrugio.

was a serviceable piece of dramatic machinery, since it enabled the playwright to place his audience in possession of the preliminary data—the most difficult of all a dramatist's tasks—in an arresting fashion. Lodge's reference in *Wit's Miserie* (1596) to "the ghost which cried so miserably at the Theator like an oister wife, Hamlet reuenge" sufficiently indicates that the ghost of the pre-Shakespearian *Hamlet* was of the Senecan brand, as also was clearly the roistering puppet of *Der bestrafte Brudermord*, the German *Hamlet*, a spook which boxed the sentinels' ears and stood in the centre of the stage opening and shutting its jaws, no doubt to the intense edification of the groundlings. Shakespeare's Ghost is both a revenge-ghost and a prologue-ghost, that is to say from the technical point of view it corresponds with its Senecan prototype. But there the likeness ends; for it is one of Shakespeare's glories that he took the conventional puppet, humanised it, christianised it,[1] and made it a figure that his spectators would recognise as *real*, as something which might be encountered in any lonely graveyard at midnight.[2] There is a tradition that Shakespeare "writ the scene of the Ghost in *Hamlet*, at his House which bordered on the Charnel-House and Church-Yard".[3] The legend may or may not be true, but it at any rate points us along the right path. The Ghost in *Hamlet* comes, not from a mythical Tartarus, but from the place of departed spirits in which post-medieval England, despite a veneer of Protestantism, still believed at the end of the sixteenth century. And in doing this, in making horror

[1] I.e., as Christianity was then understood.
[2] Cf. Creizenach, *English Drama*, pp. 114–15.
[3] *Vide* E. K. Chambers, *William Shakespeare*, II, 261.

more awesome by giving it a contemporary spiritual background, Shakespeare managed at the same time to lift the
whole ghost-business on to a higher level, to transform a
ranting roistering abstraction into a thing at once tender and
majestical.

The outward symbol of this transformation is the change
in costume. The royal figure walks the battlements of his
castle, not "in foul sheet or leather pilch", but in

> the very armour he had on,
> When he the ambitious Norway combated,

while when he appears in the Queen's chamber, it is "in his
habit as he lived", that is, as the First Quarto tells us, "in his
night-gown".[1] Time and again Shakespeare insists upon this
feature of the apparition, and the first act is full of references
to the armour, which obviously makes the greatest possible
impression upon all who see the Ghost. His "fair and warlike
form", his "martial stalk", his "portentous figure" which
"comes arméd through our watch" are notes in the recurrent
theme of the opening scene, which is continued in 1.2, when
Horatio and the gentlemen of the guard give their report to
Hamlet.

> Arméd at point exactly, cap-a-pe,

explains Horatio to the amazed Prince, who seizes upon it:

> *Hamlet.* Armed, say you?
> *All.* Armed, my lord.
> *Hamlet.* From top to toe?
> *All.* My lord, from head to foot.
> *Hamlet.* Then saw you not his face.
> *Horatio.* O yes, my lord, he wore his beaver up.

---

[1] I.e., dressing-gown. Cf. below, p. 250 n[3].

And when the witnesses have left him, it is the first thought that comes uppermost in Hamlet's mind:

My father's spirit, *in arms*, all is not well.[1]

King Hamlet was a spirit, but the spirit of a "majestical" king and a great soldier, and withal the wandering soul of a loving and much wronged husband, seeking reparation at the hands of his son. How astonishing all this must have seemed to the Elizabethans, how new, how overwhelming in its realism! It is not Shakespeare's fault that ghosts are at a discount in the twentieth century, or that the bright spectral armour which he first put upon the stage has rusted with time and the weather-changes of the human intellect. Dr Greg, at pains to throw discredit upon the Ghost's speech, compares it with "a grotesque fresco—gridirons, pitchforks, sulphurous flames, decomposition and decay—a thing we ridicule even while...our gorge rises at it".[2] Just so; we in this sceptical age, ridicule; but most assuredly Shakespeare's audience, "judicious" or "generality", did not. To them, as to Dr Johnson, the next world was an intense and ever-present reality; and they would have agreed with him that "the apparition...in the first act chills the blood with terror". But theirs was an even keener appreciation and intenser realisation than his; for the ghost scenes came upon them with all the force of a fresh and unexpected revelation of the spirit world. The spectre which seems so absurd and antiquated to Dr Greg was the first of its kind to appear in the English theatre, and the Senecan ghost that it superseded

[1] The italics are virtually Shakespeare's since he places the words in brackets which denote a change of voice.
[2] *The Modern Language Review*, XII, 412–13.

must have seemed equally absurd and antiquated to Shakespeare. He wrote for all time; but to cast our historic sense behind us as we read him is to do him much wrong.

And how admirably he planned the whole business! All his cunning is employed to make the Ghost a dramatically convincing figure. We hear that it has appeared to Barnardo and Marcellus on two separate nights before the play opens, when as Horatio tells us,

> thrice he walked
> By their oppressed and fear-surpriséd eyes
> Within his truncheon's length.

These previous appearances are the first link in the chain of evidence. The two soldiers are convinced of its reality and of its identity with the dead king. It appears again twice in the first scene, on both occasions so unexpectedly as to make the spectators jump, and with beaver up so that Horatio and the others can clearly see its face. They recognise the armour, the beard, even the play of features. Horatio is a new-comer, a scholar and a sceptic. He too is convinced, against his daylight judgment. Next night there is one more addition to the watch—Hamlet himself. But it is not he who first sees the Ghost when it appears; it is Horatio. Nor does the Prince at once hold conference with the spirit of his father. An impassioned appeal for certainty and an excited dialogue upon the subject of the apparition intervene before Hamlet throws his would-be protectors from him and follows the Ghost from the platform.

Four appearances, three witnesses and one of them a sceptic—why this minute detail, why this accumulation of circumstantial evidence, if not to assure us of the Ghost's objectivity, before it encounters Hamlet? Such an assurance, indeed, is vital to Shakespeare's purpose. For Hamlet, and I believe the audience also, are later to entertain doubts about the Ghost, not of its reality but of its nature; and it was of great importance that such doubts should not be confused with those of the sceptical Horatio before they were dispelled by "the sensible and true avouch" of his own eyes.

Problems of Elizabethan spiritualism

The Ghost in *Hamlet* raises, indeed, problems of Elizabethan spiritualism, which are very different from those which present themselves to the mind of Sir Oliver Lodge. To understand to the full the scenes in which it appears we must acquaint ourselves not only with the current superstitions regarding ghosts in Shakespeare's day but also with the current philosophical and theological opinions concerning them. Shakespeare was not the man to introduce a new and startling type like this into the theatre without relating it closely to contemporary thought and feeling on such matters. He rejected the Senecan spook just because it was unrelated to Elizabethan belief, and when he brought a real ghost on to the boards he was careful to stress its actuality by exhibiting the effect of the apparition upon characters holding different opinions about the spirit world, opinions which would be entertained by different parts of the audience.

Thus the first act of *Hamlet*, though far less diffuse, possesses something of the character of a Shaw discussion drama —without the discussion. One can well imagine how Mr Shaw would deal with the apparition of a deceased parent, did he elect to introduce such a phenomenon into one of his plays; how he would bring together a number of characters representing a variety of attitudes of mind—the parson, the sentimental woman, the man of common sense, the rationalist and the professed spiritualist; and how he would make them talk about the business, for three or more acts. Shakespeare does the same thing, up to a point. The Ghost is seen by four different persons, standing for three typical points of view on the question of apparitions, and their words and actions show them reacting in different ways under the spell of the visitor from the other-world. There is of course little or no discussion, since the opinions are introduced to set off the Ghost, and not the Ghost to precipitate a flood of opinion. Shakespeare has filled in this background with the greatest possible artistic delicacy and economy of effect, so much so that very few even notice its existence. Yet to pass it over is to lose much of the subtlety and beauty of the scenes in which the Ghost figures. A brief excursion into the realm of Elizabethan theology will help us to appreciate it all more fully.

Broadly speaking there were three schools of thought in the sixteenth and seventeenth centuries on the question of ghosts. Before the Reformation the belief in their existence, which was of course much older than Christianity, had offered little intellectual difficulty to the ordinary man, since the Catholic doctrine of Purgatory afforded a complete explanation of it in theological terms, though thinkers like St Thomas Aquinas might indulge in speculation which anticipated in a measure later Protestant theory. In fact doctrine and popular belief, in this case, found mutual support. Thus most Catholics of Shakespeare's day believed that ghosts might be spirits of the departed, allowed to return from Purgatory for some special purpose, which it was the duty of the pious to further if possible, in order that the wandering soul might find rest. But for Protestants the matter was not so easy. The majority of them accepted the reality of apparitions without question; but how were they to be explained? That apparitions occurred was, indeed, not to be doubted by reasonable persons. Universal testimony was in their favour. Still more important, they received support from Scripture, which could not be gainsaid, the most striking instance being the apparition of Samuel conjured up by the witch of Endor at Saul's behest. Yet it was not possible that they were the spirits of the departed, for Purgatory being an exploded tradition, the dead went direct either to bliss in heaven or to prison in hell, crossing in either event a "bourn from which no traveller returns". The dilemma gave rise to lengthy and sometimes heated discussions in theological circles on the nature and provenance of spectres: and the orthodox Protestant conclusion was that ghosts, while occasionally they might be angels, were generally nothing but devils, who "assumed"—such was the technical word—the form of departed friends or relatives, in order to work bodily or spiritual harm upon those to whom they appeared.

King James I gives expression to this view in his *Daemonologie* (1597)[1] and it is exceedingly common in Protestant

---

[1] *Vide* reprint by G. B. Harrison in "The Bodley Head Quartos" (1924). James (pp. 65–6) expressly dissociates himself from those who believe in angelic apparitions, on the ground that since the time of Christ and the Apostles the age of miracles has ceased, a point he borrows, without acknowledgment, from Scot.

writers of the time. The most comprehensive treatise upon it, so far as I am aware, was a book by Ludwig Lavater, published in Zürich in 1570, of which a certain R. H. made an English translation, printed in 1572 under the title *Of Ghostes and Spirites walking by Nyght*, a second edition of which appeared in 1596.[1] Spalding shows no knowledge of this important volume in his *Elizabethan Demonology*, but Moorman rightly insists upon its first-class interest in relation to *Hamlet*. Indeed, the book is so germane to the ghost scenes that there seems to me a high probability that Shakespeare had read it. In any case, Hamlet himself is clearly steeped in the opinions which Lavater expounds, and his attitude towards his father's spirit cannot be comprehended without taking these views into account. In 1586 an immense and learned reply to Lavater from the Catholic standpoint was published by a French lawyer, Pierre Le Loyer, under the title of *IIII Livres des Spectres ou Apparitions et Visions d'Esprits, Anges et Demons se monstrans sensiblement aux hommes*, a book less illuminating than Lavater's, but nevertheless, as I shall show, not without relevance to *Hamlet*.

There was, moreover, a third school of thought on the subject, of which we get a glimpse in the attitude of Horatio at the opening of the first scene. Reginald Scot is its most famous exponent, and his *Discoverie of Witchcraft* (1584), to which he appended a *Discourse vpon Diuels and Spirits*, is recognised by all as one of Shakespeare's source-books. Scot's view is frankly and entirely sceptical. As a Christian,

[1] A reprint edition by Miss Yardley and myself with Introduction and Appendix was published by the Shakespeare Association in 1929, cf. p. 9 above.

he does not of course deny the existence of spirits. What he contests is the possibility of their assuming material form, and he is even bold enough to attempt to explain away apparitions in Holy Writ, like that at Endor. As for the idea that devils can assume the bodies of the dead, it appears to him no less idle and profane than the purgatorial theory which it superseded. In a word, apparitions are either the illusion of melancholic minds or flat knavery on the part of some rogue. It is worthy of note that all the writers, whatever their point of view, declare that persons subject to melancholy, as Hamlet was, were peculiarly prone to spectral visitations.[1] Scot had few followers in print, and his book was publicly burnt by the hangman soon after the accession of the author of *Daemonologie*, which indeed was written, in the words of the royal preface, "against the damnable opinions of two principally in our age, wherof the one called Scot an Englishman, is not ashamed in publike print to deny, that ther can be such a thing as Witch-craft: and so mainteines the old error of the Sadducees, in denying of spirits". But the "old error" lived on, though men might be chary of expressing it in public. Sir Thomas Browne, writing about forty years later than King James, echoes his words:

It is a riddle to me...how so many learned heads should so far forget their Metaphysicks, and destroy the ladder and scale of creatures, as to question the existence of Spirits. For my part, I have ever believed, and do now know, that there are Witches: they that doubt of these, do not onely deny *them*, but Spirits; and are obliquely and upon consequence a sort not of Infidels, but Atheists.[2]

[1] Cf. p. 74 below.
[2] *Religio Medici*, I, xxx (Golden Treasury, pp. 49–50).

This sounds like a direct reply to Scot, while the following passage,* from the same section of *Religio Medici*, is also worth quoting in connection with *Hamlet*:

I hold that the Devil doth really possess some men, the spirit of Melancholy others, the spirit of Delusion others....I do think that many mysteries ascribed to our own inventions have been the courteous revelations of Spirits...and therefore believe that those many prodigies and ominous prognosticks, which fore-run the ruines of States, Princes, and private persons, are the charitable premonitions of good Angels, which more careless enquiries term but the effects of chance and nature.[1]

Spiritualism, in short, formed one of the major interests of the period. As Le Loyer puts it:

Of all the common and familiar subjects of conversation, that are entered upon in company of things remote from nature and cut off from the senses, there is none so ready to hand, none so usual, as that of visions of Spirits, and whether what is said of them is true. It is the topic that people most readily discuss and on which they linger the longest because of the abundance of examples, the subject being fine and pleasing and the discussion the least tedious that can be found.[2]

And when Milton describes the midnight studies of "Il Penseroso" in his "high lonely tower" he significantly gives demonology pride of place next to philosophy and before tragedy, ancient and modern. Plato helps his scholar

> to unfold
> What Worlds or what vast Regions hold
> The immortal mind that hath forsook
> Her mansion in this fleshly nook;

[1] *Religio Medici*, I, xxx–xxxi (pp. 50–1).
[2] Lavater, *op. cit.* p. 222.

metaphysics leads to speculation concerning spirits:

> And of those Dæmons that are found
> In fire, air, flood, or underground,
> Whose power·hath a true consent
> With Planet or with Element;

and demonology, in turn, suggests the tragedies of Æschylus and Sophocles,

> Or what (though rare) of later age
> Ennobled hath the Buskined stage.

In these last two lines we may, I think, perceive a glance at *Hamlet* and *Macbeth*. At any rate, we could hardly find a better statement at once of the importance which thinkers of that age ascribed to the question of spirits and of the position they assigned it among other enquiries and pursuits. It was on the one hand a branch of philosophy and on the other a familiar element of tragic drama.

The four witnesses

Yet there was nothing certain or determined about it; all was in dispute. And while the doctors thus debated together, what was the plain man to believe? To ask this question is to reveal one of the principal attractions of *Hamlet* for serious minds in Shakespeare's generation, since the play is a perfect reflection of the vacillation, not to say confusion, of thought on the problem. Of the four persons who see the Ghost, two—Marcellus and Barnardo—are officers of the guard, and presumably little touched by philosophical and theological speculation. They typify the ghost-lore of the average unthinking Elizabethan, and Shakespeare uses Marcellus as

the mouthpiece of the traditional point of view which was
that of pre-Reformation England. He joins in the scuffle to
prevent the Ghost's departure at the end of the first scene,
but immediately after repents, declaring

> We do it wrong being so majestical
> To offer it the show of violence,
> For it is as the air, invulnerable,
> And our vain blows malicious mockery—

a sentiment which finds Catholic support in the words of Le
Loyer:

It is certain that Souls cannot return in their body, which lies
in the grave, reanimating it and giving it the movement and life it
has lost. And hence, if they return perchance to this world by the
will of God and appear to us, they take not a real but a phantasmal
body. And those who believe that they return in their true body
deceive themselves greatly, for it is only a phantom of air that they
clothe themselves in, to appear visibly to men.[1]

It is Marcellus again who utters the beautiful lines, which
follow, on the peace of Christmas-tide, lines that perhaps do
more than any other speech in the scene to give a religious
background to its supernatural happenings. Yet he seems to
be sufficiently familiar with scholars to have heard of the
great ghost controversy; for, though his views are medieval
in the first scene, he is prepared to entertain different notions
in scenes 4 and 5.

It is when we turn, however, to the other two witnesses
of the apparition that contemporary speculation becomes
really important. Horatio and Hamlet are students, so that
their views will naturally be highly sophisticated by reading.

[1] *Vide* Lavater, *op. cit.* pp. 240–1.

Moreover, they are scholars of a university renowned for a particular school of theology. They have been studying together at the university of Wittenberg, Luther's university, the very cradle of the Reformation. They are in fact Protestants, and the point has no small bearing upon our interpretation of the play. Nor is the mention of Wittenberg the only indication that Shakespeare intended his audience to think of Denmark as a Protestant country. The Hamlet-saga derives from a remote pre-Christian past, and Shakespeare shows his consciousness that the whole thing happened a long time ago, by making England a tributary of the Danish crown. But, though here he is no doubt using material borrowed from his source, he takes care to strike the Christian note in the very first scene, in order to make it clear that his Ghost is a Christian one. I refer to the lines just mentioned, spoken by Marcellus:

> Some say that ever 'gainst that season comes
> Wherein our Saviour's birth is celebrated
> This bird of dawning singeth all night long,
> And then they say no spirit dare stir abroad,
> The nights are wholesome, then no planets strike,
> No fairy takes, nor witch hath power to charm,
> So hallowed, and so gracious is that time.

And if the Denmark of *Hamlet* is Christian, the audience would assume it also to be Protestant. Shakespeare's Denmark, as I have already shown, was Elizabethan England, and in any case contemporary Denmark was known as a bulwark of the Lutheran Church. Moreover, there is a religious service in the play—the funeral of Ophelia—which is certainly not Catholic, though the modern text surrounds it with all the paraphernalia of the Roman ritual. The *Globe Shakespeare*, for example, reads:

> *Enter* Priests, &c. *in procession; the Corpse of* OPHELIA, LAERTES *and* Mourners *following;* KING, QUEEN, *their trains, &c.*

which suggests a crucifix and censers at the very least. Yet the whole thing is editorial gloss, for which there is not an atom of authority in either the Folio or the Second Quarto text. Indeed, all this pomp and circumstance is ridiculous in view of Hamlet's remark about "maiméd rites" and the indignant demand of Laertes for more "ceremony". The Second Quarto gives a very different entry:

> *Enter K. Q. Laertes and the corse.*

It is difficult to dress these bare bones in elaborate ecclesiastical millinery. Is the pomp absent, because the rites are maimed? Partly, but partly for another reason. The Second Quarto, though the fact has hitherto escaped notice, tells us the character of the officiant whom Laertes addresses as "churlish priest", and who seems so unsympathetically to stand upon the letter of ecclesiastical regulation. His two speeches are headed "*Doct.*", which I take to stand for "Doctor of Divinity", and this in an Elizabethan play can mean nothing but a Protestant minister. The heading is probably an indication of costume and may be translated "black gown", while I think it likely that the surly face Shakespeare caught sight of in imagination was that of a clergyman of the Church of England.[1] In any case, it is obvious that he saw the whole scene in contemporary perspective, and that an established

---

[1] *Vide* Appendix B, "The funeral of Ophelia", for further discussion.

Protestant Church was a feature of his Denmark. It is beside the point to quote

> Unhouseled, disappointed, unaneled

as evidence to the contrary;[1] for these words are the Ghost's and the Ghost *is* Catholic: he comes from Purgatory.[2]

The two students of Wittenberg, then, are Protestants, and share the Protestant philosophy of spiritualism. Yet there is a difference between their points of view. Horatio, as I have already said, comes on to the stage as a disciple of Reginald Scot, or at any rate as a sceptic in regard to the objectivity of spectres. The guards are terrified out of their wits, but he greets them with a jest upon his lips, the contemptuous question

> What, has this thing appeared again to-night?

and the confident assertion "Tush, tush, 'twill not appear". The apparition, of course, very rapidly converts him; but it leaves his ghost-philosophy a ruin, and his utterances for the rest of the scene display a mind tossing between the medieval and the Protestant points of view, with here and there as in "Stay, illusion!" a gleam of his old scepticism. Like Marcellus, however, in the encounter on the following night, he seems to come down more or less definitely on the side of Lavater, though Hamlet clearly still suspects him of disbelief and rallies him upon the shallowness of his "philosophy". Hamlet also halts between two opinions, but his problem is different from that of Horatio. Let us look at it closely.

---

[1] For the nunnery to which Hamlet would consign Ophelia *vide* below, p. 134.

[2] *Vide* below, pp. 79–80, 84.

Hamlet is no disciple of Scot; it is true that he professes more than once to have doubts about the Ghost, but they do not concern its objectivity. He accepts it as a spirit, and never shows the slightest sign of hesitation in this belief. What he doubts is the identity of the Ghost and the nature of the place from which it comes. Is it his father's spirit indeed, or a devil, or even possibly an angel? That is his problem. Thus he does not pooh-pooh Horatio's story, as Horatio had pooh-poohed the story of Marcellus and Barnardo. Yet his perplexity is very evident in the questions he puts to them, and the nature of it in the declaration he makes at the end of his catechism:

> If it *assume* my noble father's person,
> I'll speak to it *though hell itself should gape*
> And bid me hold my peace.

This is the scholar of Wittenberg, the reader of Lavater. But the armour of which they tell him in such detail has arrested his attention; it seems so real, so unlike the conventional spook. Thus in

> My father's spirit (in arms!) all is not well,
> I doubt some foul play, would the night were come,

we have the son, full of horrible suspicion, longing to meet the only being who can tell him the truth.

When again he is face to face with the awful apparition itself, it is his theological prepossessions which at first find utterance:

> Angels and ministers of grace defend us!
> Be thou a spirit of health, or goblin damned,
> Bring with thee airs from heaven, or blasts from hell,

> Be thy intents wicked, or charitable,
> Thou com'st in such a questionable shape,
> That I will speak with thee. *I'll call thee* Hamlet,
> King, father, royal Dane.

In form, this may be blank verse of Shakespeare's best vintage; in matter, the merest commonplace of Protestant demonology. Cast it into prose, and it runs: "This portentous figure is devil or angel, for aught I know. But it has assumed my father's person and I cannot refuse to speak with it. The matter must be put to the test, whatever the risks." While it lasts, the terrible interview itself seems entirely to convince him that he is actually holding converse with his father's spirit. Indeed, as I have said already, it is scarcely possible to overestimate the grandeur, power and terror of that interview to minds of Shakespeare's time. And the solemn oath of dedication would place the seal upon those impressions. But how reconcile them with all that Hamlet has hitherto believed? His imagination begins to occupy itself with the problem immediately after the Ghost has vanished. It is only a glimpse we get, but what a glimpse! That noble and most sovereign reason is tottering upon its throne; it clutches for reality. The stars that wheel above him in the firmament, this solid earth upon which he kneels—they are surely real, if anything is real; and he invokes their aid in a loud and bitter cry. But *that* with which he has just been speaking! Is it not also real, and if so what is the nature of its reality?

> O all you host of heaven! O earth! what else?
> And shall I couple hell? O fie!

Heaven, earth—and what? Purgatory? He knows nothing of Purgatory; he never even mentions the word from beginning to end of the play, though he once hints at it in the cellarage scene, in a whisper to Horatio.[1] Yet if not Purgatory, then Hell. He shuts down the half-uttered thought with an exclamation of fierce self-accusation; but the thought is there, to be fed by what happens immediately after, and as time passes to grow stronger than the dwindling impressions of the interview.

I shall return to the cellarage scene in a moment; but let me first pursue the general tenor of Hamlet's speculation about the apparition up to the play scene, when he puts the matter to the proof and so lays his doubts for ever to rest. At the end of act 1 he leaves his companions of the night-watch to go and pray, prayer accompanied with fasting, according to the recognised precepts of Protestant pastors, since as Lavater writes: "It behoueth them which are vexed with spirits, to pray especially, and to giue themselves to fasting, sobrietie, watching, and vpright and godly liuing."[2] All this drew upon him the attention of the court, for Polonius later marks this period as the initial stage of his distemper.[3] But prayer and fasting bring him no peace, no solution of his problem; and when we see him two months later, doubt still has him by the throat. This doubt he voices plainly enough in the words:

> The spirit that I have seen
> May be a devil, and the devil hath power
> T'assume a pleasing shape, yea, and perhaps
> Out of my weakness and my melancholy,
> As he is very potent with such spirits,
> Abuses me to damn me—

[1] *Vide* below, pp. 79–80.
[2] *Op. cit.* p. 193 (heading of Ch. vi, pt. iii).
[3] *Vide* 2.2.147–51 and below, p. 211.

words which again echo the demonologists, who all agree, as we have seen,[1] that melancholy folk were specially liable to be plagued with spirits. A few hours after this, in a moment of deep despondency, the devil-theory seems triumphant; for it is clear that in the "To be or not to be" soliloquy he has either through "bestial oblivion" forgotten all about the Ghost or for the time at any rate given up the idea that it can have been his father's spirit, and that Shakespeare makes him speak of

> The undiscovered country, from whose bourn
> No traveller returns,

in order to inform the audience of this. Thus, what to the "historical" critics and others is a stone of stumbling, falls into its place as a detail in the dramatic structure.[2] Hamlet can, however, afford the luxury of relaxation at this moment, because he is about to put the Ghost and his story on trial. The Gonzago play is toward, with his uncle as witness. As he explains to Horatio:

> if his occulted guilt
> Do not itself unkennel in one speech,
> It is a damnéd ghost that we have seen,
> And my imaginations are as foul
> As Vulcan's stithy.

The interlude follows, and Claudius's conduct thereat resolves all uncertainty. Hamlet can "take the ghost's word for a thousand pound".

Not only is the Ghost, then, the instrument for setting the plot in motion, but Hamlet's doubts about it form a highly

---

[1] *Vide* p. 64.
[2] Cf. Introduction (pp. lii–liii) to my *Hamlet*.

important element of the plot during the whole of the first part of the play. I have no desire, let me repeat, to prejudge the question of Hamlet's "character". His doubts are certainly not the sole cause of his procrastination. Indeed, he seems to admit in the Hecuba soliloquy that he has no real right to delay at all. But he assuredly has more *excuse* than any critic has yet perceived; and the excuse at least provides a strong motive for the introduction of the Gonzago play, which the critics have hitherto been at pains to explain as the mere device of a shuffler.

Other superstitions

All the typical contemporary conceptions of the spirit world were, therefore, represented among the characters to whom Shakespeare introduced his Ghost, a fact which, when once realised, gives a new colouring to the events of the first part of the play. But Shakespeare did more; he framed his apparition with all sorts of references to superstitions connected with the subject. When Marcellus says (1.1.42): "Thou art a scholar, speak to it, Horatio", he explains why the soldiers have asked the student of Wittenberg to share their watch. First, ghosts could not speak until addressed by some mortal; a notion which lasted down to the time of Dr Johnson, who remarked to Boswell on one occasion: "Tom Tyers described me the best: 'Sir (said he) you are like a ghost: you never speak till you are spoken to.'"[1] Thus Barnardo, following up the request of Marcellus to the

[1] Boswell's *Life of Johnson* (ed. Birkbeck Hill, III, 307). I owe this reference to Dowden.

trembling Horatio, exclaims: "It would be spoke to" (l. 45). Secondly, ghosts could only be safely addressed by scholars, seeing that scholars alone were armed with the necessary weapons of defence, in the shape of Latin formulae for exorcism should the spirit prove to be an evil one. Horatio had, therefore, been brought both as a precaution and as an aid to further enquiry "touching this dreaded sight" already seen by the guards two nights in succession.

Another superstition, as I think, is represented in a stage-direction of the Second Quarto which modern editors ignore: "I'll cross it though it blast me. Stay, illusion!"[1] exclaims Horatio at the second appearance. And the margin of Q2 here reads *It spreads his armes*, which I take to be a misprint of *He spreads his armes* and interpret as an attempt by Horatio to stop the Ghost by spreading out his arms to bar his passage. Now, "to cross" denoted in common parlance "to obstruct" or "to encounter adversely", and that is clearly Horatio's primary meaning here. But, as Blakeway notes, "Whoever crossed the spot on which a spectre was seen became subject to its malign influence"; and Ferdinando Stanley, at one time patron of Shakespeare's company, died in 1594 after encountering "a tall man, who crossed him twice swiftly" and whom many supposed to have been an evil spirit.[2] Horatio, therefore, took grave risks in thus crossing the Ghost's path.

Again, the scuffle between the men with their partisans and the repentant words of Marcellus, already paralleled with words from Le Loyer, also find support in the following passage in Lavater:

[1] 1.1.127.
[2] *Vide* Furness, *Variorum Hamlet*, 1.1.127.

Some others, when spirits appeare vnto them, will by and by set on them, and driue them away with naked swords: and sometimes throwe them out of the windowes, not considering with themselues, that spirites are nothing hurte with weapons.[1]

Then there is the crowing of the cock, the mention of buried treasure, the idea that the apparition is connected with "something rotten in the state of Denmark", Marcellus's reference to popular, and Horatio's reference to classical, beliefs, in which the distinction between the soldier who knew his ghosts by hearsay and the scholar who has read of them in books is once again brought out. Indeed, Horatio's speech (1.1.112–25) reads almost like a paraphrase of the following passages in Lavater:

Before the alterations and chaunges of kingdomes and in the time of warres, seditions, and other daungerous seasons, ther most commonly happen very straunge things in the aire, in the earth, & amongst liuing creatures clean contrary to the vsuall course of nature. Which things men cal wonders, signes, monsters, and forewarnings of matters to come. There are seene in the aire, swords, speares, & suche like innumerable: there are heard and seene in the aire, or vppon the earth whole armies of men encountering togither, and when one part is forced to flye, there is heard horrible cries, and great clattering of armour.[2]

Many signes and wonders happen before the deathe of greate Princes. It is wel knowen by histories, what signes went before the deathe of Iulius Caesar, amongest the whiche, a great noyse was hearde in the night time, in very many places farre and neere.[3]

Further, Horatio's fear that the Ghost may lead Hamlet "to the dreadful summit of the cliff" and there drive him

---

[1] Lavater, *op. cit.* p. 214.
[2] *Ibid.* pp. 80–1.   [3] *Ibid.* p. 164.

mad gives utterance to a common belief of the time, a
belief of which Edgar makes use in *King Lear* after his eyeless
father has fallen from the imaginary cliffs of Dover,[1] and to
which King James subscribes in his *Daemonologie*.[2]

The cellarage scene

There remain certain problems connected with the Ghost
which deserve more extended treatment. One group of them
belongs to the apparition in the Queen's bedroom, which
must be deferred;[3] another to the cellarage scene, a scene in
which Shakespeare draws most strikingly upon the popular
and learned spiritualism of his age, which Scot and Lavater
illuminate for us in surprising fashion, though it has perplexed
all the commentators.[4] We marvel at Hamlet's levity with
his father's spirit, and do our best to explain the strange
epithets "boy", "truepenny" and "old mole" as the hysterical utterances of a mind on the borderland of insanity, an
explanation which is in part the truth. But there is more
behind. For one thing, Hamlet has a purpose in his levity.
His urgent need at the moment is secrecy. He must seal the
mouths of the witnesses. He can trust Horatio and is about

---

[1] *Edg.* Upon the crown o' the cliff what thing was that
Which parted from you?
    Glo.   A poor unfortunate beggar.
    Edg. As I stood here below, methought his eyes
Were two full moons; he had a thousand noses,
Horns whelked and waved like the enridgéd sea:
It was some fiend.   *King Lear*, 4.6.67–72.
[2] P. 63.   [3] *Vide* pp. 249–55.
[4] Tschischwitz (1869) alone seems to have caught glimpses of its true
significance, *vide* his notes quoted in Furness's *Variorum* and in my edition
of *Hamlet*.

to tell him all; but Marcellus must, at any cost, be prevented from talking about the night's experiences. All this is clear enough if we follow the dialogue closely.

When they come upon him after the Ghost's departure, Hamlet at first tries to parry their natural curiosity by a piece of "wonderful" news which tells them nothing; after which he takes an abrupt farewell. But the words and manner of Horatio show him a little hurt at this treatment; and, as Hamlet is anxious not to offend the only friend he has in the world, he takes him aside to tell him something of the truth. Here are the words of the text:

> *Hamlet.* I am sorry they offend you, heartily,   134
> Yes, faith, heartily.
>   *Horatio.*   There's no offence, my lord.
>   *Hamlet.* Yes, by Saint Patrick, but there is, Horatio,
> And much offence too—touching this vision here,
> It is an honest ghost that let me tell you—
> For your desire to know what is between us,
> O'ermaster't as you may. And now, good friends,   140
> As you are friends, scholars, and soldiers,
> Give me one poor request.

And then follows the business of the threefold oath. It seems to me that in the second speech Hamlet is on the point of revealing the secret to Horatio, but that finding Marcellus drawing near them in the hope of sharing their confidence, he breaks off at l. 139 with a blunt injunction to mind his own business, and then in l. 140 turns to address them both. "Yes, by Saint Patrick" is an important clue to Hamlet's intentions at the beginning of the speech; for Saint Patrick was "the keeper of Purgatory". In the late middle ages the patron saint of Ireland was regarded as the chief witness to the existence of an intermediate state, since according to legend he found an entrance thereto on an island in Lough Derg, and so was able to convince the doubting Irish.[1] The first three lines of the speech, therefore, are an intimation to the Protestant "philosopher" Horatio, who does not believe in Purgatory, that the Ghost is associated with Saint Patrick not the Devil, i.e. that he is a real ghost, and no demon masquerading in human form. At this point, Marcellus comes within earshot, and though Hamlet's final words to Horatio alone appear rude, an actor playing the part should, I think, make it clear to the audience that the rudeness is assumed out of policy and that Horatio is to be told all directly Marcellus is out of the way.

Meanwhile Marcellus, with his curiosity, is a problem to be dealt with; and that he most decidedly was not meant to overhear the reference to Saint Patrick and the "honesty"of the Ghost is proved by the fact that for the rest of the scene Hamlet does all in his power to persuade him that the Ghost is anything but honest. He addresses the Ghost in the "cellarage" as if it *were* a devil, a "familiar" with whom he has just been holding converse.* He calls it "boy" and "truepenny", that is "trusty fellow" or "faithful servant", and he makes Horatio and Marcellus swear with the devil, as the latter at any rate will believe it to be, beneath their very feet. Perhaps the most remarkable thing—the most terrifying, if we adopt the Elizabethan standpoint—about the whole episode is that the idea is suggested to Hamlet by the

[1] I owe the interpretation of this point to a review of Lavater (*op. cit.*) in *The Times Literary Supplement*, Jan. 9, 1930. Cf. also T. Wright, *St Patrick's Purgatory*, O.E.D. "purgatory", 1 *b*, and O'Connor, *St Patrick's Purgatory* (Burns and Oates).*

Ghost itself; for it is not until the Ghost says "Swear" that Hamlet begins his amazing performance. In a word, father and son seem to be playing into each other's hands in order to hoodwink an inconvenient witness. That this is the true meaning of the strange scene no candid reader of Lavater and the other writers will, I think, deny. Take two passages from his book:

Pioners or diggers for mettal, do affirme, that in many mines, there appeare straunge shapes and spirites, who are apparrelled like vnto other laborers in the pit. These wander vp and down in caues and vnderminings, & seeme to besturre them selues in all kinde of labour, as to digge after the veine, to carrie togither oare, to put it into baskets and to turne the winding whele to drawe it vp, when in very deede they do nothing lesse (p. 73).

Be not dismayde, though thou heare some spirit stir and make a noyse, for in case hee rumble onely to make thee afrayde, care not for him, but lette hym rumble so long as he wyll, for if he see thee wythout feare, hee wyll soone depart from thee (p. 191).

The noises and rumblings that spirits and devils were supposed to make in the bowels of the earth is a point to which both Lavater and Scot return again and again. Scot tells us further that the "worser moiety of devils" were divided into Aquei, Subterranei and Lucifugi, and declares that the Subterranei "assault them that are miners or pioners, which use to worke in deepe and darke holes under the earth".[1] We may remember too that Sir Toby Belch speaks of the Devil as a "foul collier".[2] After all this is it not clear that Hamlet's words—

Well said, old mole! canst work i'th'earth so fast?
A worthy pioner!—

[1] *Discourse*, ch. III.   [2] *Twelfth Night*, 3.4.121.

identify the mutterings of the Ghost with the rumblings of one "of those demons that are...underground", to quote Milton once again? Horatio will be told later on; but inquisitive Marcellus to his dying day will believe that he has sworn an oath thrice in the hearing of a powerful fiend,* and will hold his tongue.

Once we have the key to the puzzle a number of other little pieces fall into their places. Hamlet appears to act the part to perfection. The Latin tag—*Hic et ubique?*—is a scrap from the conjuror's repertory, as we have seen.* The dismissal —"Rest, rest, perturbéd spirit!"—is capable of a similar explanation, though apt enough to an honest ghost. The threefold oath finds once more a parallel in Scot, who speaks of "promises and oths interchangeablie made betweene the coniuror and the spirit", oaths which were sworn three times, and for the violation of which eternal penalties were exacted.[1] The oaths, it will be observed, are not mere repetitions: the first is concerned with what the witnesses have seen, the second with what they have heard, and the third with the "antic disposition". Moreover, the shifting or removing from place to place, as the oaths are taken, is also common form, and occurs again in Fletcher's *Woman's Prize*.[2]

In all this, I say, Hamlet appears to be acting a part. Is it only acting? The presence of the Ghost in the cellarage is most convenient for the shutting of Marcellus's mouth; but what does Hamlet himself make of it? With his Protestant upbringing, with the possibility of deception by a visitant from Hell so present to his mind that it peeps out, as we have

[1] *Discoverie of Witchcraft*, Bk. 15, ch. XVII.
[2] Act 5, sc. 3, noted by Bradley, *Shakespearean Tragedy*, p. 413.

seen, the moment his father's form sinks into the earth beneath his eyes,[1] what is he to think when the spirit *behaves* exactly like an underground demon? When he whispers to Horatio, he has made up his mind as to the honesty of the Ghost; but the voice from the cellarage is enough to shake any man's faith. Le Loyer writes: "Since the Souls do not appear so often as do Angels and Demons, it is necessary to examine diligently the Souls which appear, to discern if they are truly Souls or if it is an ambush of the enemy of the human race":[2] and he goes on to prescribe "conjuration of the spirit" as one method of testing its character, "for then the spirit cannot disguise its origin".[3] This is exactly what Hamlet does; he plays the conjurer. And the Ghost responds! Shakespeare does not tell us in so many words that the cellarage scene breeds new doubts in Hamlet's mind; but he gives us a very plain hint of Hamlet's despondency as the scene closes:

> The time is out of joint, O cursèd spite,
> That ever I was born to set it right!

The couplet is an important piece of self-revelation, a tacit confession of personal inadequacy, as all have noted; but the immediate occasion which prompts its utterance is the return with redoubled force of misgivings concerning the provenance of the apparition.

It was not necessary for Shakespeare to underline all this, to dot the i's and cross the t's of Hamlet's suspicions at this juncture, because he knew that they would be shared by the

---

[1] The vanishing in 1.5 is by means of the trap on the front stage, to which the Ghost leads Hamlet from "the platform" or upper stage where, as I think, 1.4 is performed.

[2] Lavater, *op. cit.* p. 245.　　　　[3] *Ibid.* p. 247.

spectators in his theatre, that there would be disciples of Le Loyer, of Lavater, and even of Reginald Scot among them. His patron, the Earl of Southampton, was a declared Catholic and many others were Catholics at heart, while Protestants, of course, would form a large proportion. It paid him dramatically to let all three schools of thought have their views considered. And the audience, of whatever school, would be swayed hither and thither in their opinion, as Hamlet himself was swayed, by the events of the ghost scenes. Like him they would wonder what to think before the vision appears; like him they would be overwhelmed by its apparition and accept it as the genuine spirit of the dead king while it is actually before their eyes; like him too they would be left baffled and bewildered by the cries from the cellarage. At the end of the first act, the Elizabethan audience could no more be certain of the honesty of the Ghost and of the truth of the story it had related, than the perplexed hero himself. Thus for the first half of the play the character that was on trial with them was not Hamlet's but the Ghost's. The troubles of modern critics, the need to explain the "antic disposition" and the Gonzago play later, were no troubles for them, since they found them arising naturally and inevitably out of the situation in which Hamlet was placed. But they had problems of their own. Chief among these, we may guess, was the fact that the only non-Protestant in the play was the visitor from the other world, although in life he had been King of Lutheran Denmark. Catholics would accept this as a matter of course; obdurate Protestants would refuse to admit him anything but a devil even after the play scene had proved the truth of his story: and most would stand in doubt between the two, shaking their heads and echoing Hamlet's words

> There are more things in heaven and earth, Horatio,
> Than are dreamt of in your philosophy.

As to Shakespeare's own attitude, that was, as ever, his secret.

Gabriel Harvey, in his famous marginalia written on the leaves of Speght's *Chaucer* about 1599, notes that "the younger sort takes much delight in Shakespeares *Venus, & Adonis*: but his *Lucrece*, & his tragedie of *Hamlet, Prince of Denmarke*, haue it in them, to please the wiser sort". Is it not likely that the Cambridge scholar had the Ghost particularly in mind in this reference to *Hamlet*? To his own generation, one of the most astonishing things about Shakespeare must have been his power to appeal to the "generality" and the "judicious" at one and the same time. To the groundlings holding crude views of spectral appearances, to the more enlightened burghers of the Marcellus school of thought, and to the students and philosophers among the inns-of-court men and the nobility; to all and to each according to his peculiar outlook the ghost scenes made their profound and thrilling appeal. But it was the appreciation of the judicious which Shakespeare was most anxious to secure, and which we to-day are most likely to overlook. The nature and origin of wandering spirits was one of the great questions of the time among thinking people, and the Ghost in *Hamlet* was a real contribution to the subject.

Imagine one of the scholar-courtiers of Elizabeth's retinue (and there were many such) at a performance of *Hamlet*. With what extraordinary interest will he watch the student-

prince of Denmark confronted with an unmistakable apparition, with what sympathetic curiosity will he follow the
workings of a mind under the stress of events which (as he
imagines) might not impossibly occur to himself, how keen
will be his appreciation of the variety of opinion and incident
which the magician-dramatist introduces! There can be no
doubt at all about it; the Ghost in *Hamlet* was a far more
arresting and prominent figure to the Elizabethans than he
can ever be to us. We may deplore our loss—and it is great
indeed. But it is something at least to realise its existence.
Critics who read *Hamlet* in ignorance of it are in danger of
misconceiving Shakespeare's art altogether.

IV

ANTIC DISPOSITION

O, 'tis most sweet
When in one line two crafts directly meet.

ANTIC DISPOSITION

Its origin, purpose and character

The Ghost and his message form the main theme of act 1. But the closing scene of that act, as we have just observed, leaves both Hamlet and the audience in grave doubt, doubt which is not resolved until the play scene in the middle of act 3. Thus the pivot of the plot during the next two acts is the testing of the Ghost's story, or to put it in other words, Hamlet's attempt to probe the secret guilt of Claudius. On the other hand, Hamlet's knowledge, or at any rate strong suspicion, of this guilt is *his* secret, which he cloaks beneath the "antic disposition", and which Claudius and Polonius with the aid of Rosencrantz and Guildenstern in their turn seek to probe. The second and third acts, therefore, are occupied, and most thrillingly occupied, with a double intrigue: Hamlet trying to sift Claudius; Claudius and Polonius trying to sift Hamlet. Hamlet, however, for reasons to be discussed later, makes no endeavour to "catch the conscience of the King" before the play scene itself, whereas Claudius is found actively at work on his side at the very beginning of act 2. And this "lag" on Hamlet's part means that most of the second act is taken up, not only by the efforts of his enemies to bring him to book, but also by Hamlet's own response to those efforts. That is to say, the main theme of this act is the "antic disposition", the attempts to get behind it by spying upon Hamlet, and the manner in which

Hamlet, who is (as I shall show) soon fully conscious of what is going on, plays up to the various theories concerning his supposed madness. The second act of *Hamlet* is comedy; a comedy of masks. But the comedy does not stop there; it runs right on into the act that follows. For we shall find that a due understanding of this intrigue and of Hamlet's attitude towards it will explain all sorts of details in the play scene which would otherwise puzzle us. In the play scene the comedy of masks reaches at once its climax and finale. After Lucianus has poured the mock-poison into the Player-King's ears, both Hamlet and Claudius know each other for what they are; and masks are henceforth useless.

In approaching this section of the play our first consideration must be Hamlet's reasons for assuming the "antic disposition". It will have to be considered eventually in its bearings upon the problem of his character. But no psychological theory, such as might occur to a spectator at the end of the play in casting back his mind and reflecting upon the personality of the hero, can be accepted as an adequate dramatic explanation. To be fully satisfactory the explanation must exhibit the initial impulse arising naturally out of the occasion on which it takes place and must relate it to the task which Hamlet has in hand. I do not mean that spectators should see at once for what purpose Hamlet decided to act the madman. What I mean is that none of them should consider it absurd, and that they should feel Hamlet could hardly have done anything else under the circumstances. The notion entertained by some writers that the original spectators accepted the "antic disposition", together with the rest of the plot, because they were familiar with the story before

Shakespeare handled it, seems to be hardly worth discussing. Elizabethan spectators were not students of Shakespearian sources; nor is it at all likely, as I shall point out later,[1] that in the theatre of that time, with its rapidly changing repertory, the audience (apart from one or two here and there perhaps) would recollect the details of the old *Hamlet* when they saw Shakespeare's revision of it several years later. To them it would be a new play, and its effects would have to justify themselves as in a new play; that is, they would have to be self-explanatory. And after all it is a simple business enough. To see how it came about we must return to the cellarage scene for a moment, and follow the movement of Hamlet's mind under the stress of circumstances and emotion, which, obvious enough to the Elizabethans, have taken me two chapters to expound.

The Ghost, departing after the delivery of his mission, leaves his son in a pitiable condition. He is beaten to the ground, distraught and half-paralysed; and as he tries to rise, he presses his hand first to his throbbing heart and then to that "distracted globe" his head. There follows the "tables" speech, which begins with an ardent promise of remembrance, breaks out into unbalanced hilarity at the recollection of his uncle's smiling face at the Privy Council and concludes with a solemn oath of dedication to the quest which the Ghost has laid upon him.[2] As Horatio and Marcellus come from the castle Hamlet is still upon his knees in the darkness, and to the former's anxious prayer "Heaven secure him!" he

---

[1] *Vide* pp. 147–8.
[2] *Vide* notes 1.5.107–9, 110, in my edition of *Hamlet* for a fuller exposition of this speech.

mutters a fervent "So be it!" Yet, a second later he is on his feet, mockingly echoing the cry of Marcellus by converting it into a falconer's call. And when they come up with him he is apparently in the highest spirits:

Mar. How is't, my noble lord?
Hor.   What news, my lord?
Ham. O, wonderful!
Hor.   Good my lord, tell it.
Ham. No, you will reveal it.
Hor. Not I, my lord, by heaven.
Mar. Nor I, my lord.
Ham. How say you then, would heart of man once think it?
But you'll be secret?
Hor. Mar.   Ay, by heaven, my lord.
Ham. There's ne'er a villain dwelling in all Denmark
But he's an arrant knave.

Once again, however, the hilarity vanishes as quickly as it had come. For the next speech, in reply to Horatio's expostulation, though beginning in the same tone, suddenly changes to solemnity, as the words "business and desire" remind Hamlet of the task that lies before him, and ends with the pathetic "Look you, I will go pray". No wonder Horatio is disturbed at such behaviour and by such "wild and whirling words". Yet the see-saw goes on. An hysterical jocularity, wilder and more whirling than ever, returns as the voice speaks from the cellarage; and, once the threefold oath is completed, it is succeeded by the utmost despondency of spirit.

In short, this passage of a hundred lines exhibits Hamlet in a state of extreme emotional instability, and with an intellect tottering on its seat. Furthermore, the "antic disposition" has manifested itself on three separate occasions before Hamlet ever refers to it at all: in the "table-book" speech, at Horatio and Marcellus's entry, and in conjuring the "worthy pioner" underground. The second of these is as typical an example of its use as may be found anywhere else in the play; and like the other two it is clearly partly deliberate and partly involuntary: that is to say, the mood comes unsought but is welcomed as affording relief when it does come, and is accordingly purposely elaborated and prolonged. In a word, Shakespeare wishes us to feel that Hamlet assumes madness because he cannot help it. The tragic burden has done its work, and he is conscious that he no longer retains perfect control over himself. What more natural than that he should conceal his nervous breakdown behind a mask which would enable him to let himself go when the fit is upon him?

Not that we are to suppose Hamlet thought it out in these or any other terms. It is one of his characteristics, as we shall see, that he never thinks anything out. All that actually happens is that, realising he had displayed intense and uncontrollable emotional excitement in the presence of Horatio and Marcellus, he pretends that he has been acting a part, and warns them that it may occur again;[1] at the same time exacting an elaborate oath from them that, if it does so occur, they will not hint by word or gesture that they know anything

---

[1] Dowden anticipates me here. "Hamlet's madness", he writes, "is not deliberately assumed; an antic disposition is, as it were, imposed upon him by the almost hysterical excitement which follows his interview with the Ghost, and he ingeniously justifies it to himself by discovering that it may hereafter serve a purpose" (Introduction to *Hamlet*, "Arden edition", p. xxvi).

whatever about it. The oath, in the case of Marcellus at least, is a very necessary precaution. For any confession of knowledge about Hamlet would be dangerous: if he hinted that the madness was genuine he would be drawn on to speaking of the interview with the Ghost from which, as he would assume, the madness sprang; if he asserted that it was pretended, he would expose Hamlet still more perilously.

As for the relation of the "antic disposition" to Hamlet's task, that is surely equally natural and obvious. However urgent the command of the Ghost, the difficulty of executing it without injuring the Queen, and the perplexity concerning the Ghost himself, forbid immediate action: Hamlet needs time for consideration. Meanwhile, the assumption of insanity would enable him, as Dr Bradley puts it, "to give some utterance to the load that pressed on his heart and brain",[1] and would also give him a freedom of speech and action he could not otherwise obtain. The fact that it makes the King extremely uneasy about him, so that he sets his spies to work, a fact which some put down to the weakness of the inherited plot, is with more discrimination attributed by Dr Bradley to the weakness of Hamlet's character. Yet I cannot believe that this either was Shakespeare's intention. Discussing the two months' interval between act 1 and act 2, Dr Bradley writes: "Beyond thus exciting the apprehensions of his enemy Hamlet has done absolutely nothing; and...we must imagine him during this long period sunk for the most part in 'bestial oblivion' or fruitless broodings, and falling deeper and deeper into the slough of despond."[2] This, however, overlooks the fact that it is Hamlet's state of mind which

[1] Bradley, *op. cit.* p. 121.   [2] *Op. cit.* p. 130.

drives him to pretend madness, a state of mind which he could not conceal and which, in any case, would have excited comment and suspicion. It ignores, too, that recklessness which is a marked trait of Hamlet throughout. Why should Hamlet care what Claudius thought about him? a man he was always just about to kill.

Furthermore, Dr Bradley's words illustrate a fallacy that impairs a good deal of his Shakespearian criticism, brilliant and subtle as it is, viz., the fallacy of regarding separate episodes of the play, especially episodes early in the play, in the light of his knowledge of the whole. In the first place, at the beginning of act 2 no spectator knows, or ought to know, that two months have elapsed, seeing that he is not informed on that head until the middle of the third act.[1] He is vaguely aware that some weeks have elapsed, that is all. In the second place, though this sense of the passage of time may make him a little uncomfortable when he finds that Hamlet has done nothing meanwhile, he is certainly not at this stage fully alive to the dangers of delay or perplexed about its cause; while it is quite impossible for him to imagine Hamlet "sunk in 'bestial oblivion' or fruitless broodings". And if, looking back from the beginning of act 4, by which time he has grown thoroughly alarmed at the delay, he should ask himself whether Hamlet had been wise to assume the "antic dis-

[1] And then only by inference. At 3.2.126 Ophelia says that King Hamlet has been dead "twice two months", and it is only by comparing this statement with that of Hamlet at 1.2.138, which tells us that his father had been dead not quite two months, that we deduce a two months' interval between acts 1 and 2. Such calculations do not take place in the theatre! Indeed, I now feel that even the stage-direction *Some weeks pass*, which I insert at the end of act 1 in my edition, stresses the interval overmuch.*

position", his answer is quite as likely to be in the affirmative as in the negative, since, as we shall see, by act 3 Hamlet was exciting his uncle's suspicions of set purpose, and the pretence of madness might be explained as an early indication of this purpose. Such speculation, however, is extremely risky; and I do not myself think that it entered into Shakespeare's calculations at all. The "antic disposition" was assumed on a sudden impulse, the first of many, on Hamlet's part; it was obviously prompted by his hysteria at the moment; and it would be accepted as a convenient disguise while he was maturing his plans. To consider it more curiously than this is to treat *Hamlet* as history not drama.

A point, which some who reprehend the pretended madness as an ill-assimilated legacy from the old saga are apt to overlook, is that Shakespeare had every inducement to retain it if he could, and that, at any rate, until the middle of the fourth act, it is the very salt of his play. He saw that it possessed immense dramatic possibilities and he took full advantage of them. Imagine *Hamlet* without it, and most of the wit together with all the fun, except for Osric and the Grave-diggers, and Polonius playing the fool "in's own house", would be lost. Hamlet's quibbles, in particular, are the fruit of it. True, he begins to quibble in 1.2 before he sees the Ghost; but the native gift thus vouched for is exercised with much greater freedom after the assumption of the "antic disposition". "Mad Hamlet" is indeed the fool of the play that takes its name from him. By acting the natural, he usurps the natural's privileges, and Touchstone-like uses his madness "like a stalking-horse, and under the presentation of that he shoots his wit". Far too little has been made of this aspect of the play; but lack of space forbids treatment of it here, and I must refer the reader to the Introduction and Notes of my recent edition of *Hamlet* for further discussion.

Another aspect of the "antic disposition" not sufficiently reckoned with by modern commentators is its expression in Hamlet's costume. Ophelia tells us that before his madness Hamlet had been

> The glass of fashion and the mould of form;

and though we never see him except in mourning, his black doublet was no doubt rich enough and the points of his hose well tied in the Privy Council scene at the beginning of the play. In the second scene of act 2, however, we hear from Claudius that

> nor th'exterior nor the inward man
> Resembles that it was;

and this merely confirms the description given of him by Ophelia in the previous scene, as he appears suddenly before her in her closet,

> with his doublet all unbraced,
> No hat upon his head, his stockings fouled,
> Ungart'red, and down-gyved to his ankle,
> Pale as his shirt.

I shall have more to say about this episode in a moment, but as far as concerns Hamlet's disorderly attire, I cannot do better than quote the words of Professor J. Q. Adams, who is the first I think to perceive its true significance. He writes:

This slovenliness in costume has usually been interpreted as the pose of the forlorn lover. It is true that literary artists of the seventeenth century sometimes represented a disappointed lover as adopting a melancholy pose accompanied by a certain carelessness in dress.[1] But Hamlet's physical appearance cannot be explained on this score. He has "no hat upon his head"; the sad lover is invariably represented with his hat plucked low over his eyes. Hamlet's doublet is "all"—that is, entirely—unfastened, a most indelicate form of dishabille. His stockings are down-fallen to his ankles; since men's stockings reached to or above the knee, Hamlet was thus bare-legged. And the stockings are actually "fouled", which takes away the fine sentimentality of the lover-pose. Most significant of all, perhaps, is the allusion to his shirt. This part of a man's costume was not supposed to be visible; yet Hamlet appears in public in his shirt; it is almost as though, as we should say to-day, he appeared in his undershirt. None of these things can be explained on the score of the sentimental, lovesick youth.

He then goes on to cite the well-known lines from *Diaphantus* (1604), a poem by Anthony Scoloker, the hero of which

> Puts off his clothes, his shirt he only wears,
> Much like mad Hamlet;

lines which clearly preserve for us the contemporary stage-effect of Burbadge's impersonation. He also quotes a passage from *The Revenger's Tragedy* (c. 1607), a play obviously inspired in part by *Hamlet*, which runs:

> Surely we are all mad people, and they
> Whom we think mad are not: we mistake those;
> 'Tis we are mad in sense, they but in clothes.

And he concludes that "Hamlet's madness, as it impressed the audience of the Globe, was conspicuously a madness 'in clothes'".[2]

---

[1] Cf. *As You Like It*, 3.2.365–75.
[2] *Hamlet*, ed. by J. Q. Adams, Houghton Mifflin Company, 1929, pp. 222–4.

I do not doubt that when Hamlet appeared on Shake-speare's stage before the eyes of Claudius, Gertrude and Polonius in 2.2 he was not only "reading on a book" but apparelled exactly as Ophelia had depicted him to her father a few moments earlier. Her speech was, therefore, partly designed to prepare the audience for this entry, while in the exclamation of the Queen,

But look where sadly *the poor wretch* comes reading,

we catch a glimpse of the supposed madman through his mother's eyes. Nor do I doubt that he retained the same admired disorder until his departure for England under guard.* It was, indeed, the visible token of his pretended madness; and was theatrically of first importance since it kept the "antic disposition" constantly before the mind of the audience. Whether it should be regarded as deliberate or involuntary is a question which I shall take up later.

The "antic disposition" excites the suspicions of Claudius; and these suspicions and the explanation which Polonius furnishes provide, as I have said, most of the action in the second and third acts. Critics have been so preoccupied with problems of character that they have neglected this feature of the plot. Yet if we run rapidly over the scenes in these two acts, it will be seen how large a part of them is taken up with it. Half the first scene of act 2 is devoted to talk between Ophelia and Polonius about the incident just spoken of, which convinces the old man that unrequited passion for his daughter is the cause of the Prince's insanity, and so leads to Ophelia being used as the decoy in the trap of the eaves-droppers. The second scene opens with the audience given to Hamlet's schoolfellows, Rosencrantz and Guildenstern, who have been sent for by the King, as he puts it,

> to gather
> So much as from occasion you may glean
> Whether aught to us unknown afflicts him thus,
> That opened lies within our remedy;

which, as we soon learn, is only a polite way of requesting them to spy upon him. No sooner have they retired than Polonius comes in, bursting with the story Ophelia has just given him, and roundly declaring that he has found

> The very cause of Hamlet's lunacy;

to which Claudius replies

> O speak of that, that do I long to hear,

displaying an eagerness greater, I think, than he shows upon any other occasion in the play, except when he thirsts for Hamlet's death in 4.3.

The arrival of the ambassadors from Norway postpones the telling of Polonius' news for about thirty lines. In the interval, however, there takes place a brief but very significant colloquy between husband and wife:

> *King.* He tells me, my dear Gertrude, he hath found
> The head and source of all your son's distemper.
> *Queen.* I doubt it is no other but the main,
> His father's death and our o'erhasty marriage.
> *King.* Well, we shall sift him.

Shakespeare wrote this to make us realise that Hamlet's madness was a source of grave anxiety and much discussion on the part of Claudius and his consort, and that the former was preoccupied rather with his own safety than with Hamlet's health. The word "sift", together with the advent of

Rosencrantz and Guildenstern, shows that the King suspects Hamlet to be concealing something dangerous to the throne behind his "transformation". The theory of Polonius is different. Ophelia's account of the closet scene leaves him positive that the Prince has gone mad because she repelled his advances. The notion flatters his family pride; he explains it all to their majesties, at tedious length and with many "limbs and outward flourishes"; and the upshot is that the King determines to "try it further" by throwing Ophelia in Hamlet's path and listening to conversation between them from a place of concealment. Meanwhile Rosencrantz and Guildenstern take their turn and attempt to catch Hamlet in his talk, not very successfully. They report their failure at the beginning of act 3, and immediately after comes the nunnery scene with Claudius and Polonius behind the arras.

Thus from the end of act 1 right up to the play scene, Hamlet's "antic disposition" and the theories accounting for it form the main theme of the play. These theories, be it noted, are three in number: (1) the explanation of Polonius, given above, (2) that of Claudius, the nature of which we shall explore later, and (3) that of Gertrude, who attributes the disorder to

His father's death and our o'erhasty marriage.

We hear little about the last after 1.2 until the play scene; but there it becomes important, since in that scene Hamlet toys with the three theories like a conjurer with coloured balls, keeping them all in the air at once by a brilliant display of wit. Until then, he is mainly concerned with those of his uncle and would-be father-in-law, to what effect we must now examine. And since the theory of Polonius is given the first innings by Shakespeare, we may begin with that.

Hamlet and Ophelia

The attitude of Hamlet towards Ophelia is without doubt the greatest of all the puzzles in the play, greater even than that of the delay itself, a fact which should long ago have created suspicion that in the course of three centuries Shakespeare's original intentions have somehow been obscured. The difficulty is not that, having once loved Ophelia, Hamlet ceases to do so. This is explained, as most critics have agreed, by his mother's conduct which has put him quite out of love with Love and has poisoned his whole imagination. The exclamation "Frailty thy name is woman!" in the first soliloquy, we come to feel later, embraces Ophelia as well as Gertrude, while in the bedroom scene he as good as taxes his mother with destroying his capacity for affection, when he accuses her of

> such an act
> That blurs the grace and blush of modesty,
> Calls virtue hypocrite, *takes off the rose*
> *From the fair forehead of an innocent love*
> And sets a blister there.

Moreover, it is clear that in the tirades of the nunnery scene he is thinking almost as much of his mother as of Ophelia.

The word "blister" in the passage just quoted introduces us to the real problem; for it refers to the branding of a harlot. Why brand "an *innocent* love" thus? Gertrude had played the harlot with Claudius; why pour abuse which might be appropriate to her upon the unoffending head of Ophelia? As Dr Bradley notes: "The disgusting and insulting grossness of his language to her in the play scene...is such language as you will find addressed to a woman by no other hero of Shakespeare's, not even in that dreadful scene where Othello accuses Desdemona."[1] And that Shakespeare intended us to interpret Hamlet's speeches here, together with some of those in the nunnery scene, as, like Othello's, belonging to the brothel is, I think, incontestable. We may try and palliate this conduct by dwelling upon Hamlet's morbid state of mind, by recalling that manners were ruder and speech more direct with the Elizabethans than with ourselves, by noting that since Ophelia and the rest thought he was mad they would be ready to extenuate his behaviour on that ground (as for instance Ophelia's outspoken song in 4.5 is generally regarded as a pathetic symptom of her condition), and by emphasising the fact that she had jilted him and that he had therefore a grievance against her. Yet all will not do; Hamlet's treatment of her remains inexcusable on the ordinary reading of the story, and as such it endangers the very life of the play.

For, whatever weakness we may be expected to find in Hamlet's character, however severely Shakespeare judges him and asks us to judge him also, it is vital to his purpose that we should retain our interest in him and admiration for him right up to the end. Rob us of our respect for the hero and *Hamlet* ceases to be a tragedy; yet that is just what his unexplained behaviour to Ophelia threatens to do. There is a savage side to Hamlet, which comes out in his ruthlessness towards Rosencrantz and Guildenstern, and in the speech as

[1] *Op. cit.* p. 103.

the King kneels in prayer, a speech that Dr Johnson found "too horrible to be read or to be uttered". Yet this savagery, discordant as it is with our scale of values, does not detract from our general sense of the nobility and greatness of the man. But savagery towards a gentle and inoffensive child, one whom he had loved and whose worst crime towards him is lack of understanding and inability to disobey her father's commands, is a very different matter. It is, in fact, irreconcilable with everything else we are told about him.

Hamlet treats Ophelia like a prostitute; and the only possible defence for him is to show that he had grounds for so doing. What can they have been? The answer came to me, late in this enquiry, when after trying many solutions of the Hamlet-Ophelia tangle I had given the whole thing up and had ceased thinking about it. I was making the first draft of my Notes for *Hamlet* in the edition recently published by the Cambridge University Press, and asking questions, as an editor must, about the meaning of word and situation at each step I took. Presently I arrived at the point, early in 2.2, at which Polonius and Claudius devise the plot of listening to Hamlet and Ophelia behind the arras, when my attention was arrested by this line in the speech of Polonius:

> At such a time I'll loose my daughter to him.

The expression was not new to me. I had met it before in *The Tempest* at 2.1.124, where the cynical Sebastian sneers at Alonso because he would not marry his daughter to a European prince,

> But rather loose her to an African;

and in *The Merry Wives* at 2.1.163, where the confident

Master Page declares of Falstaff that "if he should intend this voyage towards my wife, I would turn her loose to him; and what he gets more of her than sharp words, let it lie on my head". I had met it also, listening to present-day farmers in the north of England discussing the breeding of horses and cattle; and that this was the meaning intended, a meaning that would assuredly not escape an Elizabethan audience, was confirmed to my mind by Polonius speaking of "a farm and carters" five lines later, in accordance with Shakespeare's habit of sustained imagery.[1]

But to understand the point of it and its connection with what follows, we must have the whole context before us. I quote from the Second Quarto text:

> *King.* How may we try it further?
> *Pol.* You know sometimes he walkes foure houres together 160
> Heere in the Lobby.
> *Quee.* So he dooes indeede.
> *Pol.* At such a time, Ile loose my daughter to him,
> Be you and I behind an Arras then,
> Marke the encounter, if he loue her not,
> And be not from his reason falne thereon
> Let me be no assistant for a state
> But keepe a farme and carters.
> *King.* We will try it.

> *Enter Hamlet.*

> *Quee.* But looke where sadly the poore wretch comes reading.
> *Pol.* Away, I doe beseech you both away, *Exit King and Queene.*
> Ile bord him presently, oh giue me leaue, 170
> How dooes my good Lord Hamlet?

---

[1] *Vide* Introduction (pp. xxxv–xxxix) to my *Hamlet.*

Ham. Well, God a mercy.
Pol. Doe you knowe me my Lord?
Ham. Excellent well, you are a Fishmonger.
Pol. Not I my Lord. 175
Ham. Then I would you were so honest a man.
Pol. Honest my Lord.
Ham. I sir to be honest as this world goes,
Is to be one man pickt out of tenne thousand.
Pol. That's very true my Lord. 180
Ham. For if the sunne breede maggots in a dead dogge, being
a good kissing carrion. Haue you a daughter?
Pol. I haue my Lord.
Ham. Let her not walke i'th Sunne, conception is a blessing,
But as your daughter may conceaue, friend looke to't.

Everything that Hamlet here says is capable of an equivocal
interpretation reflecting upon Polonius and Ophelia. "Fishmonger", as many commentators have noted, means a pandar or procurer;[1] "carrion" was a common expression at
that time for "flesh" in the carnal sense;[2] while the quibble
in "conception" needs no explaining. And when I asked
myself why Hamlet should suddenly call Polonius a bawd
and his daughter a prostitute—for that is what it all amounts
to—I could discover but one possible answer to my question,
namely that "Fishmonger" and the rest follows immediately
upon "loose my daughter to him". Nor was this the end of
the matter. For what might Hamlet mean by his sarcastic
advice to the father not to let the daughter "walke i'th Sunne",
or by the reference to the sun breeding in the "carrion"
exposed to it? Bearing in mind Hamlet's punning retort "I

[1] *Vide* note 2.2.174 in my *Hamlet*.
[2] *Vide* O.E.D. "carrion", 3, and *Merchant of Venice*, 3.1.32–4.

am too much in the 'son'", in answer to Claudius's unctuous question at 1.2.64,

> And now my cousin Hamlet, and my son,
> How is it that the clouds still hang on you?—

and recalling Falstaff's apostrophe to Prince Hal: "Shall the blessed sun of heaven prove a micher and eat blackberries? a question not to be asked. Shall the son of England prove a thief and take purses? a question to be asked",[1] is it not obvious that Hamlet here means by "Sunne" the sun or son of Denmark, the heir apparent, in other words himself? And if so, "let her not walke i'th Sunne" is to be paraphrased "take care that you do not loose your daughter to me!"

What then? *Hamlet must have overheard what Polonius said to the King.* The context allows no escape from this conclusion, inasmuch as what Hamlet says to Polonius is only intelligible if the conclusion be allowed. It remains to examine the text in order to discover, if possible, what Shakespeare's intentions, clearly impaired in some way by corruption, may have been. We are left, of course, to conjecture, but even so we are not entirely without clues. Says Polonius:

> You know sometimes he walks four hours together
> Here in the lobby;

and as he speaks we may imagine him jerking a thumb over his shoulder towards the inner-stage before which the three plotters stand, their faces to the audience. Words and the action are a direct invitation to the spectators to look in that direction; and, as they do so, Hamlet enters the inner-stage from the door at the back, his eyes upon his book, quite

[1] 1 *Henry IV*, 2.4.449–53.

unconscious at first that his uncle, his mother and Polonius are on the outer-stage, which stands for the audience-chamber of the castle. In short, "Here in the lobby" is equivalent to a stage-direction, and marks with practical certainty the moment at which Hamlet comes in and the place of his entry. And it is the right moment; for the entry should seem un-questionably accidental, lest the audience should suspect him of deliberate spying. It would never do, for example, to let him linger in his place of concealment. Between the King's question "How may we try it further?" and his resolve "We will try it" there lie eight lines of dialogue. They just give Hamlet time to enter the lobby, grow conscious of voices in the larger chamber beyond, pause for a moment beside the entrance thereto, compose his features, and come forward. But brief as the period is, it is long enough for him to take in the whole eavesdropping plot and to implicate Ophelia beyond possibility of doubt in his ears as one of his uncle's minions.*

Nor does the textual aspect of the matter present any insuperable difficulties. If things are as I contend, there must have been two entries for Hamlet in Shakespeare's manuscript at this point: one for the inner-stage at l. 159 or l. 161 and the other for the outer-stage at l. 167 where it now stands. Such a double-entry would have been puzzling to a compositor or a transcriber, and it is not at all surprising to find the first one absent in both the Second Quarto and First Folio texts, seeing that it might easily have been mistaken as a prompt entry,[1] while the Queen's words "But look where sadly the

---

[1] In preparing manuscript play books for performance prompters occasionally repeated entries in the margin a little in advance of those in the original with the intention of bringing "the characters on at the back

poor wretch comes reading" would be accepted as showing which was the entry intended by the author. The omission is rendered all the more probable by the fact that both texts tend to omit important stage-directions, and that on more than one occasion such omissions occur at the same place in both editions.[1]

Hamlet's accidental discovery of the intention to spy upon him has a bearing much wider than his attitude towards Ophelia. Indeed, the manner in which it eases the general working of the plot is strong testimony in its favour. As we shall find, it constitutes the mainspring of the events that follow in acts 2 and 3; it renders the nunnery scene playable and intelligible as never before; it adds all kinds of fresh light and shade to the play scene. In a word, its recovery means the restoration of a highly important piece of the dramatic structure. For the moment, however, let us confine our attention to the matter in hand; and see what it tells us about Hamlet's relations with the daughter of Polonius. Here its value is at once obvious, since it casts its light backward as well as forward and enables us for the first time to see these relations in proper perspective and as a connected whole.

That Hamlet was at one time genuinely in love with Ophelia no serious critic has, I think, ever questioned. Furthermore, she herself tells us that, complying with the warning of Laertes and the commands of Polonius, she

> did repel his letters, and denied
> His access.[2]

of the stage a few moments earlier in order that they may be able to enter into the dialogue at the correct point". Cf. W. W. Greg, *Elizabethan Dramatic Documents*, p. 217.

[1] *Vide The Manuscript of Shakespeare's Hamlet*, II, 186.   [2] 2.1.106–7.

So far all is plain enough; but after this darkness descends, and the commentators grope for a path without a clue. Dr Bradley, the most discerning of them all, having declared that when in doubt a critic ought to say so honestly, goes on: "This is the position in which I find myself in regard to Hamlet's love for Ophelia. I am unable to arrive at a conviction as to the meaning of some of his words and deeds, and I question whether from the mere text of the play a sure interpretation of them can be drawn."[1] He perceives that the love was "mingled with suspicion and resentment, and that his treatment of her was in part due to this cause".[2] Furthermore, he detects "signs that Hamlet was haunted by the horrible idea that he had been deceived in Ophelia as he had been in his mother; that she was shallow and artificial, and even that what had seemed simple and affectionate love might really have been something very different".[3] But when he casts about for the cause of all this he finds nothing but her "rejection" to account for it, and the inadequacy of such an explanation is clearly the root of his perplexity.

Take again his interpretation of the earliest glimpse we get of the two together, the interview in Ophelia's closet. On this he writes:

When Hamlet made his way into Ophelia's room, why did he go in the garb, the conventionally recognised garb, of the distracted *lover*? If it was necessary to convince Ophelia of his insanity, how was it necessary to convince her that disappointment in *love* was the cause of his insanity? His *main* object in the visit appears to

[1] *Shakespearean Tragedy*, p. 153.
[2] *Op. cit.* p. 157.   [3] *Op. cit.* p. 155, n. 2.

have been to convince *others*, through her, that his insanity was not due to any mysterious unknown cause, but to this disappointment, and so to allay the suspicions of the King. But if his feeling for her had been simply that of love, however unhappy, and had not been in any degree that of suspicion or resentment, would he have adopted a plan which must involve her in so much suffering?[1]

The paragraph, written for the sake of the last question which is left unanswered, displays the acumen we look for in its author. For who before Dr Bradley has noticed that Hamlet is in 2.2 alive to the suspicions of his uncle concerning the "antic disposition" and takes steps to furnish an explanation of it? Nevertheless, he is obviously uncomfortable about the suggestion that Hamlet's main purpose in seeking out Ophelia was to hoodwink his uncle, though once again, if that were not his purpose, what was it? he seems to ask.

The double entry for Hamlet at 2.2.159 makes all clear. In marking the exact point at which Hamlet first becomes aware of the suspicions of Claudius and begins himself to grow suspicious of Ophelia, it enables us to take his previous interview with her at its face value without any reading between the lines. The disordered attire was intended, as we have seen, to denote "antic disposition" and has no reference to her rejection of him, though she and her father naturally suppose that it has. On the other hand, Hamlet is of course deeply hurt by her refusal to see him and by the return of his letters; and this explains his silence and the passionate scrutiny of her face: he will not speak unless she first speaks to him. Yet, though she had "denied his access", he has forced himself into her presence. Why? Put aside all preconceived

[1] *Op. cit.* pp. 155–6.

notions of Hamlet, derived from Shakespeare's critics and not from Shakespeare; think of Hamlet as we last saw him, in the cellarage scene, his mind tottering on the verge of insanity; and the meaning of his invasion of her closet is patent enough. Here is the full picture of him, as she gives it:

> Lord Hamlet with his doublet all unbraced,
> No hat upon his head, his stockings fouled,
> Ungart'red, and down-gyvéd to his ankle,
> Pale as his shirt, his knees knocking each other,
> And with a look so piteous in purport
> As if he had been looséd out of hell
> To speak of horrors—he comes before me.

The first three lines prepare us, we have noted, for Hamlet's "antic" appearance in the next scene. But the rest! There can surely be nothing assumed or pretended here. The idea that the interview has been sought by Hamlet in order to suggest that his madness is due to his jilting by Ophelia is out of the question. Love, even "disprized love", does not cause a man's knees to knock together, or give him the look of one fresh from gazing upon all the horrors of Inferno. The lines describe the after-effects of some terrible dream or overpowering delirium, such as was known to attack melancholic subjects; and Shakespeare wrote them, I am convinced, to show us that the mental instability obvious in the cellarage scene, so far from being temporary, had grown more intense meanwhile.

In this state of mind Hamlet turns to Ophelia, the woman he thought loved him, until his mother taught him the value of woman's love and Ophelia herself seemed to confirm the lesson by returning his letters and refusing to see him; turns in the desperate hope of finding even now some comfort and help in her company. But she has nothing for him; and though, as she tells us,

> He falls to such perusal of my face
> As a' would draw it,

her face reflects fear alone, the fear that is still upon her as she relates the story to her father. And so, after a long pause waiting for the help that never comes, he takes his leave:

> At last, a little shaking of mine arm,
> And thrice his head thus waving up and down,
> He raised a sigh so piteous and profound
> As it did seem to shatter all his bulk,
> And end his being; that done, he lets me go,
> And with his head over his shoulder turned
> He seemed to find his way without his eyes,
> For out adoors he went without their helps,
> And to the last bended their light on me.

As a picture of appeal, an appeal extended to the latest possible moment of the meeting, these lines are almost unbearably poignant. To suppose that Shakespeare intended them to represent play-acting on Hamlet's part is absurd. In "sore distraction" of spirit Hamlet instinctively turns for support to the only being left who might give it him. She fails; and the "piteous" sigh shows that he realises her failure, and that all is over between them. Thus she has rejected his love, and proved unresponsive to an appeal of extreme need. He is not yet suspicious of her; but the ground of his mind is ready for suspicion should the seed fall.

Half an hour later Polonius is retailing the scene after his own fashion to the King and Queen, and reading aloud to them one of Hamlet's love-letters. In the general bewilderment concerning the relations between Hamlet and Ophelia some have even believed that this letter is intended to be ironical, and have fastened upon the word "beautified" as evidence of this, comparing it with "I have heard of your paintings", etc., at 3.1.145–7. But (i) the letter must have been written before Ophelia "repelled" Hamlet's correspondence, and (ii) Polonius's condemnation of "beautified" is sufficient to show that it is an innocent word. As a matter of fact it simply means "beautiful" or "endowed with beauty" and is so used by Shakespeare himself in *The Two Gentlemen of Verona*[1] and elsewhere. We may take it, therefore, that the letter is a genuine, if characteristic, love-letter, perhaps one of the earlier ones of the series. It begins, as Dowden remarks, "in the conventional lover's style, which perhaps was what Ophelia would expect from a courtly admirer; then there is a real outbreak of passion and self-pity; finally, in the word 'machine',[2] Hamlet indulges, after his manner, his own intellectuality, though it may baffle the reader; the letter is no more simple or homogeneous than the writer".[3]

Hamlet has little cause to love Polonius, whom he despises as a "tedious old fool", to whose friendship with Claudius he owes the loss of the crown, and who as he is no doubt aware is responsible for Ophelia's jilting of him. When therefore he overhears his proposal to loose his daughter to him, he is consumed with a savage anger. From behind his "antic" mask he lashes out at him, as we have seen; accusing him of playing the pandar, and hinting that the daughter he

[1] 4.1.55–6: "Seeing you are beautified With goodly shape."
[2] Cf. Appendix E, pp. 314–15.
[3] Note on 2.2.116–24 in the "Arden" *Hamlet*.

has been so carefully guarding from him had better not now be left in his path. But everything he says only makes Polonius the more certain that he is mad for love of Ophelia. Hamlet notes the effect of his words, and it is this, I think, which first gives him the idea of feeding Polonius's theory as an explanation of the "antic disposition". For when the old man next enters he harps upon his daughter in his reference to Jephthah, and continues doing so until the play scene is over.

The "fishmonger" episode is, I say, a savage attack upon Polonius; but it does not, except indirectly, reflect upon Ophelia herself. What Hamlet has heard shows him that she is to be used as a decoy; it reveals nothing of her own attitude towards the scheme. That can be tested when the moment comes; and unfortunately Ophelia's conduct then confirms his worst suspicions. But before we consider the nunnery scene itself, and what happens therein, the second theory of the "antic disposition" must be examined, the theory of Uncle Claudius. For there are two men behind the arras when Polonius looses his daughter, and Hamlet's words to her are meant for the ears of them both.

Thwarted ambition

The relations between Hamlet and Ophelia have interested critics far more than those between Hamlet and the King; but the latter are, on the ordinary reading of the play, hardly less obscure. It is generally agreed that Hamlet's apparent madness excites the suspicions of Claudius, but no one seems to ask what these suspicions exactly amount to. Probably this is because, in a vague kind of way, most modern readers of *Hamlet* assume that the King fears his guilty secret may somehow have come to Hamlet's knowledge. But this cannot have been intended by Shakespeare. Dead men tell no tales, unless they return from beyond the grave, which of course they cannot do. Claudius is a practical man; he had no accomplices; the secret is perfectly safe. We can be certain that it is not *that* which troubles him.

Nor is there any real difficulty in perceiving the cause of his suspicions, once the political implications of the play have been grasped. King Claudius is a usurper;[1] and, having stolen the precious diadem and put it in his pocket, he naturally keeps a wary eye upon the rightful owner. On the first occasion they are seen together, he gives the young man much excellent advice on the subject of his "unmanly grief" and politely crosses his purpose to return to Wittenberg; for it is best to keep dangerous persons under direct observation.[2] But he employs all the arts of blandishment upon him; he thrice greets him with the name of "son" (to Hamlet's extreme discomfort); and, as we have noted, he makes a bid for his acceptance of the *fait accompli* by announcing in full Council that he regards him as his heir. The policy is not successful. On the contrary, not only does Hamlet pointedly ignore his advances but the melancholy, which he first ascribes to "unprevailing woe", deepens as time goes on until it develops into a complete "transformation" of

---

[1] *Vide* pp. 30 sqq. above.
[2] Dr Bradley (*op. cit.* p. 130) writes that the King is "so entirely at ease regarding him that he wished him to stay on at Court". I suspect policy in everything Claudius does. Cf. 3.1.191: "Madness in great ones must not unwatched go."*

behaviour. What is Claudius to make of all this? Let the opening words of Bacon's essay "Of Ambition" provide an answer:

Ambition is like choler; which is an humour that maketh men active, earnest, full of alacritie and stirring, if it be not stopped. But if it be stopped, and cannot have his way, it becommeth adust, and thereby maligne and venomous. So ambitious men, if they finde the way open for their rising, and still get forward, they are rather busie then dangerous; but if they be check't in their desires, they become secretly discontent, and looke upon men and matters with an evill eye; and are best pleased when things goe backward; which is the worst propertie in a servant of a prince or state.

Compare this with the King's own diagnosis a little later in the play:

there's something in his soul,
O'er which his melancholy sits on brood,
And I do doubt the hatch and the disclose
Will be some danger[1]—

and it will be seen that the same thought informs both passages.

As I shall point out when I come to discuss Hamlet's character, it is a mistake, of which some modern critics are guilty, to try to fit Shakespeare's creatures and his conceptions of human nature into the procrustean bed of Elizabethan psychology; his vision altogether transcended such limitations. But it is equally unfortunate to leave contemporary notions of the kind out of our reckoning in estimating his dramatic situations. Elizabethan psychology helps us little to solve the mystery of Hamlet; but some

[1] 3.1.167–70.

knowledge of it is essential to the full understanding of what the other characters in the play think about him and his behaviour.* At this time, the usual explanation of melancholy, or the madness which sprang therefrom, was, as Bacon implies, the choking or stopping of "the nimble spirits in the arteries".[1] These vital spirits according to the psycho-physiology of the middle ages, still accepted in Shakespeare's day, were the vehicle of the soul itself and the link between soul and body; so that if they "be impaired, or let of their working in any work, the accord of the body and soul is resolved, the reasonable spirit is let of all its works in the body; as it is seen in them that be amazed, and mad men and frantic, and in others that oft lose use of reason".[2] It follows that the passions, which were motions of the soul, were dependent upon and accompanied by the agitation or activity of the vital spirits; so that if the one were checked the others were checked also.

We may see then what views were likely to be held about Hamlet's distemper by the other characters in the play, by Hamlet himself, and by Shakespeare's audience. They would suppose some stoppage or impairment of his vital spirits, which had caused them to become "adust", that is burnt or dried up, "and thereby maligne and venomous", and had in turn given rise to melancholy, which was technically a morbid condition of the bile. And they would naturally attribute this stoppage to the frustration of some strong passion. Polonius puts it down to disappointed love;

[1] *Love's Labour's Lost*, 4.3.302.
[2] Bartholomew Anglicus quoted in *Mediaeval Lore*, ed. by Robert Steele, p. 31.

Claudius, for his part, ascribes it to thwarted ambition. He does not, be it observed, deny the existence of Hamlet's melancholy, or think it assumed, at any rate at first. He accepts it as genuine enough. What his suspicions centre upon is the cause of the melancholy; seeing that a prince of the blood royal who became melancholy through ambition would grow "secretly discontent and looke upon men and matters with an evill eye...which is the worst propertie" he could have, and so would threaten danger to the state.

At his reception of Rosencrantz and Guildenstern the King does not allow anything of this to appear. As a matter of fact his view is never hinted at in the Queen's hearing, though it is legitimate, I think, to detect its presence behind the words:

> What it should be,
> More than his father's death, that thus hath put him
> So much from th'understanding of himself,
> I cannot dream of.

But that Hamlet's schoolfellows understand the situation well enough is clear from their first interview with the Prince.* When he sees them unexpectedly before him, Hamlet is overjoyed. They are friends of long standing; they are not of Elsinore; and they are a diversion from his thoughts.

> My excellent good friends! How dost thou, Guildenstern?
> Ah, Rosencrantz! Good lads, how do you both?

The greeting is almost as warm as that which he gives to Horatio and Marcellus in 1.2. But he soon cools. After a little young-mannish bawdy talk, recalling their student days together, he asks, as friends did when they met in those days without newspapers, "What's the news?" "None, my lord", replies Rosencrantz, "but that the world's grown honest." An honest world! It seems a monstrous notion to the son of Gertrude, who had himself a few minutes earlier declared that "to be honest, as this world goes, is to be one man picked out of ten thousand."* Nor is it an altogether tactful remark to the dispossessed heir of Denmark. It, therefore, arrests his attention and excites his suspicion, easily awakened after his recent experience in "the lobby". "Then is doomsday near", he remarks drily; and goes on:

But your news is not true. Let me question more in particular: what have you, my good friends, deserved at the hands of Fortune, that she sends you to prison hither?

Guildenstern. Prison, my lord!

Hamlet. Denmark's a prison.

Rosencrantz. Then is the world one.

Hamlet. A goodly one, in which there are many confines, wards and dungeons; Denmark being one o'th'worst.

Rosencrantz. We think not so, my lord.

Hamlet. Why, then 'tis none to you; for there is nothing either good or bad, but thinking makes it so: to me it is a prison.

Rosencrantz. Why, then your ambition makes it one: 'tis too narrow for your mind.

Hamlet. O God! I could be bounded in a nut-shell, and count myself a king of infinite space; were it not that I have bad dreams.

Guildenstern. Which dreams, indeed, are ambition: for the very substance of the ambitious is merely the shadow of a dream.

Hamlet. A dream itself is but a shadow.

Rosencrantz. Truly, and I hold ambition of so airy and light a quality, that it is but a shadow's shadow.

Hamlet. Then are our beggars bodies, and our monarchs and outstretched heroes the beggars' shadows....Shall we to th' court? for, by my fay, I cannot reason.

So he breaks off; and almost immediately afterwards rounds upon them and forces them unwillingly to admit that they have been sent for by "the good king and queen". He does not need to be told "to what end". Nor does he show any further friendliness towards them. He takes the hands they hold out to him because "th'appurtenance of welcome is fashion and ceremony"; but he hints that he prefers the company of the players. And he concludes with the quibble about the hawk and the handsaw, which implies that he is not quite so mad as they and his "uncle-father and aunt-mother" imagine.

Clearly the key-passage in this long word-fence, from which Hamlet emerges victorious, is the thirty lines concerning prison Denmark and Hamlet's ambition just quoted, lines which the commentators appear to have entirely passed over,* though Mr Granville-Barker tells me he never had a doubt about their meaning, while actors and audiences of the seventeenth century tumbled to it readily enough. Of this we have interesting proof in the First Quarto of *Hamlet*, a garbled text based upon notes got together by someone, whether actor or spectator, present at original performances of the play, as all critics are now agreed. This person failed to recall the actual lines in question, and even their general tenor had escaped him, but he was quite clear as to their dramatic significance: they had something to do with the succession in Denmark. Accordingly, his mind consciously or unconsciously reverted to the only other occasion when

Hamlet and his "friends" directly refer to the topic, viz. the dialogue at 3.2.338–44, which runs:

Rosencrantz. Good my lord, what is your cause of distemper? you do surely bar the door upon your own liberty, if you deny your griefs to your friend.
Hamlet. Sir, I lack advancement.
Rosencrantz. How can that be, when you have the voice of the king himself for your succession in Denmark.

This dialogue he reproduced, as best he could, and set down here, as the text of the First Quarto witnesses:

Ham. Nay then I see how the wind sits,
Come, you were sent for.
Ross. My lord, we were, and willingly if we might,
Know the cause and ground of your discontent.
Ham. Why I want preferment.
Ross. I thinke not so my lord.

The report is clumsy and crude, and it is misplaced; yet Shakespeare's intentions, so subtly expressed in the genuine version that modern readers have overlooked them, shine through the distortion all the more unmistakably. The change from "distemper" to "discontent" is a good illustration of what I mean: psychology has become politics.

The thirty lines about ambition are political also. The passage shows us what the King suspects and puts Hamlet completely on his guard. The two friends, acting under instructions, are sifting him "to gather as much as from occasion they can glean". But it is Hamlet himself who leads them on to the subject of ambition. For directly their declaration of belief in the world's honesty has arrested his attention he arrests theirs in turn by calling Denmark a

prison. The epithet is true enough: Denmark *is* a prison for
him.[1] But they swallow the bait with avidity. "Prison, my
lord!" exclaims Guildenstern, with a meaning glance at
Rosencrantz. When the heir apparent calls his heritage a
prison, something must be seriously wrong; and it is not
difficult to guess what the something is. In a moment they
are swooping at him like a couple of untrained hawks, with
clumsy suggestions about his ambition. Hamlet eludes them
every time, and in the end bluntly changes the conversation;
but he leaves them with something to ponder over, not only
in the talk of the prison, but in his insistence upon his
disinheritance.

As we have seen, Hamlet is not insensible to the loss of the
throne; and he expresses dissatisfaction with his lot both in
the two direct outbursts against the "cutpurse" who has
robbed him[2] and in references elsewhere. For example, at
the end of the scene in which Horatio and Marcellus tell him
of the Ghost, he says "I will requite your loves", that is he
will, after the manner of princes in that age, recompense
them for the trouble they are taking; and he repeats the
promise at the end of the cellarage scene in these words:

> And what so poor a man as Hamlet is
> May do t'express his love and friending to you
> God willing shall not lack.

Here he is clearly hinting at his loss of the throne, which is
again referred to in the jocular suggestion to Horatio, after
the success of his Gonzago-play, that he might join a company of players, if the rest of his fortunes turn Turk with
him.[3] And so in the dialogue before us, when Rosencrantz

[1] *Vide* Appendix E, p. 318.   [2] *Vide* above, p. 30.   [3] 3.2.275–8.

and Guildenstern obsequiously offer to "wait upon" him at
court, he replies: "No such matter: I will not sort you with
the rest of my servants; for to speak to you like an honest
man, I am most dreadfully attended." Editors have interpreted this as referring to his "bad dreams". But that he
intends his interlocutors at any rate to take it in the literal
sense is proved by what follows. The speech continues: "But,
in the beaten way of friendship, what make you at Elsinore?"
"To visit you, my lord," replies Rosencrantz, "no other
occasion." To which Hamlet, identifying himself with the
real men of his earlier speech as distinguished from the
"monarchs and outstretched heroes" which are their shadows,
ironically retorts: "Beggar that I am, I am even poor in
thanks, but I thank you."

They will remember these hints later no doubt, but for the
moment they are nonplussed, as appears from their report to
Claudius in the following scene. The latter's question to
them,

> And can you by no drift of conference
> Get from him why he puts on his confusion,
> Grating so harshly all his days of quiet,
> With turbulent and dangerous lunacy?—

indicates the nature of the mission he has entrusted to them,
since "drift of conference", which the Second Quarto reads
in place of the colourless "drift of circumstance" that all
modern editors have taken over from the Folio text, means
"leading him on in cunning talk".* Clearly, too, the only
"drift" they had attempted was that leading in the direction
of his ambitions. They conceal the fact that he has succeeded
in unmasking *them* and has forced them to admit themselves

agents of "the good king and queen". But they acknowledge defeat:

> *Rosencrantz.* He does confess he feels himself distracted,
> But from what cause a' will by no means speak.
> *Guildenstern.* Nor do we find him forward to be sounded,
> But with a crafty madness keeps aloof
> When we would bring him on to some confession
> Of his true state.

Once again, these words can only refer to the talk about ambition which Hamlet had so adroitly evaded. And his attitude towards them, together with the blend of reserve and apparent readiness to talk, as in the long speech describing the symptoms of his distemper, is reflected in what follows:

> *Queen.* Did he receive you well?
> *Rosencrantz.* Most like a gentleman.
> *Guildenstern.* But with much forcing of his disposition.
> *Rosencrantz.* Niggard of question, but of our demands
> Most free in his reply.

As often elsewhere, Shakespeare in his report of what happens in a previous scene furnishes exact instructions for the acting of it, instructions which have here been generally overlooked by both players and critics. Yet the mission of the two spies has not been entirely fruitless. The news of the players and of the intended play pleases Claudius greatly; he will attend with all his heart,

> and it doth much content me
> To hear him so inclined.
> Good gentlemen, give him a further edge,
> And drive his purpose into these delights.

The words once again emphasise that to him Hamlet, though dangerous, is an invalid, and that it is his policy to cure him of his melancholy so that he will cease to brood over his wrongs.[1]

We are left, then, at the end of the episode with the knowledge that the King is no nearer his objective, and that his sifting process has so far proved of no avail. It is, therefore, the turn of Polonius to try his hand. Hamlet, on his side however, has scored heavily. He has learnt all he needs, and will make much capital out of it. How he does so in the nunnery scene and the play scene we are now to examine.

The nunnery scene

Rosencrantz and Guildenstern go out, and the scene begins to shape itself for the eavesdropping. The King bids the Queen leave him with Polonius and Ophelia; and tells her of their purpose. He insists, and she accepts the point without question, that they are "lawful espials". The innocent little scheme is justified in the interests of Denmark, and of Hamlet himself; and she expresses the hope that the outcome will bring happiness for them all, Ophelia included. Gertrude is always hoping for the best. The King's words,

> For we have closely sent for Hamlet hither,
> That he, as 'twere by accident, may here
> Affront Ophelia,

should be carefully noted in passing, if we wish to understand exactly what follows. Hamlet is not coming to the lobby of his own motion; he has been sent for. Not, of course, ostensibly by Claudius, but "closely", that is privately or

[1] *Vide* above, p. 118.

without his knowledge of the real sender of the message. Nevertheless some kind of pretext has been given; and, when he arrives, he will find, not what he expects, but Ophelia. There would be no flaw in this expedient, if the object of it had not happened to overhear the whole plot the day before.

The snare is now laid; the decoy made to appear at once innocent and tempting; and the fowlers take cover. Polonius gives Ophelia a prayer-book, and says "walk you here"; "here" being, of course, the lobby at the back of the stage. There is, however, a theatrical tradition that she should be kneeling when Hamlet enters,* which is I think a sound one; for, if she is only walking up and down with a book in her hands, how does he know that she is at her "orisons"? I presume, therefore, that some kind of prie-dieu stood in the lobby. Finally, before actually "bestowing" himself behind the arras, Claudius utters an aside, which it is also important not to miss. "Read on this book", says the moralising father to his daughter,

> That show of such an exercise may colour
> Your loneliness; we are oft to blame in 'this,
> 'Tis too much proved, that with devotion's visage
> And pious action we do sugar o'er
> The devil himself;

upon which the King comments to himself:

> O, 'tis too true,
> How smart a lash that speech doth give my conscience.
> The harlot's cheek, beautied with plast'ring art,
> Is not more ugly to the thing that helps it,
> Than is my deed to my most painted word:
> O heavy burden!

It is the first indication in the play that Claudius possesses a conscience; and it leads up to the "blenching" in the play scene and to the prayer that follows. But there is more in it than this. The reference, after "devotion's visage", to

> The harlot's cheek, beautied with plast'ring art

is leitmotiv on Shakespeare's part. The linked images hark back to the "fishmonger" and his "good kissing carrion"; and reopen a theme which Hamlet will presently elaborate.

Hamlet walks into the trap in complete unconsciousness. As he enters, his mind is not on the plot, his uncle or Ophelia. If he remembers the Ghost at all, it is to write it off as a snare of the evil one. He is back again where he was when we first had sight of his inner self; back in the mood of the soliloquy which begins

> O that this too too sullied flesh would melt,
> Thaw and resolve itself into a dew,
> Or that the Everlasting had not fixed
> His canon 'gainst self-slaughter.

But he is no longer thinking of his own "sullied flesh", still less of the divine command. By constantly turning it over he has worn the problem to the bone:

> To be, or not to be, that is the question.

A like expression of utter weariness is not to be found in the rest of human literature. Sleep, death, annihilation, his whole mind is concentrated upon these; and the only thing that holds his arm from striking home with "the bare bodkin" is the thought of "what dreams may come", "the dread of something after death". For he is without the consolations of Lucretius. He believes in immortality, which means that by death he may exchange one nightmare for a worse.

Eternity has him in a trap, which dwarfs the little traps of Claudius and Polonius to nothingness. No one but Shakespeare could have interrupted an exciting dramatic intrigue with a passage like this. The surprise and the audacity of it take our breath away, and render the pity of it the more overwhelming.

As the meditation finishes, Hamlet sees Ophelia behind him upon her knees. The sight reminds him of nothing except "the pangs of disprized love", and those have long been drowned in "a sea of troubles". "The fair Ophelia!" he exclaims; the words have no warmth in them. And, when he addresses her, he speaks in irony:

> Nymph, in thy orisons
> Be all my sins remembered.

Romantic actors interpret this as gushing tenderness; and even Johnson calls it "an address grave and solemn, such as the foregoing meditation excited in his thoughts". Dowden, however, sees "estrangement in the word 'nymph'"; and I find deliberate affectation in that word and in "orisons".* They are both pretentious expressions, while the reference to "all my sins", the sins for which she has jilted him, the sins he will enlarge upon later in the scene, surely indicates a sardonic tone. In any event, it is certain that most critics have completely misunderstood the dialogue that follows, because in their sympathy with Ophelia they have forgotten that it is not Hamlet who has "repelled" her, but she him.[1] She had refused to see him and had returned his letters; she could not even speak a word of comfort when in deep trouble he forced his way into her room with mute pitiable appeal.

[1] Professor J. Q. Adams is an exception (*op. cit.* pp. 253–4).

After that he had done with her; and the Ophelia he now meets is a stranger. Stranger indeed! For listen:

> Good my lord,
> How does your honour for this many a day?

Is she implying that *he* has neglected *her*? It was only yesterday he had been with her despite her denial of his access. But at first he takes small note of her words and answers with polite aloofness:

> I humbly thank you, well, well, well.

It is a form of address he employs later with people like the Norwegian Captain and Osric,[1] while the repeated "well" sounds bored.[2] Nevertheless, she continues:

> My lord, I have remembrances of yours,
> That I have longed long to re-deliver.
> I pray you now receive them.

What should that mean? Once again, however, he brushes it aside: "I never gave *you* aught,"—the woman to whom I once gave gifts is dead. Yet still she persists:

> My honoured lord, you know right well you did,
> And with them words of so sweet breath composed
> As made the things more rich. Their perfume lost,
> Take these again, for to the noble mind
> Rich gifts wax poor when givers prove unkind.
> There, my lord.

And here she draws the trinkets from her bosom and places them on the table before him.

---

[1] 4.4.29; 5.2.83.
[2] Dowden, whose notes are very suggestive at this point, interprets the repetition as "impatience".

The unhappy girl has sadly overplayed her part. Her little speech, ending with a sententious couplet, as Dowden notes, "has an air of being prepared". Worse than that, she, the jilt, is accusing him of coldness towards her. Worst of all, Hamlet who has been "sent for", who meets her in the lobby "by accident", finds her prepared not only with a speech but with the gifts also. She means no harm; she has romantically arranged a little play scene, in the hope no doubt of provoking a passionate declaration of affection, which perhaps

Will bring him to his wonted way again,

as the Queen had remarked just before Hamlet's entrance, and will at any rate prove to the King that she and her father are right in their diagnosis of the distemper.[1] But the effect upon Hamlet is disastrous. Until that moment he had forgotten the plot; it is a far cry from thoughts of "the undiscovered country" to this discovery. But he is now thoroughly awake, and sees it all. Here is the lobby and the decoy, playing a part, only too unblushingly; and there at the back is the arras, behind which lurk the Fishmonger and Uncle Claudius. His wild "Ha, ha!" the fierce question "are you honest?" that is to say "are you not a whore?" together with a significant glance round the room, are enough to show the audience that he realises at last, and warn them to expect "antic disposition". Everything he says for the rest of the scene is intended for the ears of the eavesdroppers. As for the daughter who has been "loosed" to him, she will only get what she deserves. For play-acting has completed her downfall in his eyes. First the abrupt breaking-off of all

[1] J. Q. Adams (*op. cit.* pp. 254–5) suggests that she acts under her father's orders; but this seems going too far.

intercourse between them, without any reason given, then the failure to meet his last appeal, then the overhearing of the plot in which she was to take a leading part, and last this willing and all too facile participation: is it surprising that to an imagination "as foul as Vulcan's stithy" such things should appear in the worst possible light, or that he should treat her from henceforth as the creature he believes her to be? He puts her to one final test before the scene is over; but the dice are loaded against her. Thus, through a chain of misconceptions, due to nothing worse than narrowness of vision and over-readiness to comply with her father's commands, Ophelia blackens her own character in her lover's eyes. The process has been obscured hitherto owing to the absence of one important link in the chain; but the link now in place makes all clear, explains Hamlet's attitude, and shows her fate as even more pathetic than we had supposed.

Everything he says, I repeat, for the rest of the scene is intended for the ears of Claudius and Polonius, whom he knows to be behind the arras. The restored entry at 2.2.159 happily rids us of the traditional stage-business of Polonius exposing himself to the eye of Hamlet and the audience, which has hitherto been the only way open to stage-managers of putting any meaning at all into the scene.[1] It is a trick at once crude and inadequate: crude, because the chief councillor of Denmark is neither stupid nor clumsy, and to represent him so, as producers are apt to do, is to degrade intrigue to

---

[1] I refer to the common practice of causing Polonius to stick out his head; some producers adopt the subtler device of a mere movement of the arras, sufficient no doubt for a modern audience which knows its *Hamlet* but not, I think, for Elizabethans.

buffoonery[1]; inadequate, because it only tells Hamlet of one, whereas his words clearly lose a great deal of force if he is not known to be conscious of the presence of two. He speaks at both; but he speaks, of course, to Ophelia, while as he speaks he has yet a fourth person constantly in mind, his mother. If this be remembered, and if we also keep in view Hamlet's habitual lack of self-control once he becomes excited, the dialogue is easy to follow.

I return to it:

Hamlet. Ha, ha! are you honest?
Ophelia. My lord?
Hamlet. Are you fair?
Ophelia. What means your lordship?
Hamlet. That if you be honest and fair, your honesty should admit no discourse to your beauty.

If, that is, you were the chaste maiden you pretend to be, you would not allow your beauty to be used as a bait in this fashion. Ophelia, of course, misunderstands and, supposing him to mean that her beauty and his honesty ought not to discourse together, wonderingly enquires: "Could beauty, my lord, have better commerce than with honesty?"* To which he, twisting her words back to his own meaning, replies:

Ay truly, for the power of beauty will sooner transform honesty from what it is to a bawd, than the force of honesty can translate beauty into his likeness. This was sometime a paradox, but now the time gives it proof.

[1] Perhaps the most memorable feature of the never-to-be-forgotten performances of *Hamlet* in modern dress by the Birmingham Repertory Company was the playing of Polonius as a dapper and exceedingly shrewd diplomatist, a worthy "assistant for a state", but ageing and allowing his shrewdness to o'er-reach itself.

To paraphrase again: "physical Beauty is stronger than virtue, and will make use of Virtue herself as her procuress. People used to think this incredible, but your conduct proves its truth." He refers to "devotion's visage" and the "pious action" with which Ophelia had tried to "sugar o'er" her designs upon him. But he is probably also thinking of his mother's conduct, as is suggested by the talk of "our old stock" that follows. Indeed, from this point onwards Ophelia becomes identified in his mind with the Frailty whose name is Woman, and that in turn leads to thoughts of his own "sullied flesh". He goes on: "I did love you once", that is, before my mother took off the rose

> From the fair forehead of an innocent love.

But a son of Gertrude is "rank and gross in nature" and capable of nothing except lust; so that I did not really love you. "Conception is a blessing", but what children could a man like me and a woman like you hope for save a brood of sinners? Better a nunnery!★

So far Hamlet's talk has been in fishmonger-vein, and is meant for the Jephthah behind the arras. But now is the turn for Uncle Claudius. The mention of corrupt stock leads by natural transition to an elaborate confession of criminal propensities on Hamlet's part which *we* know to be ridiculous, but which is intended to make the King's blood run cold. "I am very proud, revengeful, ambitious" is the gist of it. Could any other three epithets be found less appropriate to Hamlet? But Claudius says he is ambitious; and Claudius is a reasonable man. The following, too, sounds terrible:

with more offences at my beck, than I have thoughts to put them in, imagination to give them shape, or time to act them in:

—until we scan it and find that it amounts to nothing at all, since the same might be said of any mortal.

At this point Hamlet gives Ophelia her last chance with his sudden "Where's your father?" She answers with a lie, as it would seem to him, though of course she is observing the most ordinary precautions and, as she thinks, humouring a madman. But it is this crowning proof of her treachery, I suggest, that provokes the frenzy with which the episode closes. He goes out, perhaps in the hope that the rats may emerge from their hole and that he may catch them in the act of so doing. Twice he rushes from the room and with each return his manner grows more excited. His two final speeches are mainly food for fishmongers, and he concludes by coming very near to calling Ophelia a prostitute to her face. The repeated injunction "to a nunnery go" is significant in this connection, since "nunnery" was in common Elizabethan use a cant term for a house of ill-fame.[1] And that this was the traditional interpretation of Hamlet's meaning on the seventeenth-century stage is shown by the *Der bestrafte Brudermord* which makes him say "go to a nunnery, but not to a nunnery where two pairs of slippers lie at the bed side".[2]

As he leaves for the last time he throws his uncle one more morsel to chew: "I say we will have no mo marriage—those that are married already, *all but one*, shall live, the rest shall keep as they are." Why, it may be asked, does Hamlet deliberately and recklessly threaten the King in this way? Partly, as I have already suggested, because Hamlet always acts as if he

---

[1] *Vide O.E.D.* "nunnery" 1 *b*, quoting Fletcher's *Mad Lover*, 4.2 ("There's an old nunnery at hand. What's that? A bawdy-house."), Nashe's *Christ's Tears* (McKerrow's edition of *Nashe*, II, 152), etc.

[2] *Vide* Furness, *Variorum Hamlet*, II, 128.

were just on the point of killing his uncle, and partly for reasons which will become clear later. In any event, these threats show that the Prince has thoroughly grasped the hints about ambition dropped by Rosencrantz and Guildenstern; and is now posing as the discontented heir thirsting for revenge, a rôle he will play to remarkable purpose in the next scene.

After Hamlet's final departure, Ophelia is given twelve lines of lamentation over his fallen state, before the espials steal warily from their hiding place, a circumspection natural after his repeated exits, but surely enough to warn us that Polonius, with whom caution is almost a disease, could never have revealed his presence to Hamlet, as the traditional stage practice makes him do.* The discussion of what they have heard shows that their points of view have in no way converged. Claudius scornfully dismisses the forlorn love theory; nor does he think that melancholy has yet developed into utter madness. But Hamlet has said enough to prove himself to be in a very dangerous frame of mind; too dangerous to remain any longer near the royal person:

> He shall with speed to England,
> For the demand of our neglected tribute.
> Haply the seas, and countries different,
> With variable objects, shall expel
> This something-settled matter in his heart,
> Whereon his brains still beating puts him thus
> From fashion of himself.

At present Claudius thinks of England as a health-resort; it is only after the play scene that he sees it as a grave. Polonius agrees with the scheme but cannot subscribe to his royal master's diagnosis of the disease. "But yet I do believe", he mutters while assenting to the projected voyage,

> The origin and commencement of his grief
> Sprung from neglected love;

and he urges that the theory shall be put to one more test before the voyage takes place. This obstinate clinging to his own opinion is to have, we shall find, important dramatic consequences in the play scene which now follows.

V

THE MULTIPLE MOUSE-TRAP

Make mad the guilty and appal the free,
Confound the ignorant, and amaze indeed
The very faculties of eyes and ears.

THE MULTIPLE MOUSE-TRAP

The parallel sub-plots

The play scene is the central point of *Hamlet*. It is the climax and crisis of the whole drama. Yet it remains almost wholly unintelligible to the modern reader and playgoer. Three points alone are clear: that Hamlet treats Ophelia in a very offensive manner, that the dialogue between the Player King and Queen has direct reference to the second marriage of Gertrude, and that the speech of the murderer leaves Claudius "marvellous distempered". For the rest, the dumb-show is usually omitted on our stage, the Gonzago-play seems long-winded and tedious, most of Hamlet's comments are delivered as the more or less incomprehensible ravings of pretended madness, and the actor who represents him is obliged to sustain the interest of the audience by the vulgar trick of wriggling across the boards to Claudius's feet like a snake. In short, everything is done to belittle and obscure the interlude upon the inner-stage, to slur over the cryptic utterances of the Prince, and to concentrate the whole attention of the spectators upon two *faces*, those of Hamlet and Claudius. These faces play an important part in the scene, and Shakespeare undoubtedly intended us to watch them carefully. But to make them the only thing worthy of notice, as is done in the modern theatre, is to reduce an incomparable piece of dramatic literature to the level of pantomime.

I would ask those who think they understand the play scene to read over Shakespeare's pages again, and then to find answers to the following questions: How is it that the players bring with them to Elsinore a drama which reproduces in minute detail all the circumstances of the King's crime? What is the dramatic purpose of the long conversation between Hamlet and the First Player immediately before the play begins? Why is the play preceded by a dumb-show? Why does not Claudius show any signs of discomfiture at this dumb-show, which is a more complete representation of the circumstances of the murder than the play which follows it? What is Hamlet's object in making the murderer the nephew and not the brother of the king? Why should the courtiers, who know nothing of the real poisoning, assume later that Hamlet has behaved outrageously to his uncle and even threatened him with death?[1] These are questions which vitally affect the scene as a whole, and without a satisfactory answer to each one of them it is impossible even to know what is happening. A few, on minor points, may be added by way of showing how far we are as yet from appreciating this, the most exciting episode in Shakespeare's greatest drama. What is the exact significance of Hamlet's "I eat the air, promise-crammed"? Why does he lead Polonius on to speak of the assassination of Julius Caesar? To whom and what does "miching mallecho" refer? For what reason does Shakespeare introduce the Prologue, with his ridiculous jingling posy? Why does Hamlet preface the speech of the murderer with that extraordinary remark, "The croaking raven doth bellow for revenge"?

[1] Cf. pp. 164 sqq.

Here are eleven queries about a scene of some 180 lines in length, and not a single one of them can be answered with any certainty on the accepted reading of the play. Is Shakespeare, therefore, a bungler, a slipshod dramatist, who leaves loose ends and banal obscurities thickly scattered over the central scene of his most famous drama? Previous chapters have shown that apparent obscurities may be explained and elucidated through the recovery of elements in the plot which have been lost or forgotten. Owing to its crucial character and its central position, the play scene is the point at which all the threads of the plot may be expected to meet. An examination, therefore, of the play scene should not merely confirm the clues already discovered but bring fresh ones to light.

We shall do well to start with a collection of problems which may be described as technical—problems that affect the construction of the play as a whole, and lead us into the workshop of the master-craftsman himself. Chief among these is the parallelism between the Gonzago-play and the circumstances of Claudius's crime. It is curiously detailed and precise. The garden scene, the afternoon nap, the nature of the drug, the method of the poisoning, the wooing of the queen, the seizure of the crown: all are duplicated. The Ghost's story and the Gonzago story are one, except in three apparently trivial particulars: the place of action is in the one case Elsinore and in the other Vienna; Baptista, unlike Gertrude, is not guilty of adultery; and Lucianus is the nephew, not the brother, of the king. Now it is surely clear that this coincidence is deliberate and purely structural; the two inner plots, so strangely alike, are two main pillars of the play, which run up into a great arch and meet in the play scene; remove them, or disturb their balance by alterations, and the whole drama would come toppling down. That the parallelism is fundamental, and has no bearing on the characters and the dramatic plot, is proved by the fact that we were not intended to dwell upon it at all. Once we begin to do so, we are faced with the fact that the players arrive at Elsinore with an item in their repertory which embodies a detailed account of the assassination of King Hamlet, an account which must have been written before that crime actually took place. And yet three centuries of spectators and readers have found no difficulty in swallowing the coincidence; they have been conscious of it, otherwise the play scene would have lost the last shred of its meaning, but they have seen nothing strange or incredible in it. In fact, the first critic to bring out the point clearly was Dr W. W. Greg, in the article spoken of in my first chapter.

How it was all contrived will be seen if we run over the references to the Gonzago-play before the play scene. They are strikingly meagre. The idea of having a play was a sudden inspiration on Hamlet's part; as ever, when he acts, he acts on impulse. He knows nothing of the advent of the players at court until Rosencrantz informs him at 2.2.320; and they enter shortly after in the course of the same scene. The First Player, at Hamlet's invitation, then recites the Pyrrhus speech; and it is during this recitation that the Gonzago scheme takes root in Hamlet's brain, for, as the rest of the actors go out with Polonius, the Prince stops the First Player; asks him if he can play *The Murder of Gonzago*; tells him to have it ready by "to-morrow night"; and bids him "study a speech of some dozen or sixteen lines" which he will in the meantime "set down and insert in't". The working of Hamlet's mind during all this is made clear by the "rogue and peasant slave" soliloquy which follows. What could not the actor effect, he asks,

> Had he the motive and the cue for passion
> That I have? he would drown the stage with tears
> And cleave the general ear with horrid speech,
> Make mad the guilty and appal the free.

And later we have the scheme revealed[1] in the words:

> I'll have these players
> Play something like the murder of my father
> Before mine uncle, I'll observe his looks,
> I'll tent him to the quick, if a' do blench
> I know my course.

In the following scene the King and Queen hear of the projected play and promise to attend; while, at the opening of the

---

[1] A friendly correspondent enquires "how it is that in 2.2.541 Hamlet asks the players to play *The Murder of Gonzago* (and to be allowed to insert certain lines), and only after the players are gone hits on the idea of so doing".* The reply is, that we are to suppose Hamlet "hitting on" the Gonzago scheme while the First Player recites the Pyrrhus speech and that Shakespeare communicates this to us by means of an expository soliloquy, a soliloquy, that is, which recapitulates Hamlet's emotions as the Player's recitation proceeds: his amazement at the force of the simulated passion, his shamed recollection of his own comparative lethargy and dulness, his hysterical and overwrought fury against his uncle, his sudden inspiration to use the players in order to bring the matter to a final test. Thus, though the soliloquy is actually uttered after the players have gone out, it is in effect a dramatic reflection of what has already taken place and as such is an interesting example of one use of the soliloquy convention, for which *vide* M. Bradbrook, *Themes and Conventions of Elizabethan Tragedy*, pp. 111–36.

next scene after that, we find the stage all ready for the play, and Hamlet giving the First Player his final directions how his inserted speech should be spoken. The players then go out to dress for the performance; and Hamlet has his conversation with Horatio, in the course of which he informs him

> There is a play to-night before the king,
> One scene of it comes near the circumstance
> Which I have told you of my father's death,

and bids him, when he sees that act afoot,

> Observe my uncle—if his occulted guilt
> Do not itself unkennel in one speech,
> It is a damnéd ghost that we have seen.

Immediately after this the play scene itself begins.

Thus, before the play scene opens, the audience in the theatre knows nothing of the interlude except that it is called *The Murder of Gonzago*, that it is "something like the murder" of the late king, and that Hamlet himself has inserted a short speech in it, which will presumably make the likeness still clearer. Obviously we are here confronted with a piece of dramaturgy. The idea of having a play within the play, we can imagine Shakespeare saying to himself, is attended with certain difficulties. To serve its dramatic purpose, the actors' play must come as close as possible to the situation at the Danish court; for not only has Hamlet to catch the King's conscience, but I have to catch and rivet the attention of my audience. "Something like" will not do at all; it must be identical or, at least, differing only in such a way as will indicate that it is another story, without impairing the overwhelming dramatic effect of its similarity upon the minds of

Claudius and my spectators. But if the differences are small, as they must be for the scene to effect its purpose, might not the audience begin asking themselves how it comes about that the actors should have a play, the plot of which is to all intents identical with what had taken place at Elsinore? To avoid such questions it will be necessary to cover up my tracks, to throw them off the scent. They shall be told that the Gonzago story is "something like the murder" of the late king, that "one scene of it comes near the circumstance" of the actual poisoning, that Hamlet has adapted it; but they shall know nothing more about the matter until they see the play itself. Thus they will be prepared for similarity, part of which they will assume due to Hamlet's adaptation, while in the excitement of the play scene itself, when the almost complete identity of the two plots breaks upon them for the first time, their minds will be far too busy with other things to be enquiring where the actors got the play from.

The problem of the dumb-show *

The parallelism between the Gonzago-play and the circumstances of Claudius's crime, as revealed by the Ghost, is therefore part of the architectural scheme of the play as a whole, which Shakespeare never intended us to observe. He throws the audience off the scent by keeping them in ignorance of the details right up to the play scene. But he does more than this. Like an honest craftsman he conceals his structural design, not so much by covering it up as by letting his lines run off into all kinds of tracery and foliation, which catch the eye of the onlooker and, once again, prevent him prying into the secrets of the structure. The key-stone of the Ghost–Gonzago arch is the dumb-show of the play scene, framed with the most beautiful and delicate carved work. Nevertheless, the dumb-show itself is no mere ornamental flourish; it is as essential to the stability of the edifice as the arch of which it is the key-stone. For remove it, and what happens? The play scene is ruined. The players' play without the dumb-show consists of seventy lines of dialogue between a king and a queen about second marriage, followed by six lines uttered by an entirely unexpected character, who thereupon without warning of any kind proceeds to poison the sleeping king. It is not a play; it is not even a scene; it is a piece of a scene, terminated by Claudius at the very moment when the only action which occurs in it is about to take place.

There are several reasons why Shakespeare was obliged to truncate and obscure his players' play in this fashion. In the first place, as I have just said, it could not be given as a whole because it was to be interrupted before the end. It was necessary, again, to confine most if not all the dialogue to the theme of second marriages, because, as we shall see, part of Hamlet's intention is to test his mother. But the chief reason was that there was Claudius to think of. The play is a Mouse-trap, the jaws of which must snap upon the imprisoned victim suddenly, unexpectedly, overwhelmingly. Had there been too much parallelism in the spoken play, or indeed any clear hint of the coming murder, the King would have seen the trap, and would either have prematurely taken fright or have had an opportunity of screwing himself up to endure the spectacle of his crime and so perhaps have avoided giving himself away in Hamlet's eyes. He must be lured gradually and unconsciously into the trap, and then caught—squealing. In other words, the audience must feel satisfied that he knows nothing of what awaits him, until the jaws snap; if they do not feel this, the sport of the great Claudius-drive will be spoilt.

He must know nothing, but they must know everything. How, then, was Shakespeare to make the parallelism plain to the spectators? Neither before nor during the play can he *tell* them what is going to happen. Yet somehow he must take them into his confidence, for, unless the identity of the Gonzago story and the speech of the Ghost is made absolutely clear, the dramatic effect of the play scene may altogether miscarry with the generality. Not only will they fail to anticipate the climax and so miss the keen pleasure of watching, with Hamlet, the unconscious Mouse drawing nearer and nearer the trap; they will not fully understand what is taking place at all. It seems at first sight a pretty dilemma; how did Shakespeare get out of it? Stage-craft offered him the means of escape. *He put the whole plot into a dumb-show.* "Belike this show", remarks Ophelia, who gives us the clue not for the last time in this scene, "imports the argument of the play." It does; and it imports so successfully that we do not notice anything wrong about the play while it is being acted. The dumb-show is, as it were, a flash of revelation, which discloses to even the stupidest member of the audience all the facts he needs to know at the earliest possible moment of the scene; and then fades as suddenly as it has come.

That such was the technical purpose of the dumb-show is borne out by the fact that there appears to be no other example in Elizabethan drama of a dumb-show setting forth an argument.[1] The device, which was a common one and by no means growing old-fashioned by the date of *Hamlet* as some suppose,* was normally employed either (i) to foreshadow the contents of a play (or an act) by means of a *symbolical* or *historical* tableau, as when for example, to quote Creizenach, "in *The Spanish Tragedy* the fearful termination of the wedding feast is prefigured in dumb-show, in which torch-bearers enter, followed by a black-robed Hymen who blows out their torches"; or (ii) to save the dramatist the trouble of composing dialogue for part of the action by representing it in pantomime, which was often then "explained by some one acting as intermediary between performers and audience, this person being usually designated as Chorus, but sometimes as Presenter". The dumb-show in *Hamlet* belongs to neither category; it is an anticipation in full action of the spoken scene that follows, and as such would be entirely superfluous in any ordinary drama. For his Gonzago-play Shakespeare could not do without an argument in pantomime; and he is careful to inform the spectators, through the mouth of Ophelia, that the show is intended to perform this unusual function lest any doubt should linger in their minds about the parallelism. He also makes amusing use of the convention of the presenter, as we shall see later.

It may here be objected that a dumb-show which is generally omitted on the modern stage can hardly be as dramatically essential as I claim. The omission, however, is only feasible because the modern producer thinks he can

[1] Creizenach, *English Drama in the Age of Shakespeare*, pp. 388–90; cf. also Hunter *apud* Furness, *Variorum Hamlet*, note 3.2.127.

safely assume that the bulk of his audience "know their *Hamlet*" before they enter the theatre, having read the play at school or elsewhere; that in fact they already possess the information which the dumb-show was designed to communicate to them. Moreover, the assumption is sometimes incorrect; and I have myself, sitting in the gallery, where Shakespearian criticism is always interesting because at its most fearless and unliterary, overheard a discussion between two spectators who were mystified by the Gonzago-play simply because the story of *Hamlet* was new to them and the producer had deprived them of the assistance which Shakespeare provided. *Hamlet* was not written for ex-pupils of modern secondary schools, but for Elizabethans, many of them illiterate, who came to the theatre without any previous knowledge of the play, and for whom the outline of the story could not be made too plain. For it is the outline we are here concerned with; subtler dramatic points, intended for the "censure" of the judicious, might pass over the heads of the groundlings, as Shakespeare knew well enough.

But, I hear others object, did not Shakespeare find the dumb-show in the old *Hamlet* and just take it over as it stood without much thought about it one way or another? And is not, therefore, all talk of design on his part beside the mark? The answer to this is, first, that we do not know what the old *Hamlet* contained. The Bad Quarto text of 1603, it is true, gives us an argument-dumb-show before the Gonzago-play, but that tells us little, since it probably means nothing more than that the pirate was setting down what he remembered of the performance of Shakespeare's *Hamlet* at the Globe. And, if we enquire of the late and very corrupt *Der bestrafte*

Brudermord for evidence, we find something still less helpful,
viz. a dumb-show without any spoken play to follow. Even,
however, if we grant the premiss, if we assume that Shakespeare did borrow both dumb-show and Gonzago-play from
his predecessor, from Kyd or some other, there still remains
a second reply to the objection. A revising dramatist, who
takes over material from the play he is working upon, accepts
thereby responsibility for it. And that Shakespeare accepted
the responsibility consciously is shown by the comments of
Hamlet and Ophelia on the dumb-show immediately it is
finished, which prove it to be an integral and deliberate part
of his text. This being so, it is incredible that he, a practical
man of the theatre, would have retained so elaborate a
stage-business, which involves the provision of "a bank of
flowers"* together with pantomime by six or seven players,
unless he attached some dramatic significance to it. Those
who see no need for the dumb-show are, in effect, charging
Shakespeare with a surprising lack of consideration for his
fellows at the Globe. They do more; they impute gross
carelessness, since if they are right he must have borrowed the
dumb-show from the old play without noticing that it
creates an exceedingly awkward dramatic situation for his
two principal characters.

I come here to the most powerful of all objections to my
justification of the dumb-show. Surely it is absurd to suppose—so the objectors urge—that Shakespeare adopted or
retained this device in order to avoid divulging the point of
the spoken play to Claudius, when Claudius sits watching the
device itself which includes every circumstance of his crime,
poisoning through the ear and all? This is the crux from which,

as explained in Chapter 1, the whole present enquiry set out, the crux to which Dr Greg first directed the serious attention of critics and on which he himself erected a new and comprehensive theory of *Hamlet*. Without any doubt whatever Claudius remains on the stage while the dumb-show is proceeding; yet, though he rushes shrieking from the room when the murder is later repeated in dramatic form, he is apparently quite unconcerned by its mimic representation. There are people who will believe any crudity or carelessness of Shakespeare; but he cannot possibly have been unaware of this seeming inconsistency, as those who explain the dumb-show as unconscious borrowing are bound to assume. He must have been perfectly cognisant of the dramatic issues involved, and have seen the difficulty about Claudius and the dumb-show three centuries before Dr Greg. There is, therefore, we may be sure, some satisfactory way out of it, if only we can discover it.

Dr Greg's own solution, outlined above,[1] may be thrown into the form of the following syllogism: inasmuch as the King watched the dumb-show unmoved, he cannot have recognised it as a representation of his crime; and, if the dumb-show did not represent the crime, then the story of the Ghost must be false. I have dealt with this theory at length elsewhere,[2] and need not here repeat my arguments. I must, however, point out that the syllogism is impregnable as it stands, and that if we are to escape the conclusion we have to rebut the premiss. There are only two ways of doing this: we must show either that the King was not watching the

---

[1] *Vide* pp. 5–7.
[2] *The Modern Language Review*, XIII, 129–56.

dumb-show (which we shall later find is the true solution), or that he was not unmoved as he watched it. The second alternative, which is the explanation most widely entertained by critics who have given any thought to the matter, has been wittily described by Dr Pollard as the "second tooth" theory, since it implies that Hamlet deliberately tests the King twice, in the dumb-show and then by means of Lucianus, and that Claudius is sufficiently strong-nerved to stand the first trial but breaks down under the second.[1] Mr Granville-Barker, who accepts this interpretation, tells me that it is quite actable on the stage, and on such an issue there is no higher authority. Yet, if a layman may be so daring, I cannot help thinking that the double test is less dramatically effective than the single one, especially if the minds of the audience (but not the mind of Claudius) have been prepared for the test of Lucianus, by means of the dumb-show, which intensifies their excitement because it informs them exactly what the *dénouement* will be, in the manner described above. Indeed, I suspect that "barren spectators", whose needs Shakespeare always had to bear in mind, would fail altogether to see the point of this double-trial, would be puzzled at the King enduring the dumb-show and wonder why, having passed that test, he should fly from the second enactment of the poisoning.

But we do not need to stand upon disputable points, since we have grounds far more relative. The real weakness of the "second tooth" theory is that there is not a word in the text

[1] *Vide* Dowden's *Hamlet* (*op. cit.*), p. 116; W. W. Lawrence, "The Play Scene in Hamlet", *Journal of English and Germanic Philology*, xviii, 1–22; Percy Simpson, "Actors and Acting", *Shakespeare's England*, ii, 252–3.

that can be quoted in support of it. It gets us out of the difficulty, it is true, but there is nothing to show that this is the way Shakespeare intended us to get out of it. It would, I think, be going too far to say that an interpretation entirely lacking in textual support should be ruled out as illegitimate, but it must assuredly be considered very hazardous; more especially as Hamlet refers several times to the test before and after it takes place, without hinting in any way that the dumb-show is part of it. On the contrary, everything he says clearly shows that he has nothing in mind but the speech, his speech, and that it is this which is to "catch the conscience of the King". He asks the First Player to study "a speech of some dozen or sixteen lines" (2.2.544); and the opening words of 3.2—"Speak the speech I pray you as I pronounced it to you"—show him coaching the same player in the delivery of his lines before the play begins; while in his injunction to Horatio to be keenly on the watch he is even more explicit. Let me repeat his words:

> There is a play to-night before the king,
> One scene of it comes near the circumstance
> Which I have told thee of my father's death.
> I prithee when thou seest that act afoot,
> Even with the very comment of thy soul
> Observe my uncle—if his occulted guilt
> Do not itself unkennel in one speech,
> It is a damnéd ghost that we have seen.

"*One* scene...that act...in *one* speech"; such reiterated insistence upon a single point in the coming performance seems almost designed to make it impossible for the audience to entertain "second tooth" notions; and I suspect that this was actually Shakespeare's intention. In any event, our expectant attention having been wholly directed upon a speech, the dumb-show takes us completely by surprise. Equally pointed are Hamlet's words after Claudius and the court have departed in confusion:

> *Hamlet.* O good Horatio, I'll take the ghost's word for a thousand pound. Didst perceive?
> *Horatio.* Very well, my lord.
> *Hamlet.* Upon the talk of the poisoning?
> *Horatio.* I did very well note him.

Not, be it observed, "upon the poisoning", which might be taken as covering the dumb-show, but "upon the *talk* of the poisoning", which points to the speech of Lucianus and to nothing else. Yet, had Shakespeare meant us to accept the dumb-show as Hamlet's first attempt to tent his uncle to the quick, how easily he might have warned us of the fact! A couple of words would have been enough. The "double tooth" theory will not work: not merely is it unsupported by any authority in the text, but the references in the text to the testing of the King are indisputably confined to the speech of the murderer. Nor is this all, for I have now to prove, and prove from the text, that Hamlet cannot have planned the dumb-show, inasmuch as he disliked dumb-shows in general, is as completely taken aback by this one as we are ourselves, and is withal exceedingly annoyed at it.

Miching mallecho

Shakespeare needed a dumb-show for technical reasons, but he had to furnish a dramatic explanation for its presence. He had, that is, to lead the audience to attribute it to someone in the play. Clearly there are only two possible alternatives: either it is performed at the express command of Hamlet, the master of the ceremonies, or the responsibility for it rests upon the shoulders of the players alone. A brief review of the Prince's relations with the players will help us to see which alternative is to be preferred.

After his disillusionment with Rosencrantz and Guilden-stern, Hamlet is delighted to welcome the players to Elsinore. He selects immediately a rather bombastic passionate speech from a *Dido and Aeneas* play, and bids the First Player recite it. This is done with such fire and effect that Polonius at any rate is greatly impressed; the actor is evidently a vigorous elocutionist, and though Hamlet's comment is restrained— "'Tis well" is all he says—he appears well satisfied. The arrangements for the performance of a play are then made; and, when the First Player next appears, Hamlet is giving him careful instructions how the all-important "dozen or sixteen lines", inserted by his own hand, are to be delivered. Com-mentators have dwelt much upon this conversation, since it seems to let us into Shakespeare's own views about the methods of his craft; but in so doing they have overlooked its connection with the Hamlet story. To begin with, Ham-let's words show that his inserted speech, which is of course now written, is to be one of "passion", and that the passion referred to is not love but anger or crime—the passion of the torrential, tempestuous, whirlwind species, which the Herods and the Termagants of the old plays had so grossly exag-gerated. They show, furthermore, that, despite his general approval of the rendering of the Pyrrhus speech, Hamlet is nervous, very nervous, about the First Player's capacity to recite his lines properly. This is natural, of course, seeing that the speech is to be the chief instrument in his unmasking of the King. Yet Hamlet, it is quite obvious, is not thinking primarily about Claudius at all; he is thinking of his lines. He wants full justice done to his essay in the art of drama. Note, too, what it is particularly that he fears:

If you *mouth* it as many of your players do, I had as lief the town-crier spoke my lines. Nor *do not saw the air* too much with your hand thus, but use all gently.....O, it offends me to the soul, to hear a robustious periwig-pated fellow *tear a passion to tatters*, to very rags, to split the ears of the groundlings, who for the most part are capable of nothing but *inexplicable dumb-shows and noise*: I would have such a fellow whipped for o'erdoing Termagant, it out-herods Herod, pray you avoid it....O there be players that I have seen play—and heard others praise, and that highly—not to speak it profanely, that neither having th'accent of Christians, nor the gait of Christian, pagan, nor man, have so *strutted and bellowed*, that I have thought some of nature's journeymen had made men, and not made them well, they imitated humanity so abominably.

Surely all this sheds a very remarkable light upon what happens immediately after in the play scene? First of all we have one of those dumb-shows that Hamlet thinks fit for groundlings alone—here, alas! only too explicable. Next we have a ridiculous prologue-jingle which Hamlet treats with undisguised contempt. Is it possible to hold him responsible for either of these effects?[1]

Critics have seen that the dumb-show creates difficulties in

[1] I think it probable that Shakespeare himself held such stage-tricks in contempt. He certainly laughs at them in the comic dumb-show and presentation which precedes the Pyramus and Thisbe play in *A Midsummer-Night's Dream*.

regard to Claudius; they have not seen that it creates difficulties quite as great in regard to Hamlet himself. For what
is he to make of this premature exhibition of his mouse-trap
in all its naked outline? If he has not ordered it, will he not
be vexed at its appearance? The dialogue that follows it
between Ophelia and himself makes it quite clear, or at least
should make it quite clear if only people would read *Hamlet*
with their eyes open, that he is very angry indeed; and his
comment, "Marry, this is miching mallecho, it means mischief", shows upon whom he fastens the blame. But let us
have the dialogue before us, that we may know exactly what
we are dealing with.

> *Ophelia.* What means this, my lord?
> *Hamlet.* Marry, this is miching mallecho, it means mischief.
> *Ophelia.* Belike this show imports the argument of the play.
>
> *Enter Prologue.*
>
> *Hamlet.* We shall know by this fellow. The players cannot keep
> counsel, they'll tell all.
> *Ophelia.* Will a' tell us what this show meant?
> *Hamlet.* Ay, or any show that you will show him—be not you
> ashamed to show, he'll not shame to tell you what it means.
> *Ophelia.* You are naught, you are naught, I'll mark the play.
> *Prologue.* For us and for our tragedy,
>   Here stooping to your clemency,
>   We beg your hearing patiently.
> *Hamlet.* Is this a prologue, or the posy of a ring?

When we bear in mind the convention of dumb-shows
and presenters, explained above,[1] the situation expressed in
these lines can hardly be disputed. After the dumb-show a

---

[1] *Vide* p. 147.

chorus or presenter might be expected; and, when the traverse on the inner-stage hid the dumb-show and a player thereupon appeared before it, Shakespeare's audience would naturally take him for a presenter, come to explain the show that had just finished. Our text, it is true, reads "Enter Prologue", but *Hamlet* is a stage-play not a book, and neither the Prince of Denmark nor seventeenth-century spectators would recognise the player as a prologue. On the contrary, Hamlet's words "We shall know by this fellow" make it clear that he takes the player for a presenter who will explain "what this show meant"; in other words, that the audience (including Claudius) will now learn all about the play that was to follow. In short, Hamlet sees that his speech is about to be rendered superfluous, and the spring of the mouse-trap released before the moment has arrived. His anxiety is evident in the sentence that follows the one just quoted: "The players *cannot* keep counsel, they'll tell all!" It is evident too, surely, in the dialogue that takes place immediately after the dumb-show, which exhibits Ophelia's attention concentrated upon the meaning of the pantomime and Hamlet's upon something quite different, viz. the conduct of the players, conduct which "means mischief". For the words "miching mallecho" I take to refer, not to the crime of Claudius, as most commentators seem vaguely to imagine, but to the *skulking iniquity* of the players, who have introduced this unauthorised and ridiculous dumb-show, and so have almost ruined the whole plot. "Mallecho" is a Spanish word, current in England at the time, meaning misdeed or wickedness,[1] while

---

[1] Dowden quotes Shirley, *Gentleman of Venice*: "Be humble, Thou man of mallecho, or thou diest."

"miching" means at once lurking like an enemy or a treacherous dog, in order to attack from behind,[1] and playing truant like a schoolboy; both meanings being apt to the First Player, who had received his lesson from Hamlet before the interlude began and was now playing him false.* Yet, all's well that ends well; the dumb-show, as we shall see, passes unnoticed by the King, and the presenter, who would have "told all", turns out to be only a silly prologue.

Should any reader doubt the foregoing interpretation, let him ask himself why Shakespeare introduced the prologue. Is it possible to explain the "posy" upon any other reading than that just given? Shakespeare could not have penned a seemingly idiotic jingle like this without some deliberate purpose in mind. It is a gimcrack from the players' box of tricks; and Hamlet's question, "Is this a prologue, or the posy of a ring?" vents at once his scorn and his relief.

Thus the dialogue between Hamlet and Ophelia which follows the dumb-show means that the show itself is entirely unexpected by him and exceedingly displeasing. This explanation, however, carries with it a point of greater significance than any yet noticed. Hamlet's anxiety concerning what the supposed presenter may reveal, his cry "The players cannot keep counsel, they'll tell all", would be pointless if Claudius had been watching the dumb-show, which reveals every circumstance of his crime and "tells all" with a vengeance. In a word, that anxiety is altogether incompatible with the "second tooth" theory. Not only does Hamlet not plan to test his uncle twice, but his uncle has not been subjected to a first test at all. We are, accordingly, thrown back

---

[1] *O.E.D.* cites a good illustration from 1609: "A miching curre, biting her behinde, when she cannot turne backe."

upon the alternative theory; the only other way, as we have seen above, in which the apparent indifference of the King to the dumb-show can be accounted for, viz. that the show has somehow escaped his notice. That this is the true state of affairs is, indeed, clear from another passage of the text not yet quoted. "Belike this show imports the argument of the play," little Ophelia had remarked to Hamlet. The interlude then proceeds, and at the end of the dialogue between Player King and Player Queen, Claudius, who has grown restive under the glaring references to second marriages, rounds on Hamlet at the latter's pointed question to his mother and sharply enquires, "Have you heard the argument? is there no offence in't?" The query, unconsciously repeating Ophelia's word, unheard by the questioner because spoken aside to Hamlet, makes it certain that the King cannot have seen the dumb-show, which *is* the argument of the play, as every member of the audience is now aware. In short, the repetition of the word "argument" was designed by Shakespeare to underline for us the King's ignorance of the dumb-show. And "no offence"! Is it really credible for a moment that, if he had sat watching that detailed revelation of his crime in pantomime a minute or two earlier, he could have uttered those words—to Hamlet of all people?[1]

The King was not looking at the dumb-show; he was doing something else. What was he doing? Halliwell-Phillipps long ago suggested that he missed seeing the show because he was talking to the Queen while it was going on. This is in part the true explanation, but it is not satisfactory

---

[1] The "second-tooth" school will, of course, seek to explain this as acting; an explanation which I hope at this stage of the argument my readers will not find it easy to entertain.

as Halliwell-Phillipps states it, inasmuch as he says nothing about the subject of the conversation, is unable to show how the business is made clear to the audience—an essential point —and fails to observe that the episode forms one of the most exciting issues of the play scene. It will be convenient to defer a full exposition of the matter until the mechanism of the play scene is all in order. Here I need only register my belief that the King's conversation begins, not with Gertrude, but with Polonius, when, as Hamlet supports the love-distraught theory by throwing himself at Ophelia's feet, the old man exultantly exclaims "O ho! do you mark that?"; that its subject is Hamlet's behaviour to Ophelia and the standing dispute between King and Chief Councillor concerning the cause of his madness; and that the Queen is forced to join in, in order to hide her own confusion, by Hamlet's cruel sally: "for look you how cheerfully my mother looks, and my father died within's two hours". It is conjecture, of course, but conjecture based upon the text, growing naturally out of the general dramatic situation, and withal—or so I venture to hold—the only possible way of playing the scene, if the previous lines of my argument are sound.

Leaving that, however, for later treatment, we must return to the players, for there are still points to be cleared up about them. Once the interlude is under way they give Hamlet no further trouble until Lucianus enters with his "vial". He comes on at line 242 and he begins to speak at line 255. What is he doing all the time? He is acting the stage-villain, making mouths, grimacing, strutting about the boards; in short, he is doing those very things which Hamlet had strictly enjoined the First Player to avoid. The Prince is stung to anger, this time more violent than before. "Begin, mur-

derer!" he shouts at him; "Pox! leave thy damnable faces
and begin! Come—the croaking raven doth bellow for
revenge." The first sentence is obvious enough in intention;
but what does Hamlet mean by the "croaking raven"?
Richard Simpson showed that the phrase is a telescoped
version of the following two lines from *The True Tragedy of
Richard the Third*:

> The screeking Raven sits croking for reuenge.
> Whole heads of beasts comes bellowing for reuenge.

But no one seems to have observed the point of the quotation
in Hamlet's mouth. *The True Tragedy*, an old chronicle play
belonging to the Queen's company of actors, is an extreme
example of Elizabethan rant, the speech from which these
lines are quoted being a particularly outrageous specimen of
its quality.[1] The purpose of Hamlet's words, therefore, is

[1] Miss Bradbrook (*Themes and Conventions of Elizabethan Tragedy*,
p. 99) describes it as "probably the most prodigious piece of epiphora in
the English drama" and again as "a part to tear a cat in and worth the
delay in the action". Here are the most striking lines (Malone Soc.
reprint ll. 1880–1895):

> Meethinkes their ghoasts comes gaping for reuenge,
> Whom I haue slaine in reaching for a Crowne.
> Clarence complaines, and crieth for reuenge.
> My Nephues bloods, Reuenge, reuenge, doth crie,
> The headlesse Peeres comes preasing for reuenge.
> And euery one cries, let the tyrant die.
> The Sunne by day shines hotely for reuenge.
> The Moone by night eclipseth for reuenge.
> The stars are turnd to Comets for reuenge,
> The Planets chaunge their coursies for reuenge.
> The birds sing not, but sorrow for reuenge.
> The silly lambes sits bleating for reuenge.
> The screeking Rauen sits croking for reuenge.
> Whole heads of beasts comes bellowing for reuenge.
> And all, yea all the world I thinke,
> Cries for reuenge, and nothing but reuenge.

clear. He is exhorting the player, in bitter sarcasm, to bellow the critical speech of the evening in the robustious, ranting manner of the old chronicle plays—in short, to "o'er-do Termagant and out-herod Herod".

And who is this Lucianus? Who but the First Player himself?[1] Hamlet had entrusted him with his "speech", and had (politely) warned him not to mouth, bellow, or strut as he delivered it. Surely we need not hesitate to assume that the warning and the sarcasm were addressed to the same person? The assumption, however, brings us up against the vexed problem of the identification of Hamlet's inserted speech, over which much paper and ink have been expended. The speech, as we have seen, was one of passion, and the only other lines in the Gonzago-play which would answer to this description are those of Baptista, which would be spoken by the boy in the cast. Moreover, it is the words of the murderer which cause Claudius to blench, and there is therefore a strong presumption that they were Hamlet's contribution. It is to them that he directs Horatio's close attention before the play begins, and to them also that he refers in his glee after the play is over. Lastly, they are the only words in the interlude which point directly at the crime of Claudius:

> Thoughts black, hands apt, drugs fit, and time agreeing,
> Confederate season, else no creature seeing,
> Thou mixture rank, of midnight weeds collected,
> With Hecate's ban thrice blasted, thrice infected,

---

[1] Mr Granville-Barker tells me that by theatrical tradition the First Player is given the part of the Player King. Such a tradition is miching mallecho, since Hamlet expressly asks the First Player at 2.2.543 ff. to "study" his inserted speech, which must, as I show, be the Lucianus speech.

Thy natural magic and dire property,
On wholesome life usurps immediately.

What are these lines but a condensation of the description of the poisoning in the Ghost's speech?

Upon my secure hour thy uncle stole
With juice of cursed hebona in a vial,
And in the porches of my ears did pour
The leperous distilment, whose effect
Holds such an enmity with blood of man,
That swift as quicksilver it courses through
The natural gates and alleys of the body,
And with a sudden vigour it doth posset
And curd, like eager droppings into milk,
The thin and wholesome blood; so did it mine.

The "secure hour", the foul nature of the drug, its swift effect upon the "wholesome" body: all are the same. These considerations, taken in conjunction with our unmasking of the First Player, should leave no doubt upon the matter. The poisoner's speech is Hamlet's echo of his father's words, and the poisoner is the rascally leader of the Gonzago troupe.

Need we hesitate any longer to assume that Shakespeare made the players his scapegoat for the dumb-show? I would go further. The temptation to guy some rival company of actors in this by-play must have been almost irresistible; and my belief is that Shakespeare did not attempt to resist it.[1]

[1] *Vide* Appendix C, "The Identity of the Gonzago Troupe".

"*Nephew to the King*"

We have now dealt with seven of the eleven questions posed at the beginning of this chapter, not to mention one or two additional problems which have cropped up on the way. Those that remain, however, are perhaps the most important of all. Let me recall them to the reader. What does Hamlet mean by his remark to Claudius "I eat the air, promise-crammed"? Why does he remind Polonius of his enacting Julius Caesar "once i'th'university"? What is his object in making the murderer of the Gonzago-play the nephew and not the brother of the king? And, lastly, why should the entire court, who know nothing of the real poisoning, assume later that Hamlet has behaved outrageously to his uncle and even threatened him with death?

Only one of these problems has, I think, been previously discussed, the last; and only one critic has discussed it.* Dr Bradley alone has perceived that something needs clearing up in the attitude of the court after the play scene. He writes:

> The state of affairs at Court at this time, though I have not seen it noticed by critics, seems to me puzzling. It is quite clear [and here he refers to passages which will presently be noted] that everyone sees in the play-scene a gross and menacing insult to the King. Yet no one shows any sign of perceiving in it also an accusation of murder. Surely that is strange. Are we perhaps meant to understand that they do perceive this, but out of subservience choose to ignore the fact?[1]

The evidence on which he relies for the existence of the "state of affairs" which he finds so puzzling consists of four passages which merit close attention. The first are the words

[1] *Op. cit.* p. 137 n.

that Rosencrantz and Guildenstern use of the King and Queen immediately after their exit in the play scene. The King, they tell Hamlet, "is in his retirement marvellous distempered", and the cause of the distemperature they take to be "choler"; while as for the Queen she is "in most great affliction of spirit" and Hamlet's "behaviour hath struck her into amazement and admiration".[1] Secondly, we find the two sycophants in the following scene closeted with Claudius himself, and discoursing to him, to quote Dr Bradley again, "on the extreme importance of his preserving his invaluable life, as though Hamlet's insanity had now clearly shown itself to be homicidal",[2] and discoursing thus in reply to words of his, which are themselves plain enough—

> I like him not, *nor stands it safe with us*
> To let his madness range. Therefore prepare you,
> I your commission will forthwith dispatch,
> And he to England shall along with you.
> *The terms of our estate may not endure*
> *Hazard so near's* as doth hourly grow
> Out of his brawls.[3]

He is suggesting to his two listeners that Hamlet is suffering from homicidal mania; and they accept the suggestion.

Thirdly, the Queen sends for Hamlet; and Polonius coaches her for her part as they await his coming:

> Tell him his pranks have been too broad to bear with,
> And that your grace hath screened and stood between
> Much heat and him.[4]

---

[1] 3.2.301, 3.2.312–3, 327–8; "amazement and admiration" may be paraphrased "bewilderment and astonishment" in modern English.

[2] *Op. cit.* p. 136.

[3] 3.3.1–7; Q2 prints "browes"; perhaps "braves" was the word Shakespeare wrote. [4] 3.4.2–4.

What pranks are these which Gertrude has so much difficulty in excusing? They clearly concern Claudius very nearly— "Hamlet, thou hast thy father much offended" are her first words—and equally clearly they are pranks of a dangerous character. For the Queen, as Dr Bradley notes, is almost as frightened as her husband. "When, at the opening of the interview between Hamlet and his mother, the son, instead of listening to her remonstrances, roughly assumes the offensive, she becomes alarmed; and when, on her attempting to leave the room, he takes her by the arm and forces her to sit down, she is terrified, cries out 'Thou wilt not murder me?' and screams for help"[1]—a scream which Polonius, who is as jumpy as the rest, echoes from behind the arras, very unhappily for himself. Gertrude's terror cannot be due to her son's madness alone, since half an hour before she feared him so little that she had begged him to come and sit beside her to watch the play. What has happened meanwhile to alarm her? Certainly it has nothing to do with the discovery of Claudius's crime. Of that she is entirely ignorant, as is proved by her words to Hamlet later in this same scene. Nor can it be supposed for a moment that Rosencrantz and Guildenstern have guessed the secret, as Dr Bradley in his perplexity half-heartedly suggests, and that "out of subservience" they pretend "to ignore the fact".

Fourthly, a few scenes later[2] Claudius has to persuade Laertes that he is himself personally not in any way responsible for the murder of Polonius. The proof of his innocence is given off the stage in the presence of witnesses chosen by the dead man's son; but something of its character is revealed

[1] *Op. cit.* p. 137.   [2] 4.5.201–18; 4.7.1–29.

by subsequent references which show that the King's main line had been to convince him

> That he which hath your noble father slain
> Pursued my life.

And his success is manifest from Laertes's reply:

> It well appears: but tell me,
> Why you proceeded not against *these feats,*
> *So crimeful and so capital in nature,*
> As by your safety, greatness, wisdom, all things else,
> You mainly were stirred up.

What then were

> these feats
> So crimeful and so capital in nature,

of which Hamlet had been guilty, as the King has proved to Laertes by witnesses? They include, of course, the murder of Polonius, but clearly they also involve the person of Claudius himself. When had that person been threatened? What does it all mean?

On the face of it, the problem seems capable of a very simple solution. The foregoing suggestions of Hamlet's homicidal mania, of his being a menace to the throne and withal a dangerous lunatic, may all be traced to King Claudius. We are not told his reasons, but tyrants do not give reasons; their words are enough. And Claudius, so the argument might run, aware that Hamlet knew his secret, would stick at nothing to discredit him in the eyes of his mother and the court. Are we not informed, indeed, that he invents "bugs and goblins" in Hamlet's life in order to blacken his character with the King of England?[1] And if he

[1] 5.2.22.

says, as he virtually does say in the speech just quoted from the opening of 3.3, that his nephew is bent upon his assassination, will not any sycophant of the court accept his statement in words very similar to those used by Rosencrantz and Guildenstern? Hamlet's motives required no explaining. He was the dispossessed heir, as everyone knew, gone mad from "ambition adust"; what more need be said?

The argument, based on the passages cited by Dr Bradley and above enumerated, looks plausible enough, until confronted with another passage, which Dr Bradley has strangely overlooked. Before Claudius says anything at all to Rosencrantz and Guildenstern about Hamlet's murderous intentions, his nephew has himself hinted at them in unmistakable fashion to the two spies immediately after the play scene is over:

> *Rosencrantz.* Good my lord, what is your cause of distemper?
> *Hamlet.* Sir, I lack advancement.
> *Rosencrantz.* How can that be, when you have the voice of the king himself for your succession in Denmark?
> *Hamlet.* Ay, sir, but "While the grass grows"—the proverb is something musty.

In short, the heir to the throne does not propose to wait his turn, but to anticipate the course of nature by action. It is Hamlet, then, and not Claudius, who first broaches the subject of assassination, and of ambition as the motive therefor. And his words, harking back as they do to the King's proclamation of Hamlet as his heir in full Council at the beginning of the play, are clearly also connected (as the pirate of the First Quarto unconsciously testifies [1]) with the previous

[1] *Vide* pp. 120–21.

talk about ambition with Rosencrantz and Guildenstern at
2.2.245–68, and with the threats in the nunnery scene of
ambition and revenge; threats of which the royal eavesdropper is quick to see the point, as his subsequent speech
shows.[1] Finally, they give the clue to the four problems of
the play scene which still remain to be solved, and to which
we may now return.

"How fares our cousin Hamlet?" solicitously asks Uncle
Claudius, as he enters to attend the play. "Excellent i'faith,"
retorts Hamlet, "of the chameleon's dish, I eat the air,
promise-crammed—you cannot feed capons so." It is a
pregnant quibble, as we shall see later, with more than one
meaning; but the surface sense is patent enough. "I am
tired," says Hamlet, "of being fed with mere promises of
the succession." And the theme of his talk with Polonius
immediately after is the death of tyrants. But hints are not
sufficient to justify the attitude of Claudius, Gertrude and the
courtiers when the play scene is over, an attitude which implies that Hamlet has threatened his uncle in a fashion so
obvious that all have seen it. We must, then, examine the
interlude itself and discover, if we can, this strange menace,
a menace which, as is now becoming obvious, will alone
explain the passages that have caused Dr Bradley such
perplexity, together with others he has passed over.

Assuming, as we ought, that none of those present at the
Gonzago-play, save Hamlet, Horatio and Claudius, know
anything of the murder of King Hamlet, or even suspect it,
let us ask ourselves how this play would strike the other
spectators, the rest of the court. The point intended for

[1] *Vide* p. 135.

Claudius will be lost upon them, and though they will no doubt feel that the references to second marriages are offensive there is nothing menacing in those. But there is a point, a very menacing point indeed, which would require no explanation. First, the play is a drama of regicide, performed at the instigation of the rightful though dispossessed heir to the throne and in the royal presence itself. "No offence in't", indeed! An Elizabethan audience—the real audience— could not fail to catch the meaning of this, conscious as they were of the sensitiveness of royalty on such matters, more especially with the Essex rising of February 1601 fresh in their minds; a rising which had been preceded the day before by a performance of Shakespeare's *Richard II* in order to incite the people of London to rebellion and to show them that princes had been deposed and might be again. But the case was even worse than this; for who was the murderer of the play? Who but the *nephew* of the king, the Hamlet as it would seem of the Gonzago-allegory? In a word, Lucianus-Hamlet poisons Gonzago-Claudius before the assembled court! Could the courtiers, Polonius, Rosencrantz, Guildenstern, the Queen herself, and the rest wonder that Claudius should break up the whole seditious business and leave the chamber? Or need we marvel that in the next scene Rosencrantz and Guildenstern should speak obsequiously but plainly of the dangers that threaten the majesty of Denmark?

But there is a still stranger thing to notice. The players' play gives no hint of the relationship between murderer and king; it is Hamlet himself who, chorus-like, supplies the information. Hamlet is therefore identifying himself with the assassin; and he underlines this in the passage about "the succession in Denmark" as he talks with Rosencrantz later. He wishes the court then to draw the deductions which, as we have seen, they did draw. In other words, he uses the play to threaten his uncle in a fashion which no one who sees it can mistake. It is a sudden *dénouement*, sudden like all Hamlet's actions, like his assumption of the "antic disposition" or his decision to have the Gonzago-play itself; and I think Shakespeare intended us to consider it unpremeditated. That is to say, Hamlet does not deliberately plan the identification before the interlude begins; it comes to him, as a stroke of genius, on the spur of the moment, when Lucianus enters.[1] But it is

> The flash and outbreak of a fiery mind,

which has already, as we have noted, been amusing itself, while uncle-father lurks behind the arras, with the notion of playing the rôle of "proud, revengeful, ambitious" nephew and of sparing "all that are married, save one". Reckless? But Hamlet, we have also seen, is always just about to kill the King—never more so than at this juncture!—so that recklessness is the natural consequence of his situation. Yet, as he says himself,

> Our indiscretion sometime serves us well,
> When our deep plots do pall.

[1] In my note on *Hamlet* 3.2.243 I wrote: "Hamlet *arranges* two meanings to the Play." This seems to me, on second thoughts, prompted by conversation with Dr Pollard, to imply too much deliberation. Further, in the same note, I suggested that the identification should be made plain by dressing Lucianus in a black doublet like Hamlet's. This, which I still think would add great theatrical force to the episode, I now fear is dramatically inadmissible, since it infers previous instructions as to costume by Hamlet, which again implies deliberate planning.

If the interlude proved the Ghost honest, Hamlet intended to finish his uncle off immediately afterwards; that may be taken for granted. But what reason was he to give the world for the assassination? The Ghost's commands, the salvation of Gertrude, the family honour of the House of Denmark forbade any disclosure of the truth. The real meaning of the Gonzago story, the King's meaning, could not be revealed, because the Queen herself was involved. To what degree she was cognisant of the murder, or even an accomplice, Hamlet did not know; but however innocent she might be, a public exposure of Claudius would inevitably implicate his consort, who had also been consort of the murdered man. The crime of the King must at all costs be kept a secret.[1] Hamlet was, therefore, obliged to furnish the court with some theory which would explain the Gonzago-play, account for the open discomfiture of his uncle which he hoped it would effect, and justify (or at any rate make explicable) the assassination that was to come after. His own rights gave him everything he required. He might have pleaded them in public or in Council after the deed was accomplished, but his sudden inspiration to hail Lucianus as his mimic shadow allows for a second interpretation of the play which it would occur to no one ignorant of his secret and Claudius's to call in question, and which would prepare the court for the execution to follow.

Hamlet's mouse-trap, then, catches both King and courtiers. For the former there is the talk of the poisoning and the act, the damning and unmistakable act, of pouring the leperous distilment into the ears of the sleeping man. For the latter

[1] *Vide* above, pp. 46–9.

there is the spectacle of a monarch being done to death by his ambitious nephew. The two points are quite distinct and there is no danger of confusion between them. Claudius notices, of course, the description of Lucianus as "nephew to the king" and makes capital out of it later; but what Lucianus says and does can leave no doubt in his mind that Hamlet has probed his secret to its deadly root. On the other hand, to Rosencrantz, Guildenstern, Polonius and the rest, who have not been privileged to talk with King Hamlet's ghost, the play will suggest no reference to his death, which was due, as all men knew, to the bite of an adder.[1] What they must see, because Hamlet takes care they shall not miss them, are the insults to the Queen in the allusions to the second marriage of widows, insults that leave them in a condition of horrified expectancy for what the mad Prince may do next. When, therefore, a murderer suddenly appears, who is announced as "nephew to the king", and then poisons him "for's estate", they cannot fail to understand for what purpose Hamlet had planned the play. The evening's entertainment is a complete success.

All the parts of the play scene are now in order, restored to their proper function according to what I believe was the design of the master craftsman. But we have not yet seen how the mechanism works. The test of our discoveries, the test which can alone ultimately justify them in the eyes of the world, is dramatic performance. Some day perhaps that test will come. For the present a bookman must do what he

---

[1] To suppose, as one of my friendly critics does, that the coincidence of a garden *mise en scène* for both deaths would arouse their suspicions is surely to find Scotland Yard at Elsinore.

can. In a word, taking the text of the Second Quarto as my guide, I shall describe the scene as I think Shakespeare intended it to be acted, as it would be acted were I producer and had instructed the actors in their parts. The description will involve here and there a little repetition of points already made above. But the reader will perhaps forgive that, for the sake of a straightforward account, undistracted by argument "about it and about".

The play scene restored

Before attempting to interpret a scene in Shakespeare there is one question which it is well to deal with first: In what mood are the principal characters when it begins?

It is not difficult to guess the mood of Gertrude. She is possessed by that indomitable placidity which seldom deserts her. She is, of course, distressed at the madness of her son, which she steadfastly attributes, whatever her husband or Polonius may say, to "his father's death and our o'er-hasty marriage"; but she comes to the play with a glad heart, for she sees hopes of Hamlet's recovery in his interest in such amusements. She is therefore entirely unsuspicious of his intentions, and little guesses what he has particularly in store for herself. Claudius also looks with favour on the idea of the play. He is as delighted as the Queen when in the preceding scene he hears from Rosencrantz and Guildenstern that Hamlet proposes to entertain them all, for it pleases him to learn that his nephew's mind is occupied with anything so healthy and innocent. He has no suspicions of the play, and no interest in it; he attends it simply to give Hamlet en-

couragement, "and drive his purpose into these delights".
Moreover, he is thinking of other things. Hamlet's talk with
Ophelia, which he has just overheard from his place of spying,
has finally convinced him that the Prince is suffering from
the disease of ambition, and that the disease may prove
dangerous to the reigning monarch. He determines therefore
to watch, not the play, but Hamlet, narrowly. With him
enters Polonius, the champion of the rival theory, who is not
in the least satisfied that the King is right, and has insisted on
a second seance behind the arras, in which Gertrude shall take
the place of Ophelia as decoy.[1]

Next of the train appears Ophelia herself, "of ladies most
deject and wretched", with the pallor caused by her recent
terrible experience still in her cheeks. All she knows is
that Hamlet, her lover, her idol, her god, is mad. After his
outrageous conduct to her in the lobby, she is prepared for
anything. Her task is to endure patiently, and to do what she
can by soothing words to calm the ravings of that once
"noble and most sovereign reason". Behind her walk
Rosencrantz and Guildenstern, commissioned no doubt by
his majesty to keep a watchful eye upon the Prince. At any
rate, in regard to Hamlet's "madness" they share Claudius's
theory.

And Hamlet himself? His mood seems calm and self-
controlled. He has just given the players the most precise
instructions about the delivery of his speech, instructions
which prove him to be for the time clear-headed and collected. In the exquisite and touching conversation that
follows with Horatio, a conversation in which Hamlet carries

[1] Cf. pp. 135–6.

on and develops the doctrine of μηδὲν ἄγαν already enjoined upon the First Player, he is at his very best. It is his one perfectly serene and untroubled moment in the whole play. Note, too, the apparent deliberation of his plans for the interlude. He entrusts Horatio with the task of fixing his eyes upon the King's face during the play, and agrees with him to compare notes afterwards. The trumpets and kettle-drums (Claudius cannot do without these heralds) cut short their talk, and Hamlet adds in a hurried whisper: "They are coming to the play. I must be idle. Get you a place." It is Shakespeare's final clue as to his state of mind. Horatio and he must separate, so as not to appear to be in collusion. Moreover he has a part to play in this scene: "I must be idle", that is to say "crazy". Hamlet is assuming his "antic disposition" consciously and of set purpose.

Indeed, he has much to do and to think of. Would his all-important lines be spoken clearly and incisively? Would the players perform the interlude as he had directed? If the play passed off well he has no anxiety about Claudius; for, had the Ghost spoken truth, there was no escape for the "conscience of the king". But "the play's the thing" for Hamlet, chiefly because it ministers to one of the cravings of his nature, his delight in plots and counter-plots. Claudius calls him "most generous and free from all contriving"; and he is so as regards men whom he trusts, like Horatio, or admires, like Laertes. But with men he hates he is very different. He takes a malicious delight in hoodwinking, fooling, and tripping up his enemies, and his love of such employment accounts in part for his delay in killing the King. He wants to play with him as a cat plays with a mouse. All this being so, how excellent a contrivance the Gonzago-play is! It will feed to the full his lust for delving a yard below Claudius's mines; it will hoist the King with his own petar. I have little doubt that Hamlet desires not merely to convict Claudius by means of the play but to put him on the rack and watch him writhing.

Claudius, however, is not his only objective. He knows the Gonzago-play and knows that it ought to catch the conscience of his mother also. He is not certain whether she is an accomplice in the crime or not. That must be tested. He will tent her to the quick, too, about her second marriage. Incest and adultery are ignored; it would be dangerous to hint at these before the assembled court, and he will have an opportunity of dealing with the matter privately afterwards. This fits in admirably with the design of making the whole thing a mouse-trap for his uncle. The King must not realise until the last moment what the play is about. He must therefore be led off the scent in the earlier part, which will deal exclusively with Gertrude. But others must be put off the scent also; the court must guess nothing of what is really afoot. How that is to be managed he does not yet know; but some device will suggest itself to his active brain.

Lastly, this interlude is his show. He is master of the revels; he has selected the scene to be played, and has even written a speech, the critical speech of the evening. He will be exceedingly anxious that the whole thing should go off well —anxious from the purely artistic point of view. Hamlet is greatly interested in drama. The players are his old friends, and he welcomes them with delight before he has even begun to think of the Gonzago scheme. He is thoroughly at home with them, and has found in their advent "a kind of joy" greater than anything he has experienced since we first saw him in his "nighted colour" at the beginning of his history. Hamlet is a patron of the stage, like Southampton, Essex, and other of Shakespeare's friends at Elizabeth's court. But he is more than this. He is an actor himself, and never so much at ease as when playing a part. Throughout almost the whole play we see him in some rôle or other. The part of madman is, of course, his main disguise, but it has many varieties: the distracted-lover variety, in two sorts at least, if not more; the variety for "tedious old fools"; and the variety of a subtler kind for his two schoolfellows, the sponges.

Nor can we doubt that this play-acting gives him intense satisfaction. It keeps his mind off that

> something in his soul,
> O'er which his melancholy sits on brood—

and which comes uppermost whenever he is left alone. It also aids him in his delving operations against Claudius and his myrmidons. And never does he obtain a more magnificent opportunity than in the play scene of displaying his great histrionic gifts, and such dramatic talent as he possessed; for since all his dupes are now gathered together watching him, he has to act all his parts at once. He "must be idle", of course—that is his habitual mask in the presence of the enemy; but he will use his madness to deadly purpose. He will shoot his poisoned arrows now at his mother, now at his uncle. He will fool Polonius, be love-distraught with Ophelia, while Rosencrantz, Guildenstern, and the rest of the court have to be hoodwinked. There is his part, too, in the play itself to be considered; here he must be "chorus", driving home the points so that not one of the varying impressions he desires to create shall miss its mark. It is a complicated and difficult task he has set himself, needing a clear head and a steady pulse.

To imagine Hamlet thinking thus helps us to disentangle the issues for ourselves; and at one time or other, no doubt, all these matters are present to his mind. But that mind does not really move in this pedestrian fashion at all. Had Shakespeare chosen to give us a glimpse of it between the nunnery scene and the play scene, in the act—shall we say?—of composing the "dozen or sixteen lines", we may be sure that it would not have been "casting beyond" itself, like the brain of Polonius, into what was about to happen or what it ought to do in the coming crisis. It would dispatch the speech for Lucianus, with the speed it later pens the "changeling letter", and would then turn to something quite remote from the purpose, something we should never have expected. Hamlet's brilliant handling of the successive situations in the play scene must be set down to genius not calculation.

The court enters for the play, and Hamlet and Horatio hurriedly break off their colloquy, Horatio taking up a place close to the seat in which Ophelia will afterwards sit, Hamlet remaining in the centre of the stage to receive the King and Queen, as befits the host. The King, Queen and Polonius enter first of the train, and Claudius, polite as ever to his "chiefest courtier, cousin and his son", enquires how he fares, eyeing him cautiously the while for further evidence of his attitude towards him. He has not long to wait. Hamlet deftly catches up the word "fares" by the wrong end, and replies: "Excellent i'faith, of the Chameleon's dish, I eat the air, Promise-crammed, you cannot feed Capons so." The commas and capitals come from the Second Quarto, and they indicate emphatic and deliberate utterance. The speech is one of those right-and-left double-barrelled shots so dear to the heart of sportsmen, hitting both marks. "Promise-crammed" and the pun upon "air" persuade Claudius that the rightful heir is still brooding over his wrongs; while "capon" has a meaning for the King also, which he misses, though we shall understand it at the end of the scene. On the other hand, the shot pierces the centre of the Polonius target, for "promise" can be taken as referring to Ophelia's broken troth, and "capon" denotes a young cock who is deprived of all capacity of love-making, or (as the popular jest of the time had it) a pullet stuffed with *billets-doux*; either way the speech points to thwarted love, and the lady's father might take his choice. Altogether, it was a good beginning to the evening.

The King parries the thrust at him by affecting not to understand it, and Hamlet with an air of contempt turns from him to his other quarry. But it is only to strike at Claudius once again; for, why, as he fools the "capital calf" about his prowess as an actor, does he lead him to speak of the scene in the Capitol, if not to remind his uncle and the court of a famous precedent for the assassination of tyrants? Nor must we miss Shakespeare's tragic irony here. Polonius will play the part of Caesar in real life, a few scenes later, when the "brute part" is Hamlet's. Rosencrantz and Guildenstern, we are also to remember, are listening intently to all this, and will recall it in the light of subsequent events. The thwarted-ambition theory is well afoot as the King moodily seats himself in his chair of state. But Hamlet has many parts to play in this strange eventful history, and it amuses him now to give the old councillor a good run for his money. To enter fully into the business, and all which it involves, we must consider for a moment how the actors are arranging themselves upon the stage.

The courtiers come in; and at once break into two groups, flanking the entrance to the inner-stage, so that the real audience may see the play properly. Claudius advances with his party, which includes Gertrude, Polonius, Rosencrantz and Guildenstern, and takes his seat right on the front of the stage, to allow the audience to watch his face carefully throughout the scene. On his inner side sits the Queen, like him half-face to the audience, while a little behind him on the outer side stands or sits Polonius. The chief of the group on the other side of the stage, which includes Horatio, is at present Ophelia, who sits opposite the King, because Hamlet is to sit at her feet, and the audience will want to watch *his* face also. Thus the characters of the play are drawn up in two confronting camps, as it were, at the beginning of this, the crisis of their history. For a moment, however, Hamlet is left standing between them, with kin on the one hand and kind on the other; and, seeing him without a seat, his mother says: "Come hither, my dear Hamlet, sit by me." She is in a tender mood; her dear boy seems mending, and she wants to pat his hand and affect an interest in this play with which he is diverting himself. But Hamlet's place is with Horatio, opposite the King and keenly on the watch. He therefore refuses her offer in words which give the thwarted-love theory an innings. "No, good mother," he says, making for Ophelia, "here's metal more attractive." The dramatic contrast between the two parties is complete; the anti-Claudius group now has its rightful leader. But the action and the words accompanying it give Polonius, the champion of the thwarted-love theory, his opportunity. "O ho!" he chuckles exultantly to the King, "do you mark that?" Claudius is strangely obtuse in regard to this matter; Polonius had been ready to wager his head upon the truth of his own theory;[1] the nunnery scene had just confirmed it; and, if further evidence were necessary, here it is in absolutely unmistakable form.

Hamlet continues to play up to Jephthah in the conversation with his daughter. His language to Ophelia, outrageous as it is, is in keeping with the part of a love-distraught swain; and her gentle forbearance of his conduct shows that she regards him as a madman and sees nothing strange in the form which his dementia takes. Her father too, so far from being shocked, is actually gleeful, for every word that is uttered in this strain establishes his theory upon a firmer basis.[2] And, as the conversation proceeds, the old man winks and nods in triumph to the King.

Hamlet, however, has yet another hare to start before the play begins, hare number three, the theory of his good mother. He lets it slip, partly to enjoy throwing the enemy into still greater confusion, partly to lead up to the dialogue

[1] 2.2.156: "Take this from this, if this be otherwise."
[2] How much of Hamlet's talk with Ophelia is meant to be overheard by others is a disputable point; I think Hamlet certainly intends his mother to hear it all and does not care who else does.

of the Player King and Queen, which he imagines is just about to begin. This dialogue is to deal with the "o'er-hasty marriage" motive, and Hamlet wants to point the moral clearly beforehand, for he is prologue as well as chorus. "Look you", he cries, "how cheerfully my mother looks, and my father died within's two hours"; and he continues fiddling on the same string for ten or a dozen lines. It is a fine piece of prologue work.

But Hamlet's "look you" is a direction, not merely to Ophelia and the court, but also to the audience in the theatre. At this point all eyes turn naturally and inevitably to the Claudius, Gertrude, and Polonius group, to see how they will take the ruthless sally. In other words, beneath Hamlet's purpose there lurks another purpose of which he is completely unconscious, since it is the purpose of his creator, of the showman who is pulling the strings of the greatest puppet-play in all literature. It is essential to Shakespeare that his audience should be fully aware of what Claudius is doing at this critical moment, *because it is the moment before the dumb-show appears*. And what is he doing? Polonius and he have been watching Hamlet for several minutes past, but this last sally complicates the matter in dispute between them, and drags in the Queen also. For it is natural to suppose that Gertrude's cheerfulness will be not a little dashed by Hamlet's words and that, as he continues in the same strain, she should, affecting not to hear him, turn away and join in the whispered conversation between her husband and Polonius. So when Hamlet invites the audience to gaze at them, they see the three with their heads together in discussion, a discussion that perhaps grows half-audible as soon as he ceases speaking.

Each is arguing in support of his favourite theory; each is eager to follow up the false trail which most flatters his judgment. It is matter for an hour's talk, especially with Polonius taking the lead. Thus they are not watching the inner-stage at all; the play is nothing to them; their whole attention is concentrated upon the problem of Hamlet's madness. The dumb-show enters, performs its brief pantomime—a matter of a few moments only—and passes out entirely unnoticed by the disputants; and when the audience turn again to see how this silent representation of his crime has affected the King, they find him still closely engaged with Gertrude and Polonius. Shakespeare's directions to his actors have gone beyond recall, and we cannot therefore be certain how he arranged this stage-business. But I am convinced that the foregoing comes near to his intentions. Halliwell's theory that Claudius was whispering to his wife during the dumb-show is unsatisfactory, because it does not go far enough; but it contains the kernel of the truth.[1]

The chief danger-spot being successfully past, it remained for Shakespeare to round off the business by explaining how the dumb-show came to be there and by preventing the audience from pondering upon it. This he does in the conversation between Hamlet and Ophelia which immediately follows.

In his talk with the First Player, barely half an hour before, Hamlet had made it quite clear that he had as little patience with "inexplicable dumb-shows" as he had with the strut-

[1] In performance, as Mr George Rylands suggests to me, the three figures will actually remain still and without by-play while the dumb-show is proceeding; since the whole attention of the audience must be concentrated upon *that*.

tings and bellowings of the average actor. The appearance of
the dumb-show, therefore, just when he had been carefully
prologuing the play itself, was exceedingly annoying to him.
But annoyance gives place to consternation when he sees that
the pantomime is likely to divulge the whole plot of the play
before it even commences. He glances anxiously at the King
as the thing proceeds (glances which are not lost upon the
audience), and observes to his relief that it has passed by him
unnoticed. He fumes, however, at the stupidity of it all, and,
when Ophelia asks him what the inexplicable show means,
he replies in an exasperated tone: "Marry, this is miching
mallecho, it means mischief." She notes his anger, attributes
it and the cryptic remark which accompanies it to a sudden
freak of madness, and soothingly suggests: "Belike this show
imports the argument of the play." Ophelia has a double
part to perform in this scene. As Hamlet's lover she has to do
what she can to calm his troubled spirit, to lend her small
assistance in nursing it back to sanity. As Shakespeare's puppet she has to provide the audience with clues. This remark
exhibits her in both rôles.

As for "mischief", there is mischief enough. The situation
has been saved for the moment by the King's unwatchfulness;
but what may not the actors do next? For, as Hamlet guesses,
there is worse behind. Yes, here comes a presenter, who
confirms his blackest fears. He is on tenter-hooks. A *dumb*-
show may slip by unobserved, but the spoken words of a
presenter, who will present the mouse-trap all too carefully,
cannot fail to reach the ears of Claudius. "We shall know
by this fellow", he cries in an anguished voice; "The players
cannot keep counsel, they'll tell all." But wondering Ophelia,

all unwitting of the true state of affairs, cannot leave Hamlet alone. "Will a' tell us what this show meant?" she persists, innocently touching him on the raw. "Ay, or any show that you will show him", retorts Hamlet savagely, breaking out into ribaldry, this time with too serious an intention, as she feels. "You are naught, you are naught", she reproves, hurt though still gentle; "I'll mark the play." But Master Presenter helps her not a whit towards the meaning of the show. To her surprise, Hamlet's joy, and the spectators' delighted amusement, he turns out to be—a prologue! And his three lines of silly jingle leave the cat still in the bag. Hamlet is safe, and he relapses into jocularity. "Is this a prologue, or the posy of a ring?" he enquires with mingled feelings of intense relief and an outraged sense of dramatic propriety. "'Tis brief, my lord", assents Ophelia, taking him back into her favour, as she notices, with relief on her side, that the storm-cloud has passed away from his mind as suddenly as it had come.

The subtlety of this is masterly in the extreme, but all the points would be readily grasped by the judicious among the audience, if the dialogue were acted as Shakespeare intended it should be. Hamlet's face of dismay at the appearance of the dumb-show, his furtive glances at the King as the panto-mime is being played, the exasperation in the tone of his comment upon it, his despair when the presenter enters, his savagery as Ophelia rubs it in, and finally his relief as the presenter turns out to be nothing but a posy-prologue—all this, together with Ophelia's part therein, is actable enough. And Shakespeare's boldness is the equal of his subtlety. For he makes all his dramatic capital out of his principal difficulty, the difficulty of rendering the unconsciousness of Claudius natural and obvious. The whole business revolves round that, and the breathless question in the minds of the spectators throughout is: Will the King find out the plot too soon? The vicissitudes of Hamlet's mood are mirrored in theirs. Their anxiety is great until the dumb-show goes off, and the appearance of the presenter revives it in full force. And, when the tension is relaxed, the dumb-show has fallen naturally into its place in the scene, the stupidity of the players is fully appreciated, and the episode is so exciting in its doubled suspense that, while taking in the complete identity which the show reveals, the spectators bother no more about it, since all their thoughts are concentrated upon Claudius. Finally, this obsession with Claudius's doings drives still deeper into their minds the fact that he has not seen anything, so that by building upon his difficulty Shakespeare has completed his triumph over it.

The interlude itself now begins, opening with the seventy lines of dialogue between the Player King and Queen upon the subject of widowhood and second marriage, lines written in a deliberately archaic style in order to distinguish them from the rest of *Hamlet*. They are deliberately commonplace also, so as to provide a rest for the audience after the excitement connected with the dumb-show and the prologue. They are not devoid of interest because they support the o'er-hasty-marriage theory and reflect upon the Queen. But the interest is a secondary one, and Shakespeare has moderated the tempo, according to his invariable custom, in order that his spectators may get, as it were, a second wind before the murderer enters and the pace becomes hot again. Moreover, after the dumb-show, which has told them just what to expect, the length and emptiness of the interlude add greatly to the tension.[1] Yet the lines give them something to think about, something unconnected with the immediate action. For the Player King concludes with a long disquisition on the subject of human instability. It is leitmotiv once more and reflects on the problem of Hamlet's character, though at this stage the audience will be hardly conscious of it.[2] And, as so often happens in Shakespeare, what serves the purpose of dramatic irony has its direct dramatic point also, a point for Hamlet and Claudius. The name of the play is " The Mouse-trap", and a mouse-trap is no use without bait. The spring of the machine lies in the speech of Lucianus at the end, but the problem is how to get the victim up to it and nosing round, so that when the trap is released he will be caught fast and squealing in its jaws. Somehow the interest of the King must be arrested and secured before Lucianus appears, must be secured by an object quite unconnected with the poisoning, since a glimpse of the spring will frighten away the game. Claudius missed the dumb-show; he must not be allowed to miss the play; he must be lured into the trap by a savoury bait. The second-marriage theme is the cheese for his majesty the mouse. Let us watch how Hamlet pushes it under his nose, how the victim sniffs at it, and finally how he swallows it.

"'Tis brief, my lord", says Ophelia. "As woman's love", caps Hamlet; and his retort, which may be taken as a reflec-

---

[1] This important point, which lends additional support to my theory of the dumb-show, I owe to Mr George Rylands.

[2] Cf. below, pp. 261–2.

tion upon her jilting of him, as one more prop to the thwarted-love theory, is also and primarily intended as an introduction to the interlude which is now, at last, about to begin. Before that wretched dumb-show usurped the stage upon which Hamlet had expected to see the Player King and Queen, he had carefully pointed the moral in two finely apt speeches on the cheerfulness of his mother's looks. But the villainous players had spoilt all that, and, now the dialogue of the play is ready to commence, he must be brief—like the superfluous Prologue who has helped to make his own prologue ineffective. Yet he tries to make up in pitch and articulation for what the phrase lacks in length, and the words go well home, to stick in the memory and be pondered upon as the dialogue progresses.

The first twenty lines afford plenty of opportunity for this pondering, since they contain nothing to interest either Claudius or anyone else. But the nine that follow, with two snap-couplets on marrying second husbands and killing first ones, spoken, we must suppose, with all the passion which the Player Queen should give them, ought to arrest attention. The reference is carefully confined to the Queen; it is wives, and not second husbands, which are hinted at as possible murderers. Hamlet is testing his mother as to her complicity in the murder; and his aside "That's wormwood, wormwood" suggests a start or a flinching on her part which would seem to him evidence of guilt. But Claudius also begins to sniff at this; for a faint aroma of the cheese is now perceptible. A long gnomic passage follows, in which the interest is again relaxed, though it has its point, just noted, for the audience. But the scent grows strong once more in the last two lines of the speech, and the Player Queen's violent oath of fidelity, together with Hamlet's comment, "If she should break it now!" brings the game right up to the bait. Player King sleeps, Player Queen leaves him, and Hamlet turns—not to Claudius, that would never do—but to Gertrude, with "Madam, how like you this play?" The inference is glaringly obvious, and she stammers "The lady doth protest too much methinks", trying to put the best face she can upon it, conscious that the eyes of the court are looking at her. Hamlet, who is almost as anxious that she should see it as that Claudius should, does his utmost to drive the point home. "O, but *she'll* keep her word", he mocks wickedly. This brings uncle-mouse fairly into the trap with the cheese in his mouth. The suspicions of Claudius are fully aroused, not about the murder—he has no inkling of that as yet—but about the second-marriage theme. What new mad prank is Hamlet up to? He arranged this play, and must be held accountable for it. "Have you heard the argument?" he asks his nephew sharply. "Is there no offence in't?" His attention is thoroughly secured; he will now watch the play out. The bait has been swallowed whole; and the first part of Hamlet's task is accomplished.

Too much "o'er-hasty marriage" business, however, may frighten the mouse before the spring is released, and if so the trap will be empty after all. Hamlet must both soothe the King and give a fresh turn to his thoughts. The chorus-talk becomes here extraordinarily brilliant and audacious, for it rivets the victim's attention by dazzling him with glints of steel—the steel of the spring itself! "No, no," replies Hamlet to his uncle's last question, stroking his prey with a gentleness which conceals exquisite malice, "*they do but jest*, poison in jest, no offence i'th'world." "Poison!" the word grates harshly on the ear of Claudius, as it was meant to do. Hamlet is playing prologue again; he is preparing the King's mind for Lucianus and his vial; he is flashing the vial in his face, but so swiftly that he cannot see what it is. The flash is disconcerting, but Claudius has no suspicion of the truth, and his thoughts are still occupied with second husbands as he asks for more information: "What do you call the play?" The answer is rapped out suddenly: "The Mouse-trap, marry how trapically."[1] Hamlet knows the quarry is caught, and he cannot resist the temptation to give vent to his glee, to cry "marry trap" like a boy who has won the game.[2] "The Mouse-trap" makes the King start, he knows not why; perhaps there is something in Hamlet's manner to cause it; a strange being, this nephew of his! "Marry how trapically" he does not catch, or, if he does, Hamlet hastily covers it up by giving it a "tropical" twist in the context that follows.

The rest of the speech, with its talk of Vienna, Gonzago and Baptista, is reassuring enough, and contains nothing more about second marriages.* It is prologue work again, however, though King Mouse is unaware of the claws in the soft paw which is caressing him, oh! so gently. "'Tis a knavish piece of work, but what of that? your majesty, and we that have free souls, it touches us not—let the galled jade wince, our

---

[1] "trapically" is the reading of Q1; Q2 and F1 give us "tropically". But in the pronunciation of the time the two words were much alike; cf. G. D. Willcock, "Shakespeare and Elizabethan English"(*A Companion to Shakespeare Studies*, p. 119. Cf. also note in my *Hamlet*).

[2] Cf. *The Merry Wives of Windsor*, 1.1.155–6: "I will say 'marry trap' with you", i.e. I will give you tit for tat.

withers are unwrung." How sweet these words and this moment must be to Hamlet! The bait is swallowed; the mouse sits, still unconscious, in the very jaws of the trap; and the spring is about to go off! Nothing now can save the King.

Yet the Prince keeps his head admirably through it all. He has others to catch as well as Claudius; and as the murderer enters he realises how they may be caught. In a loud voice, so that all can hear, he suddenly announces: "This is one Lucianus, Nephew to the King." I give the sentence from the text of the Second Quarto, which with its comma, denoting a slight pause, and its emphasis-capital for the essential word, beautifully exhibits the force which Shakespeare intended the actor to throw into his pronunciation of the all-important "Nephew". By this time the courtiers are as keenly intent upon the play as Claudius himself. The attacks upon the Queen have not escaped their notice; the cause of Hamlet's madness is, we must suppose, as hotly discussed among them as by their principals; and Rosencrantz and Guildenstern have doubtless whispered the word "ambition". When, therefore, a new character enters and is described by the master of the ceremonies as the nephew of the King, they ask whether he may not be intended for Hamlet himself. And they watch the doings of this actor with bated breath; for it is now clear to all that the interlude has a direct bearing upon the royal house, and has been selected by the mad Prince for that very reason. "You are as good as a chorus, my lord", breathes Ophelia. She speaks truth; it is the acme of his chorus-work.

Lucianus has a little business to perform before the speech; he has to take off the King's crown, kiss it, and place it on his own head.[1] Hamlet knows this, and occupies the interval with "idle" love-talk with Ophelia, in which his scorn for "presenters" is once again evident. They are his last words to her before they separate for ever. His mind is completely at ease. All his game are now in the trap—all except the Queen perhaps, and he can deal with her later. It only remains to begin those lines of his, those precious lines of which he is so proud, and the gin will go off, the jaws will snap, and the imprisoned prey will writhe in the anguish that Hamlet longs to see.

But Shakespeare has his master-stroke to play in this scene. There must be a hitch, at the eleventh hour, to raise the excitement of the audience to the highest possible point. The actor is very long with his crown-business. What in Heaven's name is he doing? Hamlet looks up, and the sight he sees freezes a half-spoken sentence to Ophelia on his lips.[2] This First Player, in whom after the Pyrrhus speech he had put his confidence—confidence grossly abused by the insertion of the dumb-show and the prologue—has once again flown straight in the face of his express commands. He is strutting and fretting about the stage, making the ludicrous grins of the conventional murderer, and sawing the air with the hand which holds the vial. He has caught, actor-like, the electric feeling of his audience, and is determined to make the most of his opportunity. All Hamlet's irritability is revived. Is this periwig-pated ruffian going to ruin everything after all, as

[1] This is what the murderer does in the dumb-show and Lucianus should, I suppose, go through the same performance, only more elaborately.

[2] The punctuation of the Second Quarto, which marks a long pause after "husbands", again brings out the point delightfully.

he so nearly ruined it at the beginning of the play? Is he going to tear the passion to tatters, to the very rags, to split the ears of all present, so that the very point of the whole evening may be missed, and the Mouse-trap fail to catch its prey? The situation is intolerable; something must be done, and that quickly, to bring the rogue and peasant slave to his senses. After a brief moment of speechless indignation, Hamlet bursts into bitter sarcasm. "'Begin, murderer!'" he shouts at him—"murderer of the Play, and now about to murder my lines. 'Pox! leave thy damnable faces and begin.' Come, tear the speech to tatters in your own sweet style. O'er-do Termagant and out-herod Herod! Let's have it in the fashion of the good old ranting chronicle plays. Quick, fellow: 'the croaking raven doth bellow for revenge'; that's your mark!"

The audience has had its third moment of breathless suspense. But all is well. Whether subconsciously or unconsciously, "revenge" is more prologue-work in Hamlet's mouth, and sounds ominously in the ears of both Claudius and the court. Hamlet, however, is not thinking of anything but the play, and the speech to the player is mock-prologue this time. Lucianus pulls himself together; the quotation from the old chronicle reminds him of Hamlet's words half an hour before; and he speaks the lines clearly and trippingly on the tongue, so that their full effect is felt. The court sees the point of the drama at last: the Player King is Claudius, and crazy Hamlet is threatening to murder his uncle and seize the crown. Claudius also sees the point, *his* point. The jaws of the deadly trap hold him in a vice. The words "mixture rank, of midnight weeds collected" bring back to his vision in dreadful detail that scene four months before, when he too was bending over a sleeping king, about to poison him with "cursed hebona in a vial". His face grows livid, he clutches the arms of his seat, his eyes start from his head. He has forgotten everything, everyone, except the hideous spectacle before him. Yes, the murderer is pouring the poison into the ears of the sleeper. The secure hour, the kind of poison, the flowery bank, the dozing king are the same. Just so, that is the way it should be done, that is how he poisoned his brother on that afternoon in the palace garden. It takes the voice of Hamlet to bring him slowly back to his senses. At first he can hardly follow the words. But he must force himself to listen; it is vital to hear what this incomprehensible, this fearful, this omniscient nephew of his is saying: "Gonzago...story extant...Italian." The words are meaningless, pointless, in their bland suavity. But what follows is not: "You shall see anon how the murderer gets the love of Gonzago's wife." Murderer, wife! wife, murderer! second husband, poison! The thing is clear. The plot of the interlude is his life's history. *Hamlet knows all!* Claudius is not safe; anything may happen. He pulls himself to his feet, and, squealing for light, he totters as fast as his trembling knees will carry him from the terrible, the threatening room. King Mouse has become a shambling, blinking paddock.

The play has made mad the guilty, but it has also appalled the free. As the murderer, the nephew, begins to administer his sham poison, a murmur of horror and indignation runs round the assembled court. Hamlet affects surprise at this and the now visible distemperature of his uncle. His cue is still "our withers are unwrung". His urbanity is imperturbable. "You are mistaken, gentlemen", he seems to protest. "'His name's Gonzago', as I told you before. 'The story is extant, and written in very choice Italian.' It has nothing whatever to do with Claudius or Denmark. Why all this fuss? You are spoiling the play. There is more to follow. 'You shall see anon how the murderer gets the love of Gonzago's wife.'" But courtiers as well as King have had enough. As their master rises at the outrage—quite properly, as they think—they break up in confusion. Hamlet sees all his enemies in full flight, a panic-stricken mob. He no longer conceals his malice, as he hurls his last shaft into the midst of them. "What! frighted with false fire!" he shouts through the clamour, though still his meaning is a double one. The Queen, good lady, ever sympathetic with those in distress, convinced like the rest that her son has "much offended" the King, sees that he is ill, and follows him out with the solicitous enquiry: "How fares my lord?" It is the very question which Claudius had asked Hamlet at the beginning of the scene. Hamlet may "eat the air" chameleon-like, but capon-Claudius is stuffed now and ready for the carving: he has had a bellyful of "fare". Polonius also has eaten of strange meat. But he is a politician, and has at last grasped the intentions of Hamlet. His daughter has been made a screen; the thwarted-love pose was a cloak for ambition; Claudius was right all the time. He sternly commands the play to stop, and hurries after the royal pair to consult with them, Rosencrantz and Guildenstern as to the steps to be taken in view of this menace to the throne. Ophelia too, like a frightened bird, has fluttered off with the throng.

And so at last Hamlet is left alone with Horatio. He throws

himself exultantly into his uncle's state seat, and chants a wild ballad snatch. Oh! the relief, the triumph, the infinite glee of that moment! He is back in the green-room of his mind, with the friend of his heart to praise him, and behind him a marvellously successful performance of histrionic art. All his disguises, his complicated and interwoven parts, drop from him. He is free, free to revel in the retrospect and to give full vent to his feelings of rapture: "Would not this, sir, and a forest of feathers—if the rest of my fortunes turn Turk with me—with two Provincial roses on my razed shoes, get me a fellowship in a cry of players, sir?" He is thinking of his acting, his lines, his admirable stage-management which saved the situation when all seemed lost. It is a characteristic outburst. Hamlet's first thoughts are of his amazing dramatic success, exceeding his wildest dreams. It is only afterwards that he remembers his uncle.

VI

HAMLET'S MAKE-UP

You would seem to know my stops, you would pluck out the heart of my mystery, you would sound me from my lowest note to the top of my compass...'Sblood, do you think I am easier to be played on than a pipe? call me what instrument you will, though you can fret me, you cannot play upon me.

HAMLET'S MAKE-UP

The turning-point

The exit of the King "marvellous distempered" is the turning-point of *Hamlet*. The comedy of masks is over, and the two mighty opposites stand face to face in full consciousness of each other's mind and purpose. The truth of the Ghost's story has been proved up to the hilt, and Hamlet is left with no shred of excuse for doubting his uncle's guilt, or for pretending to himself to doubt it. On the other hand, the scales have dropped from the eyes of Claudius. The "antic disposition" is exposed as a cover, not for ambitious designs, but for something far more deadly: Hamlet knows.

The situation is one not easy to parallel in modern life, even in the field of so-called cut-throat competition upon which our industrial and commercial magnates tilt in full panoply.[1] We are likely, therefore, to see it through a romantic haze which will obscure its significance and take off the sharpness of its detail. But both the occasion and its necessities would be evident enough to an Elizabethan "in great place", a statesman or courtier, a Cecil or a Raleigh, accustomed to move with cat-like wariness on heights where, as Bacon says (and none knew better), "the standing is slippery and the regress

[1] Since I wrote these words, political developments in Germany have restored conditions there in some ways closely approximating to those of sixteenth-century Europe. Whatever may be thought of the Nazi movement, it offers plenty of first-class material for future dramatists, or film producers.

is either a downfall or at least an eclipse",[1] where too the foothold was so narrow that one might scarcely keep it without thrusting other climbers into the gulf beneath. Such men, and indeed all who took an interest of any kind in politics, would understand the situation. As to its necessities, there could be no two opinions: Hamlet must now act, and act *at once*. "It is good", writes Bacon elsewhere, "to commit the beginnings of all great actions to Argus with his hundred eyes, and the ends to Briareus with his hundred hands; first to watch and then to speed. For the helmet of Pluto, which maketh the politic man go invisible, is secrecy in the counsel and celerity in the execution. For when things are come to the execution, there is no secrecy comparable to celerity; like the motion of a bullet in the air, which flyeth so swift as it out-runs the eye."[2] Things were now come to the execution; Hamlet can go invisible and take secret counsel with himself no longer. He must act, or Claudius will act first.

He does not act; and his failure to act is so extraordinary that his conduct at once becomes an engrossing topic and continues so for the rest of the play. Thus the unkennelling of Claudius's guilt is technically as well as dramatically the pivot of *Hamlet*. Our attention, hitherto directed to the thrilling and elaborate intrigues connected with the "antic disposition" and the testing of the Ghost's story, is now riveted upon the single problem of the hero's inaction. Plot is the main interest of the first half of the play, character of the second.

The problem of delay is a commonplace of *Hamlet* criticism. It has, however, been generally misconceived; and

[1] *Essays*, "Of great place".   [2] *Essays*, "Of delays".

for two reasons. In the first place its gravity has been under-estimated, through failure to appreciate the political stand-point, just noticed, of the Elizabethan world; in the eyes of which such inaction would appear utter madness or incredible folly. And, in the second place, the vicious habit of taking stock of the whole play at once, instead of treating it as a serial work of art in which incidents and events are arranged in a certain order and intended to be apprehended in that order, has caused many writers to overlook the fact that Hamlet's procrastination does not become really glaring until after the Gonzago-play. Shakespeare, it is not necessary to say, scores the theme with his usual skill, and the delay is not suddenly thrust at us without warning. Just as he prepares his audience for the King's discomfiture in the play scene and for the attempt to purge his soul in the prayer scene by giving him a few conscience-stricken lines in the nunnery scene, so he first of all emphasises the delay in the Hecuba soliloquy in order that we may not be altogether bewildered by Hamlet's astonishing behaviour after the play scene. But that soliloquy comes at the very end of the second act, and, though at this point spectators in retrospect may possibly begin wondering what Hamlet had been doing during the interval between his interviews with the Ghost on the battlements and with Ophelia in her closet, an interval which in 3.2—and not till then—they learn extended to at least two months, they have been given no opportunity for such speculation up to that point.[1] And even so, they are not allowed to dwell upon it; for, despite the violence of Ham-let's language, the nunnery scene and the play scene that

---

[1] *Vide* above pp. 94-5.

follow are so absorbing as to exclude all other thoughts. Thus it is only when Hamlet's neglect to crown his theatrical triumph with the act of vengeance that should follow it cries aloud for explanation that his strange outburst at the end of 2.2 begins to be appreciated.[1]

To say, however, that Hamlet's procrastination is the predominant interest of the last two and a half acts is not to say they are devoid of incident, of the "variety" which Dr Johnson praised; far from it. The King at his prayers, the shending of Gertrude, the slaying of Polonius, Hamlet's departure to England, the madness of Ophelia, the insurrection of Laertes, his unholy conspiracy with Claudius, the drowning of Ophelia, her funeral and the struggle at her grave, the comic element provided by the sexton on the one hand and by Osric on the other; all these, culminating in the fencing-match and the four deaths which result therefrom, make incident enough to supply any ordinary dramatist with stuff for half a dozen plays. Yet they form for the most part a series of detached episodes; only a few of them contribute to the mechanism of the main plot; and, though they are exciting in themselves, none except the fencing-match and what leads up to it is felt to be central. A great question overshadows them all, until the final scene: When will Hamlet exact just retribution from his uncle? and why does he not do

---

[1] Cf. A. J. A. Waldock, *Hamlet: a Study in Critical Method*, pp. 78–95. This little book, which reached my hands late in the writing of my own and with the details of which I often find myself in disagreement, contains in my judgment the wisest criticism on *Hamlet* that has yet appeared. It anticipates some of the general conclusions in the present chapter and I was encouraged to come upon a critic thinking along my own lines just as I was growing to a point.

so? Shakespeare does everything in his power to keep this question constantly before the mind of his audience, and his efforts are so successful that we remain as conscious of it when Hamlet is off the stage as when he is speaking to us.

Once we see it in this perspective, the whole play gains balance and vitality. On the traditional interpretation the fourth act sags. Occupied with the problem of delay from the very beginning, imagining Hamlet already "sunk for the most part in 'bestial oblivion' or fruitless broodings, and falling deeper and deeper into the slough of despond"[1] during "the long interval" between acts 1 and 2, we are growing a little weary of it all before the end of act 3, the very point where Shakespeare begins to insist upon it. But when, absorbed in other matters up to the end of the play scene, we only then come fully to realise the existence of the problem, it enters the field of our attention as a fresh and astonishing interest with more than sufficient life in it to keep us fascinated well into the fifth act.

Shakespeare, as everyone knows, never furnishes an explanation for Hamlet's inaction. All he does is to exhibit it to us as a problem, turning it round and round, as it were, before our eyes so that we may see every side of it, and then in the end leaving us to draw our own conclusions. Hamlet himself tries to explain it both in the Hecuba soliloquy and in the soliloquy provoked by the spectacle of the Norwegian army; but his failure to do so exhibits the attempts as part of the problem. Before we examine these attempts, before we ourselves attempt to draw the bow which has foiled the greatest Shakespearian critics, let us first of all do what

[1] *Vide* above, pp. 93–4.

Shakespeare tacitly asks us to do, let us *watch* Hamlet. Before we discuss his character let us study his behaviour.

This is to take things in their proper order, their dramatic order; for Hamlet's behaviour begins to strike us as strange long before we ought to be troubling ourselves about his delay. Almost from the outset, in fact, it presents us with another problem, which we shall find is technically associated with the delay, though dramatically distinct from it. I mean the problem of Hamlet's madness. We have already glanced at this in dealing with the "antic disposition". The time has come to consider it more carefully. Let us, therefore, retrace our steps and watch Hamlet's behaviour from his entry in the first act, gathering impressions as we proceed, that is to say, as Shakespeare reveals more and more to us; but when we come to the second half of the play reserving for convenience the question of the procrastination until we have completed a general survey of his supposed insanity.

Sore distraction

Yet we must be careful. A "behaviourist" interpretation may be as incomplete and misleading as any other purely psychological study of Hamlet.[1] For he is not a living man or an historical character; he is a single figure, if the most prominent figure, in a dramatic composition. We can no more analyse his mind than we can dissect his body. We cannot even consider him by himself, apart from the other characters, apart from the cloud of suggestion about him with which his creator constantly infects our imaginations from

[1] *Vide* below, p. 218.

beginning to end of the drama. Nothing, I have noted, is said about Hamlet's inability to act until the end of 2.2. But Shakespeare has begun to wrap him in an atmosphere of dejection long before that. The whole tone of act 1, for example, is one of despondency and failure. Nine lines from the opening of the play, before we have even heard that there is a Prince of Denmark, the sentry Francisco has struck the note of heart-sickness. To Horatio and Marcellus the apparition suggests "something rotten" or "some strange eruption" in the state of Denmark. The Ghost himself speaks ominously of

> the fat weed
> That rots itself in ease on Lethe wharf.

And Hamlet himself concludes the act with the bitter cry:

> The time is out of joint, O cursèd spite,
> That ever I was born to set it right!

But the most striking instance of Shakespeare's cunning in preparing the minds of his audience for effects he will introduce later is a speech in 1.4, the relevance of which to the theme of *Hamlet* as a whole has been somewhat neglected. I refer to the meditative lines occasioned by the braying of the kettle-drum and trumpet, heard by Hamlet, Horatio and Barnardo from the battlements as King Claudius "drains his draughts of Rhenish down". After remarking that the unhappy reputation for drunkenness, which such revelling has given the Danes, takes

> From our achievements, though performed at height,
> The pith and marrow of our attribute,

Hamlet continues,

So, oft it chances in particular men,
That for some vicious mole of nature in them,
As in their birth, wherein they are not guilty
(Since nature cannot choose his origin),
By the o'ergrowth of some complexion,
Oft breaking down the pales and forts of reason,
Or by some habit, that too much o'er-leavens
The form of plausive manners—that these men,
Carrying I say the stamp of one defect,
Being nature's livery, or fortune's star,
His virtues else be they as pure as grace,
As infinite as man may undergo,
Shall in the general censure take corruption
From that particular fault.

It is no accident of the press, as emending editors assume, that leads the speaker to pass from the plural to the singular. He is thinking of himself,* or rather Shakespeare is asking us to think of him; and though, at this stage of the play, we do not see the point, the magician is plying us with suggestion. A lesser dramatist would have placed the lines in Horatio's mouth and made him utter them as an epitaph over his dead friend; Shakespeare works them into the overture, to sound in our ears before he has shown us anything at all of the "complexion" which will "break down the pales and forts of" Hamlet's "reason". The lines end with a passage unhappily corrupt, though if we emend it, as I believe we may, it offers, by means of an alchemical metaphor, what probably takes us as near as we can get to Shakespeare's own judgment upon Hamlet:

> The dram of evil
> Doth all the noble substance often dout
> To his own scandal.

In other words, the character of the man might have been pure gold[1] but for the touch of evil or weakness which brings him to ruin. There was no spot-lighting on the Elizabethan stage, but Shakespeare knew a better way of shedding the ray of illusion upon the features of his characters, the way of poetry. Remembering, then, that Hamlet is a stage-figure and not a "real man", let us turn and look at him in the framework of the theatre.

When we first see him, at the meeting of the Privy Council, he is gloomy and sardonic, but not more so than is warranted by the loss of the crown and the marriage of his mother to the usurper, a marriage at once "o'er-hasty" and incestuous. The first soliloquy shows him trapped and defiled by the slimy coils of Gertrude's lust, his moral being shaken to its foundations, but his mind still unimpaired; for he seems perfectly normal during the conversation with Horatio, Marcellus and Barnardo afterwards. Nor in 1.4 is there anything surprising in his fierce threat to "make a ghost of him that lets" him, as he attempts to follow his father's spirit. It is only after the terrible interview, with its revelation of his mother's full iniquity and of the murder, that we begin to be aware that something is seriously wrong. Horatio's fears that the Ghost might "deprive" his "sovereignty of reason and draw" him "into madness" are seen to be not altogether baseless. In the hysterical speech about the "tables", in the "wild and whirling words" which come later, and in the unseemly hilarity followed by deep depression which marks his dealing with the "fellow in the cellarage" we have

---

[1] Gold was the "noble substance" *par excellence* to the "chemists" of that age.

evidence, as I have already indicated,[1] that his mind is finding the tragic burden too heavy for it and is beginning to give way beneath the strain. These symptoms of mental lesion, however, are dramatically connected with the assumption of the "antic disposition". Were they merely introduced for that purpose, or is the "antic disposition" later associated with real lack of balance? Did Shakespeare, in other words, intend Hamlet's conduct in the cellarage scene to represent a temporary mood arising from the tension of the moment, or had the Ghost effected that which he expressly warned his son to avoid, namely a permanent "tainting" of his mind?

The "wondrous strange" events of the cellarage scene would suggest some at least of these questions to an Elizabethan audience, upon which, be it noted, Hamlet's "wild and whirling" conduct must have made a far deeper impression than his single and parenthetical reference to the "antic disposition". Indeed, it is not until he begins palpably to play the madman with Polonius that the real point of that reference will dawn upon a spectator seeing the play for the first time. The foreshortened view of modern omniscient criticism tends to focus attention upon the "antic disposition" too early.

To answer the questions ourselves we must pass on to the second act. The talk about Laertes in Paris between Polonius and Reynaldo with which this act opens shows that some weeks have elapsed. We are therefore all the more anxious to hear how Hamlet has been faring during the interval. The first sight we get of him is through Ophelia's eyes:

[1] *Vide* pp. 50, 90–2, 130.

> Pale as his shirt, his knees knocking each other,
> And with a look so piteous in purport
> As if he had been looséd out of hell
> To speak of horrors.

It is a description of physical conditions which, as already noted,[1] can only be explained as arising from some serious mental disturbance. Dr Bradley writes, "Many readers and critics" make the mistake of imagining "that Hamlet went straight to Ophelia's room after his interview with the Ghost". Theatrical producers who cut the Reynaldo episode and so remove all indication of the passage of time between the end of act 1 and the beginning of act 2 have done much to foster this error.[2] But its source is in the lines before us, which depict a state of mind and body closely resembling and, I feel sure, intended to recall that in which the Ghost left Hamlet as he uttered the fatal words "Remember me".*

The next scene opens with the speech by Claudius to Rosencrantz and Guildenstern, which after a word of greeting begins:

> Something have you heard
> Of Hamlet's transformation—so call it,
> Sith nor th'exterior nor the inward man
> Resembles that it was.

It is plain that a "transformation" of the exterior man, visible to all the court, could not be peculiar to Ophelia's closet. The King's words are followed up by Gertrude's reference to her "too much changéd son", and by Polonius's tedious "short tale" of how Hamlet

---

[1] *Vide* p. 111.
[2] Cf. my "Elizabethan Shakespeare" (in *Aspects of Shakespeare*, pp. 214–15).

Fell into a sadness, then into a fast,
Thence to a watch, thence into a weakness,
Thence to a lightness, and by this declension,
Into the madness *wherein now he raves*,
And all we mourn for.

This last, discounted as the mere garrulity of a foolish old man by critics who miss much in *Hamlet* by underestimating the intellectual powers of Claudius's chief councillor, is evidently meant to give us a medical history of Hamlet's condition since the revelation of the Ghost. Dejection, distaste for food, insomnia, crazy behaviour, fits of delirium,[1] and finally raving madness: such are the stages of the disorder noted by those best able to watch the patient closely. For the symptoms that Polonius records are all mental, and he mentions them as facts well known to the King and Queen. Are the audience expected to attribute all this to "antic disposition"? Surely they should associate it with Hamlet's wild behaviour when they last saw him and with the report of his evident distraction of mind in Ophelia's room. They will perceive, of course, that he is acting a part at his encounter with Fishmonger Polonius, but what of the profound despondency which peeps out from behind the antic mask?

---

[1] The difference between "weakness" and "lightness" is, I take it, one between imbecile conduct during waking hours and "bad dreams" or delirious fancies. For "weakness" (= weakness of wit) cf. *Two Gent.* 1.1.69: "Made wit with musing weak"; *Temp.* 2.2.149: "A very weak monster!" *Lear*, 2.4.204: "I pray you, father, being weak seem so"; and for "lightness" (= light-headedness) cf. *Err.* 5.1.72: "And thereof comes it that his head is light"; *Oth.* 4.1.280: "Are his wits safe? Is he not light of brain?" I had not perceived the full force of these words in preparing my edition of *Hamlet*. Hamlet himself sums up the first five symptoms when he speaks of "my weakness and my melancholy" at 2.2.605.

What of the reference to walking into a grave, or of the leave-taking of Polonius?

Pol. . . . My honourable lord, I will most humbly take my leave of you.

Ham. You cannot, sir, take from me any thing that I will more willingly part withal: except my life, except my life, except my life.

No one, I believe, has ever denied that these last words express a genuine craving for death. Most critics, again, accept without question the admission about "bad dreams" and the execration of the universe as "a foul and pestilent congregation of vapours", in the talk with Rosencrantz and Guildenstern. Why then do they attach so little importance to the "turbulent and dangerous lunacy" of which Claudius speaks at the opening of the third act, echoing Polonius's earlier reference to "the madness wherein now he raves"?

We hear a good deal about such behaviour in the Amleth saga, but so far nothing of it has appeared in *Hamlet*. It is mentioned at this point, I think, to prepare us for the violence at the end of the scene, and for the assassination of Polonius later. It comes well, too, from the King's mouth, since it is his cue to insist, especially in the Queen's ear, that her son's madness is a public danger. But we have no right to treat it as false information. It fits in with the King's earlier description of Hamlet's state at the beginning of act 2, with Polonius's account of the development of his distemper, and with what we have noted concerning the disorder of his attire,[1] while Claudius would not make a statement like this if the fact were not well known to the whole court. We

[1] *Vide* pp. 96–8.

must, therefore, reckon with a "turbulent and dangerous" Hamlet. Surely, we may ask, all these indications are intended to give us information concerning his real state of mind? Indeed, when Hamlet himself speaks of his "weakness" and his "melancholy"[1] (2.2.605) he explicitly admits that he is suffering from mental disorder.

And, as a matter of fact, if we take the behaviour in the cellarage scene as the key to his behaviour for the rest of the play, we shall find that it accounts for a great deal. His outstanding characteristic in that scene, a characteristic so plain in the text that even the modern reader cannot miss it, we have seen to be one of emotional instability, an oscillation between intense excitement on the one hand and profound depression on the other. Such instability will explain all the points just noted above; it will explain too those periodic attacks of ungovernable agitation which afflict Hamlet throughout the play. These attacks have not passed unobserved by critics, but they have scarcely been made as much of as the text warrants, although they are of vital concern not only for the performance of the part but also for the interpretation of the action.

I find no fewer than seven of them. Two are those of the cellarage scene and the scene in Ophelia's closet just noticed. A third occurs when, left alone at the end of 2.2, Hamlet lashes himself into a fury of self-reproach over his delay:

Am I a coward?

Who calls me villain, breaks my pate across,
Plucks off my beard and blows it in my face,

---

[1] Both words denoted something far more definitely pathological in Shakespeare's day than they do now. Cf. p. 211 n. for "weakness" and pp. 226–8 for "melancholy".

> Tweaks me by the nose, gives me the lie i'th'throat
> As deep as to the lungs? who does me this?
> Ha, 'swounds, I should take it: for it cannot be
> But I am pigeon-liver'd, and lack gall
> To make oppression bitter, or ere this
> I should ha' fatted all the region kites
> With this slave's offal. Bloody, bawdy villain!
> Remorseless, treacherous, lecherous, kindless villain!
> O, vengeance!

So the tirade continues for another half dozen lines until at "A stallion! fie upon't! foh!" the voice breaks and Hamlet loses all control. Incidentally it is an outburst which must have given Burbadge a fine opportunity of showing how much better than his colleague, who had just been reciting the Pyrrhus speech, he

> Could force his soul so to his own conceit
> That from her working all his visage wanned,
> Tears in his voice, distraction in his aspect,
> A broken voice, and his whole function suiting
> With forms to his conceit.

The two speeches are for all the world like a theme given out by the First Violin and then repeated by the Soloist.

My fourth example comes from the nunnery scene. Here the mood of depression occurs first, with the "To be or not to be" soliloquy, and is succeeded by one of violence after the question "Where's your father?" a violence which increases as Hamlet returns for the second time. The fifth is the wild triumph which greets the King's exit in the play scene, and which Irving played in a state of frantic excitement;[1]

[1] *Vide* Mr Child's Stage-History of *Hamlet*, p. xciii of "The New Shakespeare" edition.

while the sixth and seventh may be seen in Hamlet's conduct towards his mother in the bedroom scene and in the "towering passion" of the funeral scene.

The last two we shall consider in detail later; but I may here quote a passage from the funeral scene which exactly describes the outbursts and their after-effects. Gertrude is committed by her promise to emphasise the genuineness of Hamlet's insanity; her insistence, therefore, that his outranting of Laertes by Ophelia's grave is "mere madness" should be discounted. But the rest of her attempt to explain his behaviour—

> And thus awhile the fit will work on him.
> Anon as patient as the female dove
> When that her golden couplets are disclosed
> His silence will sit drooping—

is so apt to the moods of melancholy exhaustion which alternate with those of frenzy that it must be accepted as deliberate comment on Shakespeare's part. Nor is it the only one of the kind. When Hamlet exclaims to Horatio:

> and blest are those
> Whose blood and judgement are so well co-medled,
> That they are not a pipe for Fortune's finger
> To sound what stop she please: give me that man
> That is not passion's slave, and I will wear him
> In my heart's core, ay in my heart of heart,

he is pathetically admitting that he is himself "passion's slave", and "a pipe for Fortune's finger", an admission which his creator puts into his mouth to warn the audience what to expect after the Gonzago-play is over. Hamlet owns to the same weakness, we shall find, in the moment of extreme contrition which overcomes him at sight of his father's spirit in his mother's room. But the most explicit reference belongs to that much misunderstood speech to Laertes just before the fencing-match, in which he excuses himself for the killing of Polonius on the ground that he is troubled "with a sore distraction".

The speech is so crucial that it must be quoted in full:

> Give me your pardon, sir. I have done you wrong,
> But pardon't, as you are a gentleman.
> This presence knows, and you must needs have heard,
> How I am punished with a sore distraction.
> What I have done
> That might your nature, honour and exception
> Roughly awake, I here proclaim was madness.
> Was't Hamlet wronged Laertes? never Hamlet.
> If Hamlet from himself be ta'en away,
> And when he's not himself does wrong Laertes,
> Then Hamlet does it not, Hamlet denies it.
> Who does it then? his madness. If't be so,
> Hamlet is of the faction that is wronged,
> His madness is poor Hamlet's enemy.
> Sir, in this audience,
> Let my disclaiming from a purposed evil
> Free me so far in your most generous thoughts,
> That I have shot my arrow o'er the house,
> And hurt my brother.

This is the most positive statement of Hamlet's madness by Hamlet himself in the whole play. Is it one last fling in the old game of "antic disposition" for the purpose of hoodwinking his enemies? Dr Johnson thought so and deplored it. "I wish", he writes, "Hamlet had made some other defence; it is unsuitable to the character of a brave or a good man to shelter himself in falsehood." It troubles Dr Bradley also, though he tries to extenuate it by asking "What moral difference is there between feigning insanity and asserting it?"[1] No *moral* difference perhaps, but a world of dramatic difference! It is inconceivable that Hamlet can be lying or pretending at this moment of the play, the moment when above all others his creator is anxious to secure our admiration and sympathy for him. Indeed, the whole speech is clearly designed to exhibit Hamlet as

> Most generous, and free from all contriving,

in contrast with his scheming false-faced opponent. He appeals to him first "as a gentleman" and then as "my brother"; he declares that Hamlet could "never" wrong Laertes. It is a noble and touching plea for forgiveness and for affection; to suppose it based upon a subterfuge is monstrous. It follows that when Hamlet tells us that he is subject to "a sore distraction" and killed Polonius in madness we are expected to believe him. *

The heart of the mystery

We are driven, therefore, to conclude with Loening, Bradley, Clutton-Brock and other critics that Shakespeare meant us to imagine Hamlet suffering from some kind of mental disorder throughout the play. Directly, however, such critics begin trying to define the exact nature of the disorder, they go astray. Its immediate origin cannot be questioned; it is caused, as we have seen, by the burden which fate lays upon

[1] *Shakespearean Tragedy*, pp. 420-1.

his shoulders. We are not, however, at liberty to go outside the frame of the play and seek remoter origins in his past history.[1] It is now well known, for instance, that a break-down like Hamlet's is often due to seeds of disturbance planted in infancy and brought to evil fruition under the influence of mental strain of some kind in later life. Had Shakespeare been composing *Hamlet* to-day, he might conceivably have given us a hint of such an infantile complex. But he knew nothing of these matters and to write as if he did is to beat the air. We may go further. It is entirely misleading to attempt to describe Hamlet's state of mind in terms of modern psychology at all, not merely because Shakespeare did not think in these terms, but because—once again—Hamlet is a character in a play, not in history. He is part only, if the most important part, of an artistic master-piece, of what is perhaps the most successful piece of dramatic illusion the world has ever known. And at no point of the composition is the illusion more masterly contrived than in this matter of his distraction.

In *Hamlet* Shakespeare set out to create a hero labouring under mental infirmity, just as later in *Macbeth* he depicted a hero afflicted by moral infirmity, or in *Othello* a hero tortured by an excessive and morbid jealousy. Hamlet struggles against his weakness, and the struggle is in great measure the ground-work of his tragedy. But though he struggles in vain, and is in the end brought to disaster, a disaster largely of his own making and involving his own house and that of

[1] Or, I may add, in the life history of his creator. For a criticism of Dr Ernest Jones's psycho-analysis of Hamlet and Shakespeare *vide* my Introduction to *Hamlet*, pp. xliv-xlv, and for one of Mr T. S. Eliot's application of that analysis *vide* Appendix D. See also p. vii above.

Polonius, we are never allowed to feel that his spirit is vanquished until "the potent poison quite o'er-crows" it. Had he been represented as a mere madman, we should of course have felt this; he would have ceased to be a hero and, while retaining our pity, would have forfeited our sympathy, our admiration—and our censure.[1] Ophelia exclaims,

> O, what a noble mind is here o'erthrown!

We know better: we realise that the mind is impaired, but we do not doubt for a moment that its nobility remains untouched; we see his sovereign reason often

> Like sweet bells jangled, out of tune and harsh,

yet all the while it retains its sovereignty and can recall its sweetness. There may be contradiction here; but we are not moving in the realm of logic. From the point of view of analytic psychology such a character may even seem a monster of inconsistency. This does not matter, if as here it also seems to spectators in the theatre to be more convincingly life-like than any other character in literature. For most critics have agreed that Hamlet is one of the greatest and most fascinating of Shakespeare's creations; that he is a study in genius. Shakespeare, in short, accomplished that which he intended; he wrote a supreme tragedy. In poetic tragedy

---

[1] Lear, of course, goes mad and we see his madness, though it passes away like a temporary illness. But the feelings Shakespeare claims for the two heroes are quite different. In Lear he shows us the spectacle of a Job-like being, stricken, smitten of God (for his sins) and of man, and yet winning through to a divine temper of forgiveness and reconciliation. His function is to suffer; he is not called upon like Hamlet to act. The madness, therefore, is simply the culmination of his torture; it is the effect, not the cause (as Dr Bradley notes), of the tragic conflict. Cf. *Shakespearean Tragedy*, pp. 13–14.

we contemplate beings greater than ourselves, greater than it is possible for man to be, enduring and brought to a calamitous end by sorrow or affliction or weakness of character which we should find unendurable; and we contemplate all this with unquestioning assent and with astonishment that deepens to awe. In the making of Hamlet, therefore, Shakespeare's task was not to produce a being psychologically explicable or consistent, but one who would evoke the affection, the wonder and the tears of his audience, and would yet be accepted as entirely human.

Only one critic, himself a poetic genius, has, I think, seen how it was contrived. Writing of Hamlet in *The Testament of Beauty*, Robert Bridges speaks of

> the artful balance whereby
> Shakespeare so gingerly put his sanity in doubt
> Without the while confounding his Reason;

and the point is to some extent elaborated in a passage— all too brief—of the essay entitled "The Influence of the Audience on Shakespeare's Drama". "Why", he asks, "has there been such question whether Hamlet was mad or only feigning, unless it was Shakespeare's design to make and leave it doubtful? and does not the hypothesis of such a design reconcile all?" And, he goes on to suggest that Shakespeare drew "a dramatic character purposely so as to elude analysis".[1] In a word, the solution of the problem is no abstruse psychological secret, no hidden complex, no unfathomable motive, but simply "an artful balance", a dramatic artifice by means of which the magician secures for his hero the understanding

[1] Bridges, *Collected Essays*, I, 25–7.

and indulgence which madness claims when the afflicted person is very dear or much admired, without at any moment allowing us to experience the alienation, disgust or horror which the spectacle of such madness might excite. Nor is the artifice peculiar to *Hamlet*; it is only a specially striking example of Shakespeare's general mode of working, of his tragic method. When Goethe told Zelter that he was incapable of writing tragedies because he could not tolerate discords unresolved,[1] he probably had Shakespeare in mind. And Keats, singling out the quality that goes "to form a Man of Achievement, especially in Literature, and which Shakespeare possessed so enormously", defines it as "*Negative Capability*, that is, when a man is capable of being in uncertainties, mysteries, doubts, without any irritable reaching after fact and reason".[2]

Bridges tells us that Shakespeare worked "purposely"; Keats suggests that the process was instinctive and perhaps unconscious. Whichever view be right, the balance was attained, and the technical means of its attainment are clear. In the first place, while there is much talk of Hamlet's madness, and though, as we have seen, he often yields to moods of excitement or despondency, on the stage we never see him in a condition of unmistakable insanity. It is Claudius who tells us of his "turbulent and dangerous lunacy", Ophelia who depicts his fit of delirium, or Hamlet himself who speaks retrospectively of his "bad dreams" or his "sore distraction". Furthermore, when Hamlet discusses his own condition, which he finds it impossible to explain, at the moment

[1] To Zelter, Oct. 31, 1831.
[2] Keats, *Letters*, Dec. 21, 1817.

of speaking he always seems in full possession of his faculties. Thus the soliloquies, which confirm us in our belief that there is something wrong with him because he tells us it is so, prove to us at the same time that he is fundamentally sane. A man who can describe his own mental symptoms in rational fashion is still one of ourselves. Ophelia, on the other hand, beautiful and pathetic figure as she is in the mad scenes, has passed beyond the pale of real sympathy because, her mind being completely out of control, she has ceased to be human. She is, as the King puts it,

> Divided from herself and her fair judgement,
> Without the which we are pictures or mere beasts.

We have only to think of Hamlet as a picture or mere beast to see that his derangement belongs to a different category altogether.* And I do not doubt that one reason why Shakespeare introduced these mad scenes into his play was to point this very distinction. It is true that in his request for Laertes's pardon just before the fencing-match, Hamlet uses words about himself which closely resemble those of Claudius about Ophelia:

> Was't Hamlet wronged Laertes? never Hamlet.
> If Hamlet from himself be ta'en away,
> And when he's not himself does wrong Laertes,
> Then Hamlet does it not, Hamlet denies it.
> Who does it then? his madness.

Yet there is an important difference. Hamlet can draw a line between "himself" and "his madness", a thing impossible for Ophelia; and so we gain the impression that he is usually normal but subject to occasional fits of madness. That Shakespeare never allows us to perceive exactly where the line falls is part of the artful balance. For example, the killing of Polonius, which Hamlet here attributes to his madness, is not felt to be an insane action while we witness it, not pathologically insane that is to say, though we are quite ready to accept Hamlet's word for its insanity an hour later.[1]

The fulcrum of the balance, the chief device by means of which Shakespeare prevents us seeing where sanity ends and madness begins is, as Bridges hints, the "antic disposition". We are led to suppose, I have shown, that Hamlet assumes it in the first place because he feels his mind tottering and wishes to conceal the fact from his friends. Thus the mask introduces the element of doubt from the very outset. Again, while it affords Hamlet a convenient concealment from the prying eyes of his enemies, whom it at once provokes and baffles, it is still more convenient for Shakespeare. It excites our curiosity, sustains our interest, and at the same time so effectually blurs the line for us that we can never be sure whether Hamlet oversteps it or not. We do not doubt, for instance, that he deliberately puts on the disposition when he becomes conscious of the presence of the eavesdroppers at the beginning of the nunnery scene; but who can define his real condition of mind at the end of that scene? Again, while he assumes the "idle" mask calmly and coldly in the play scene, by the time he drops it for his tête-à-tête with Horatio at the end his excitement has clearly got out of hand. Consider, even, the question of his disorderly attire. We have seen that

[1] In the theatre, that is; in the study the artifice shows a little too nakedly, and has therefore provoked question among the critics (*vide* above, pp. 216–7 and Stoll, *Art and Artifice in Shakespeare*, pp. 119–20).

one seventeenth-century spectator at least regarded this as so obviously assumed that he describes Hamlet as mad "but in clothes".[1] Was he right? We do not know; we have no means of knowing; Shakespeare did not wish us to know.

Yet while constantly putting Hamlet's "sanity in doubt", Shakespeare does it "gingerly", for two reasons, which are really one: he does not want us to become conscious of the doubt, because he does not wish to "confound his reason", that is to question his essential sanity. Doubts consciously entertained would be perplexing and distracting, while it is vital to his purpose to make us believe Hamlet fundamentally sane, because he desires us not only to admire his hero, but also to lament his defects. In a word, despite his sore distraction, Hamlet retains moral responsibility for his actions. Once again, the question is not one of psychological or ethical consistency but of the attitude of the audience. Shakespeare makes us *feel* that Hamlet is shirking a plain duty, and that he is blameworthy for this neglect. Yet at the same time he makes us realise that the procrastination is due to the distemper, is in fact part of it.

Hamlet's emotional outbursts are different in tone; they are delirious, savage, sarcastic, or merely hilarious. But they possess, we have seen, one feature in common, hysteria or lack of balance. They seem, moreover, to be generally associated with a very different mood, a mood of tenderness, solemnity or profound dejection. A similar and parallel oscillation between extremes is to be seen in the field of action, on what psychologists would now call the conative

[1] *Vide* p. 97.

side of Hamlet's behaviour. Corresponding with his attacks of uncontrollable excitement, and often accompanying them, we have impulsive or unpremeditated activity, activity in which he generally takes a keen delight, but which appears nevertheless to have very little to do with his volition. As many critics have noted, Hamlet often acts, but never upon deliberation. The assumption of the "antic disposition", the decision to test his uncle by means of the play, the murder of Polonius, the substitution of the "changeling" letter, the scene with Laertes in the grave-yard, and the killing of the King at the last are all actions taken on the spur of the moment. Shakespeare's anxiety to make Hamlet's identification of Lucianus with the "nephew to the king" in the play scene seem unpremeditated has actually concealed it from the attention of critics; to have given a hint of it beforehand would have suggested deliberation, though that Hamlet's mind is ready from the beginning of the scene to react thus is shown by his "promise-crammed" speech and his talk of the Capitol. Everything that Hamlet does, he does too readily by far at the suggestion of others; Fortune sounds the stop. Nor does he greatly care, so long as he can be *doing*. The swiftness of his decisions upon these occasions is well described in the account he gives of his mind at work when he discovers what the King's sealed commission contains:

> Being thus be-netted round with villanies—
> Or I could make a prologue to my brains
> They had begun the play;[1]

while the intense pleasure he derives from such impromptu

[1] 5.2.29–31.

activity comes out in his excited anticipation of his dealings
with Rosencrantz and Guildenstern on the voyage:

> For 'tis the sport to have the enginer
> Hoist with his own petar, and 't shall go hard
> But I will delve one yard below their mines,
> And blow them at the moon: O, 'tis most sweet
> When in one line two crafts directly meet.[1]

He does not say what he will do; he does not know what he
will do; he merely delights in the thought of doing something. On the other hand, his *in*activity, his inability to
perform that on which his mind is set, that which he wills,
corresponds with the emotional state in which he seems
drained of blood, devoid of all desire save the desire of
death, and even unable to accomplish that. At such times, as
he tells us himself, he is "dull and muddy-mettled". The
procrastination and the melancholy are all of a piece.

I call the "sore distraction" melancholy because that is the
name which Hamlet gives it,[2] and the name by which
Shakespeare and his audience no doubt thought of it. The
character of Hamlet, like that of many other dramatic characters of the period, was a study in melancholy; and
melancholy was a condition of mind to which men in
the late sixteenth century and throughout the seventeenth
gave much thought.[3] The interest found its culminating and
classical expression in *The Anatomy of Melancholy* by Robert

---

[1] 3.4.206–10.

[2] 2.2.605. The point, like other points, is much clearer in *Der bestrafte Brudermord* than in Shakespeare's *Hamlet*.

[3] Cf. J. Q. Adams, *op. cit.* pp. 195–8, 283–8, for an attempt to combine sixteenth-century and modern psychology in explanation of Hamlet's mental condition.

Burton, published in 1621, which proved melancholy to be "an inbred malady in every one of us", and so broadened out into a vast treatise upon human nature in general, considered both historically and geographically. But though Shakespeare relates his Hamlet to contemporary notions about melancholy, just as he sets his Ghost in a framework of references and allusions to the demonology of his day, neither is composed according to any prescribed pattern or recipe; and they are as greatly mistaken who seek the origin of Hamlet's character in Elizabethan psychology as those who attempt to fathom it in terms of Freudian psychopathology.

The best known text-book on psychology when he was writing *Hamlet* was *A Treatise of Melancholie* by Timothy Bright, a doctor, published in 1586, a book from which Burton is thought to have learnt a good deal and which Shakespeare himself knew, as Dowden believed and as, I hope, any candid reader of my last appendix will admit. But while Shakespeare borrows phrases here and there, and even makes use of some of Bright's notions, the *Treatise* does not I think on the whole suggest the distemper we have been considering. Bright's melancholy man is "sometimes furious, and sometimes merry in apparaunce, through a kinde of Sardonian, and false laughter";[1] he is "exact and curious in pondering the very moments of things";[2] he is "giuen to fearefull and terrible dreames".[3] These and similar points suggest Hamlet. On the other hand, "Of memory reasonable good, if fancies deface it not: firme in opinion, and hardly remoued wher it is resolued: doubtfull before, and long in deliberation: suspicious, painefull in studie, and

[1] Bright, *Treatise*, p. 102.   [2] *Ibid.* p. 130.   [3] *Ibid.* p. 124.

circumspect"[1] offers a different diagnosis. A perusal of Bright's book, in short, proves that, though Shakespeare took many hints from it, his general conception of Hamlet was his own.

I believe, as many others have believed, that this conception first came to Shakespeare from the career and personality of his patron's hero, the brilliant, melancholy and ill-fated Earl of Essex, who met his death upon the scaffold some six to twelve months before *Hamlet*, as we now have it, appeared upon the stage. Apart from the question of its probability, which I have argued elsewhere,[2] the theory has the merit of explaining why Shakespeare set out to surround his Prince with an atmosphere of mystery. The character of Essex was also a mystery, the most baffling and widely discussed of the age, and if audiences at the beginning of the seventeenth century saw the features of the Earl in those of Shakespeare's Hamlet, so far from worrying about the mystery as modern critics do, they would expect it and accept it as a matter of course. But, while the theory explains the historical origin of Hamlet's mystery, it does nothing to reveal its true nature. If Shakespeare made Hamlet mysterious partly in order to increase his likeness to Essex, he secured the effect not by psychological analysis but through dramatic illusion. Even if the historians could recapture for us the very soul of Essex and hand it over for examination to psychologists endowed with finer instruments than have yet been or are ever likely to be fashioned, the diagnosis would not help us a whit with Hamlet. For Hamlet is not Essex; he is not even Essex as

[1] Bright, *Treatise*, p. 124.
[2] *The Essential Shakespeare*, pp. 97–107.

reflected in the mind of Shakespeare; he is that reflection, sufficiently life-like to be recognisable by Shakespeare's contemporaries, but moulded, adapted and remade for the purposes of dramatic art.

In fine, we were never intended to reach the heart of the mystery. That it has a heart is an illusion; the mystery itself is an illusion; Hamlet is an illusion. The secret that lies behind it all is not Hamlet's, but Shakespeare's: the technical devices he employed to create this supreme illusion of a great and mysterious character, who is at once mad and the sanest of geniuses, at once a procrastinator and a vigorous man of action, at once a miserable failure and the most adorable of heroes. The character of Hamlet, like the appearance of his successive impersonators on the stage, is a matter of "make-up".

Dramatic emphasis

Though the illusion is produced in the main by the sustained atmosphere of doubt we have just been analysing, an important contributory cause is another dramatic artifice, closely connected with it, to which I have already referred more than once on earlier pages.[1] I mean the opportunity which the Elizabethan theatre gave its playwrights of shifting the emphasis from scene to scene. We have noted that a Shakespearian play, composed of a succession of waves through which the spectator moves like a swimmer, is liable to serious misapprehension when viewed from the aerial perspective of nineteenth-century criticism. Members of the "historical" school, rushing in reaction to the opposite extreme and tending to concentrate upon the separate waves, have missed

[1] *Vide* pp. 94 ff. and below, pp. 328 ff.

the rhythm of the total composition. They break the dramas up into detached episodes, and even hint that Shakespeare was not concerned to preserve continuity between them, provided he could secure his immediate emotional effects. This is to deny him all architectonic competence and to rank his plays with the barbaric efforts of the early cinematograph. The true point of view lies somewhere between these two. In the dramas over which he took pains there are no jolts, abrupt changes or glaring inconsistencies. The effect of lifelikeness is perfect, but this effect is itself largely due to subtle and gradual variations of stress which pass entirely unnoticed by those who experience his art under the sole conditions which he contemplated, viz. those of stage-representation.

An Elizabethan play was not a book but a drama, that is an action, a thing seen and heard in a theatre, interpreted through the voices and gestures of living performers, clad in appropriate costumes and harmonising like the members of an orchestra. Above all it was action in motion, a work of art which, unlike that of architecture, sculpture, painting, or lyrical poetry, was not to be apprehended in all its parts at one and the same moment, but conveyed the intentions of its creator through a *series* of impressions, each fleeting as the phases of a musical symphony, each deriving tone and colour from all that had gone before and bestowing tone and colour upon all that came after, and each therefore contributing to the cumulative effect which was only felt when the play was completed. The dramatist had his own perspective, his own restrictions, and his own liberty. Like the musician, while depending much upon the memory of his audience, he was free to avail himself of its limitations. So long as he could preserve the illusion of consistency, he was not obliged to adhere to it in any historical or logical sense. He knew that the incidents of the last act could not be foreseen by those who had only heard the first, and that by the time they reached the last many details of the first would have been forgotten. Thus he enjoyed a liberty denied to the novelist or the historian, whose readers can pause, ponder, and turn back the pages to check his statements. On the other hand, he had to be ever preparing his hearers for what was to come. His first act would, like that of dramatists of any other period, be largely devoted to exposition, that is to the giving of information necessary for the understanding of all that followed; but the task of exposition, of bringing the audience into a state of mind receptive to the effects he next intends, was never done till all was done. It follows that his art was, to borrow the language of theology, one of progressive revelation; and in drama, where character was the main interest, this meant that the chief personages grew more life-like and were to be viewed more and more in the round as the play moved forward.

I use the past tense, because the dramatic art of which I write belongs to the past and is now dead. Its decease was due not to any improvements in dramatic skill or deepening of dramatic appreciation: on the contrary, it is probable that the aesthetic standard of both playwright and audience[1] is

---

[1] The point is much debated, cf. Bridges, *The Influence of the Audience upon Shakespeare's Drama* (*op. cit.*) and an essay on "Shakespeare's Audience" by M. St Clare Byrne in *Shakespeare and the Theatre* (Shakespeare Association, 1927). Both Bridges and Miss Byrne, I think, tend to confuse social decency and humanity (in which the Elizabethans were far behind us) with aesthetic sensibility; *vide* my "Elizabethan Shakespeare" in *Aspects of Shakespeare* (British Academy), and cf. pp. 16–17 above.

lower to-day than it was in the age of Elizabeth. It was killed, like so many of the old art-forms, by mechanical invention. The printing-press brought about the multiplication and the cheapening of books, and, as the reading habit became general, dramatists took more and more to writing with publication in mind, until to-day plays with any pretension to literary merit appeal quite as much to the reader as to the spectator. This is one, perhaps even the chief, cause of the decline of poetic drama; for, directly a dramatist begins to keep one eye upon a reading public, he is obliged, or at least feels himself obliged, to conform to the rigid consistency which the novelist must observe. Nor dare he leave points in doubt or intentions obscure. Both the chiaroscuro and the orchestral scope of the Elizabethans are denied him. Yet modern critics, instead of envying Shakespeare the liberty of his art and praising the masterly use he makes of it, condemn him for not obeying the "law of writ" that binds an Ibsen and a Bernard Shaw![1]

A few words on the character of Horatio will serve to make the point clear and will, at the same time, I hope, remove a stone of stumbling which has offended recent critics of *Hamlet*. The best statement that I know of the difficulty is to be found in a sharp-eyed little book by Mr G. F. Bradby, entitled *The Problems of Hamlet*, from which I proceed to quote.

Horatio has no very marked individuality. He is a listener

[1] Since these paragraphs were written I have been reading Miss Muriel Bradbrook's *Themes and Conventions of Elizabethan Tragedy*. Had I done so earlier I might have enriched and strengthened this chapter. As it is, I will only say that her book seems to me the first systematic attempt to deal with Elizabethan dramatic technique on satisfactory lines.

rather than a talker, the audience for Hamlet's comments on life and people. Only once does he offer any advice, namely when in 5.2.228 he advises Hamlet to give up the fencing match with Laertes. On all other occasions he merely says ditto to his friend.

What the reader often fails to notice is that there are in the play two quite different versions of Horatio's antecedents.

(*a*) In Act I, sc. I, he is a "friend to this ground and liegeman to the Dane" (l. 15). He speaks of "*our* last king" (l. 80) and "*our* state" (l. 101). Bernardo and Marcellus treat him as an old friend. He is better informed than his companions, and can tell them the cause of the military preparations that are being made (l. 79). He is well acquainted with the history and politics of Denmark (l. 80 *et seq.*). He is appealed to as one who knew the late King well:

> *Mar.* Is it not like the king?
> *Hor.* As thou art to thyself;
> Such was the very armour he had on
> When he the ambitious Norway combated;
> So frown'd he once, when, in an angry parle,
> He smote the sledded Polacks on the ice.   (l. 58 *et seq.*)

And in Act I, sc. 2, l. 211, when he is telling Hamlet about the Ghost, he says:

> I knew[1] your father;
> These hands are not more like.

In Act IV, sc. 5, after Hamlet has set sail for England, he is still at court and in attendance on the Queen; and in Act IV, sc. 6, he is in a position to procure for the sailors an audience with the King.

(*b*) In Act I, sc. 2, ll. 161–86, and again in sc. 4 (the first 37 lines) Horatio is not a native of Denmark, and is a stranger to the court. Hamlet addresses him as "fellow-student" (sc. 2, l. 177),

---

[1] I fancy Mr Bradby misunderstands here; "knew" means "recognised" only and does not imply intimacy.

asks what has brought him from Wittenberg to Elsinore (ll. 168 and 174), and adds:

We'll teach you to drink deep ere you depart. (l. 175.)

He is ignorant of Danish customs. He hears a *flourish of trumpets and ordnance fired off within*, and asks:

What does this mean, my lord? (Act 1, sc. 4, l. 7.)

Hamlet explains: the King is "taking his rouse". Whereupon Horatio asks again, "Is it a custom?" Hamlet replies:

Ay, marry, is't:
But to my mind, though I am native here
And to the manner born, it is a custom
More honour'd in the breach than the observance.

He then proceeds to tell Horatio that the Danes have acquired a bad reputation through their heavy drinking.

Again, he is not familiar with the personal appearance of the late King, "I saw him *once*[1]", he says (Act 1, sc. 2, l. 186): "he was a goodly king". He has never heard of Yorick, King Hamlet's jester (Act v, sc. 1, l. 201); and he does not know anything about Laertes (*ibid.* l. 247) nor Osric (Act v, sc. 2, l. 82).

Such discrepancies are too glaring to be reconciled. It is almost impossible to escape the conclusion that at different times Shakespeare held two different views about Horatio, and that, like the priestly and prophetic narratives in the early chapters of Genesis, they have both been sandwiched into our text.

It is conceivable that Mr Bradby's conclusion is right, and that the discrepancies arose through revision. But if they did, the case against Shakespeare is not thereby weakened, seeing that faulty revision is no less culpable than faulty drafting. What does weaken the case, though Mr Bradby seems unconscious of it, is his own admission that "the reader often fails

---

[1] This too is open to a different interpretation, *vide* my notes in *Hamlet* and *Modern Language Review*, xxx, 348–53.

to notice" the inconsistencies he points out; and if he had said "hardly ever notices" it would not have been putting it too high. The truth is that the little points he has carefully collected and gathered into contrasted heaps do not in the least appear to conflict in the theatre itself, and cannot therefore be regarded as defects at all, if we grant Shakespeare the conditions of his own art, the only conditions which he had in mind. And when all is said, is there any need to invoke revision, or anything but the ordinary necessities of the Elizabethan playwright, to explain the discrepancies? Horatio, as I have written elsewhere, "is not a person in actual life or a character in a novel but a piece of dramatic structure. His function is to be the chief spokesman of the first scene and the confidant of the hero for the rest of the play. As the former he gives the audience necessary information about the political situation in Denmark, as the latter he is the recipient of information even more necessary for the audience to hear. The double rôle involves some inconsistency, but...only a very indifferent playwright will allow an audience to perceive such joins in his flats. And Shakespeare is able to give his puppets an appearance of life so overwhelming that his legerdemain remains unperceived not only by the spectator, who is allowed no time for consideration, but even by most readers. In the case of Horatio he secures this end by emphasising his humanity at three critical moments of the play: in the first scene, just before the Gonzago-play, and in the finale. In short, we feel we know Hamlet's friend so well that it never occurs to us to ask questions about him".[1]

[1] Introduction to *Hamlet* ("The New Shakespeare"), pp. xlviii–xlix.

I have quoted Mr Bradby's note on Horatio at length, because it is a particularly favourable example of the "historical" method, and also a warning how not to approach the problem of Hamlet's character. Horatio is a minor person, a detail in the composition, and liberties possible with him would hardly do in the delineation of Hamlet himself, the central figure of the play, upon which the full light is focussed and for whose character his creator claims from the audience an intensity of concentration without parallel in other dramas. Yet even here the emphasis shifts as the play goes forward, and unless we observe it we shall not fully appreciate the technique of his making. Something of it we have already seen in dealing with the assumption of the "antic disposition", the passage of time between acts 1 and 2, and the introduction of the delay motive; and we need not traverse that ground again. It is in the fifth act however that Shakespeare avails himself of it most fully and most audaciously. His problem there is how to reinstate Hamlet in the affections and admiration of his audience after the exhibition of his disastrous weakness in acts 3 and 4, without at the same time either condoning that weakness or suppressing it. Because he has reached the fifth act, the catastrophe of the tragedy, which involves the death of his hero, he is obliged to show us Hamlet as himself once again, greater and more admirable than ever before; otherwise the play would have ended dismally with a sense of utter frustration and inadequacy. Yet never to the last moment does he allow us to forget the fatal flaw in Hamlet's character. The feat is accomplished by means similar to those employed by musicians who wish to introduce new themes without relinquishing the old. The upper half of the score is filled with all sorts of fresh matter to arrest interest and secure sympathy, while all the time the bass throbs on "failure, failure, failure!"

In this enquiry into the dramatic make-up of Hamlet I have been doing what, of course, Shakespeare never intended us to do: I have been peeping behind the scenes of the theatre of his imagination. The impertinence has been forced upon me by the false and, as I think, degrading notions of his art current in our time. For it is only by trying to exhibit what he attempted and how he accomplished it that one can defend him from the charges of technical incompetence and slovenliness. There is nothing slovenly in *Hamlet*, whatever may be said about some other of his plays. The more one contemplates it the more flawless and subtle does its technique appear. What, then, is the general impression which Shakespeare, by means of the devices we have been examining, strove to give of Hamlet's character? Surely it is simply the impression which three centuries of spectators (apart from critics and readers, who treat the play as a book, as a novel or a chapter of history) have always received, viz. that of a great, an almost superhuman, figure tottering beneath a tragic burden too heavy even for his mighty back; or, if you will, of a genius suffering from a fatal weakness and battling against it, until in the end it involves him in the catastrophe which is at once his liberation and his atonement.

Finally, this compound of overwhelmingly convincing humanity and psychological contradiction is the greatest of Shakespeare's legacies to the men of his own quality. No "part" in the whole repertory of dramatic literature is so certain of success with almost any audience, and is yet open to such a remarkable variety of interpretation. There are as many Hamlets as there are actors who play him; and Bern-hardt has proved that even a woman can score a success. Of a rôle so indeterminate in composition almost any version is possible; with a character so fascinating and so tremendous in outline hardly any impersonator can fail.

VII

FAILURE AND TRIUMPH

That we would do
We should do when we would: for this "would" changes,
And hath abatements and delays as many
As there are tongues, are hands, are accidents,
And then this "should" is like a spendthrift sigh,
That hurts by easing.

FAILURE AND TRIUMPH

Fortune's pipe

Let us now return to the text and see how far the foregoing generalisations are borne out by Hamlet's behaviour from moment to moment of the action in the second half of the play. We left him at the end of Chapter v, it will be remembered, in a state of frantic delight at the success of his theatrical coup. Horatio, however, bears a watchful eye for his lord, and does his best to "sprinkle cool patience"

> Upon the heat and flame of his distemper.

Hamlet cries that he has earned "a fellowship in a cry of players"; "half a share" corrects Horatio. He shouts a ballad snatch; "you might have rhymed" is Horatio's comment. And the calm matter-of-fact corroboration of the King's visible disturbance is equally sober. "I did very well note him" is all he says; but the tone implies "Steady, steady; now more than ever a cool head is needed". It is only a hint; but there will be other moderating comments of the same kind later.

While Hamlet luxuriates in his triumph, Claudius is acting; and his ambassadors Rosencrantz and Guildenstern are commissioned to get the Prince to his mother's bedroom, where Polonius will listen behind the arras according to the plan suggested after the nunnery scene, and where, Claudius no doubt hopes, Hamlet will show himself so dangerous that both Gertrude and Polonius will consent to drastic action. It is clear from what follows that Gertrude is the King's difficulty, and a glimpse of her part in the unseen deliberations is given us in Polonius's words at the beginning of the bedroom scene, in which he bids her

> Tell him his pranks have been too broad to bear with,
> And that your grace hath screened and stood between
> Much heat and him.

The council of war is a hurried one and the two spies are soon back again in the hall where Hamlet lingers. He laughs at their entry, for he is expecting them; and at first he ignores their presence and calls for music. Guildenstern, however, is importunate, and does not wait to be addressed. There follows the most brilliant passage-of-arms in the whole play. An edge may be felt in what is said on both sides. The schoolfellows are still polite, but an ill-concealed menace peers through their courtesy, while Hamlet no longer troubles to keep the antic mask in place, because he now wears a second mask beneath it. Lines 336–46, which I have already quoted in part, mark the climax of the conversation. Having delivered his message and received the Prince's consent to the interview with the Queen, Rosencrantz tries a little investigation on his own account:

Ros. My lord, you once did love me.
Ham. And do still, by these pickers and stealers.
Ros. Good my lord, what is your cause of distemper? you do surely bar the door upon your own liberty, if you deny your griefs to your friend.
Ham. Sir, I lack advancement.

Ros. How can that be, when you have the voice of the king himself for your succession in Denmark?

Ham. Ay, sir, but "While the grass grows"— the proverb is something musty.

If Rosencrantz, "evil speaker, liar and slanderer" protests love, Hamlet can swear it too by his "pickers and stealers". And if Rosencrantz asks him point-blank the cause of his distemper, hinting at confinement for madmen should he refuse to answer, Hamlet will be equally direct. He gives them the answer they expect, the answer they had themselves taught him: the cause is ambition. Rosencrantz is elated, and with the play scene in mind presses further: But the King has already named you his heir in full Council, what more can you wish for? Hamlet does not shrink, or attempt to parry. He fills the cup they thirst for to overflowing: Yes, he says, but I don't propose to bide my time.

Question and answer, at this crucial moment, should convince any reader who may still have doubts that I have not exaggerated the importance of "the succession in Denmark" as a leading element in the plot and as the clue to "Lucianus, nephew to the king". They certainly convince Rosencrantz and Guildenstern that their reading of the interlude is correct, and that Hamlet seeks the King's life, as is evident from the next scene in which they speak to Claudius in no ambiguous terms of the danger that threatens the throne. It is a fine display of fence. But while it is going forward, time is passing, every second of which is precious. Hamlet threatens, threatens most cleverly and cunningly; but he does nothing. "While the grass grows" sounds ironically in the ears of the audience who are becoming increasingly uneasy at his inactivity. The proverb he refers to is "While the grass grows, oft starves the silly steed"; but there is a still mustier one about grass growing beneath men's feet. The recorders are brought in, and afford him another digression, another theme for the exercise of his wit. He presses Guildenstern hard, disarms him and completely reduces him to silence. It is a triumph of intellectual superiority; and we share all the indignation which he puts into the final thrust: "'Sblood, do you think I am easier to be played on than a pipe? call me what instrument you will, though you can fret me, you cannot play upon me." Yet the words recall an earlier speech about "a pipe for Fortune's finger". He *is* their instrument, on the which they are playing only too successfully. Polonius now enters (to see how the spies are getting on, and to help them bring him to his mother); Polonius, the tedious old fool, who has been his butt these many weeks past. The game is too easy; and in two minutes Hamlet has put him out of countenance by his cloud-camel with a weasel's back. The old man, however, is only humouring a madman, and Hamlet, whose nerves are beginning to give out, knows it well enough. "They fool me to the top of my bent" he exclaims disgustedly in a sudden fit of revulsion against all this trifling. Irony, once more! For, he is their dupe from first to last. He scores over them every time in word-play. What do they care about that? Their object is to keep him from the King and to shepherd him safely to the Queen's bedroom; and he yields to their suggestion, as a lamb to a silken string.

So successfully, indeed, have they played upon the pipe with their talk of mother...mother...mother,* that what had first been raging fury against the King is now diverted towards the Queen. Left alone, Hamlet gives utterance to his thoughts in a remarkable soliloquy, the point of which has I think escaped notice. It begins auspiciously enough:

> 'Tis now the very witching time of night,
> When churchyards yawn, and hell itself breathes out
> Contagion to this world: now could I drink hot blood,
> And do such bitter business as the day
> Would quake to look on.

At last he is going to act, we exclaim; his promise to visit his mother "by and by" means that he will visit the King *first* and "do such bitter business" as his duty demands. But what is this he is saying?

> Soft, now to my mother—
> O heart, lose not thy nature, let not ever
> The soul of Nero enter this firm bosom,
> Let me be cruel not unnatural.
> I will speak daggers to her, but use none.
> My tongue and soul in this be hypocrites,
> How in my words somever she be shent,
> To give them seals never, my soul, consent!

Not a word about his uncle! The thirst for blood, engendered by the sight of his uncle's blenching eyes and blanched face, is there, but he appears now to be at a loss to account for it. For whom is this itching dagger intended? He is going to his mother. But surely he does not intend to murder her? He is no Nero. These murderous impulses must be kept in leash. True, she deserves the worst he can find it in his heart to say to her; she may even deserve death, but it is not for him to exact it. Is Hamlet's brain incapable of entertaining two objects at the same time? His feet are set towards his mother, set by the King's minions, and he has forgotten the King altogether! It is the most glaring instance of "bestial oblivion" in the play.

Yet he is full of blood-lust; so that he may prove dangerous when he reaches the bedroom should he lose self-control. And if he were to encounter his uncle on the way, he would doubtless recollect and then be in the right mood for the deed of vengeance. He does. He finds him alone, defenceless, with his back towards him kneeling in prayer. "Now could I drink hot blood" he had declared a few minutes earlier; here is the opportunity; he is never likely to have a better. Shakespeare planned the encounter with consummate art. Yet, as Dr Bradley points out,* "Now *might* I do it," the first words Hamlet utters, "show that he has no effective *desire* to 'do it'; and in the little sentences that follow, and the long pauses between them, the endeavour at a resolution, and the sickening return of melancholic paralysis, however difficult a task they set the actor, are plain enough to a reader".[1] Dr Bradley also insists that, though the reason for delay which Hamlet gives, viz. that he prefers to wait until his father's murderer is

> about some act
> That has no relish of salvation in't

is only a pretext, it expresses a "perfectly genuine" feeling, and one, we may add, that no Elizabethan would have thought of questioning. Hamlet takes good care that Rosencrantz and Guildenstern shall be allowed no "shriving-time" (5.2.47).* Furthermore the very strength and genuineness of

---

[1] *Shakespearean Tragedy*, pp. 134–5.

Hamlet's expression of hatred, together with the satisfaction to his imagination in words like

> Then trip him that his heels may kick at heaven,
> And that his soul may be as damned and black
> As hell whereto it goes,

make the excuse more palatable to him at the moment. To adapt a well-known phrase used by Dr Johnson in another connection, he *pays* Claudius by *feeling*. Had Shakespeare put an obvious and shallow pretext into his mouth, the incident would have lost much subtlety; and we are shown immediately how illusory the pretext is by the words the King utters directly after Hamlet departs:

> My words fly up, my thoughts remain below.
> Words without thoughts never to heaven go.

After all there had been "no relish of salvation" in the King's act of prayer; Hamlet need not have hesitated, even on his own showing.[1] And so with heavy heart we follow him to his interview with Gertrude.

The bedroom scene

To understand the events at the beginning of this scene, we shall do well to remember that nephew Lucianus has revealed Hamlet as of a dangerous disposition, that he has threatened his uncle with death, and that, prompted no doubt by Claudius himself, both the Queen and Polonius now suspect him of homicidal tendencies. She takes risks, therefore; but she does not lack courage, as is seen later in her attitude

---

[1] Cf. Adams, *op. cit.* p. 277.

towards the rebellious Laertes. Moreover, Polonius will be at hand,[1] and after all Hamlet is her son. Nor does she need instruction in her part from the old councillor; she will take the high hand from the start. But Hamlet enters in one of his moods of excitement, equally determined on his side to "speak daggers". Thus she finds him more difficult than she had hoped; and, after some altercation, thinks it politic to withdraw. "Nay then, I'll set those to you that can speak", she concludes, making for the door. Words and action, I think, lead Hamlet to imagine that the King may be again eavesdropping. In any event, he does not intend to let his mother off. He seizes her by the arm, and forces her roughly into a seat.* At this she naturally takes fright, and calls out to Polonius. He, likewise terrified at Hamlet's violent tone, instead of emerging from his hiding-place, calls out for help in his turn. The shout from behind the arras confirms Hamlet's suspicions; he is ready to "drink hot blood"; and he runs the eavesdropper through, hoping it is his uncle. How easy is killing when one does not have to think about it! But the deed is even more fatal than the previous inaction. To spare Claudius was bad enough; to slay Polonius is to give his uncle just the handle he needs; not even Gertrude can any longer "stand between much heat and him".

At first, however, Hamlet seems quite unaware of all this, so intent is he upon what he has come for, the great scene with his mother, the scene already envisaged in the soliloquy before he crossed his uncle at prayers. Dr Bradley writes: "The death of Polonius sobers him; and in the remainder of

---

[1] It is clear from Polonius's words, "I'll silence me even here", that she is fully aware he is to be present during the interview.

the interview he shows, together with some traces of his morbid state, the peculiar beauty and nobility of his nature."[1] I cannot agree. The death of Polonius is at first a mere trifle, which he at once, after his lightning fashion, converts into a test for his mother:

> Queen. O what a rash and bloody deed is this!
> Ham. A bloody deed—almost as bad, good mother,
> As kill a king, and marry with his brother.
> Queen. As kill a king!

Her astonishment acquits her for us, as most critics have seen; and Hamlet, apparently satisfied for the moment, next has a word with his victim.

> Thou wretched, rash, intruding fool, farewell!
> I took thee for thy better, take thy fortune,
> Thou find'st to be too busy is some danger.

There is little sign of soberness here, certainly none of repentance, still less of nobility of nature. And when he turns again to deal with Gertrude, he is as excited as ever. Indeed, he whips himself up into greater and greater frenzy in the long speeches that follow, as the Queen's replies to them make clear. She begins with something of her former stoutness.

> What have I done, that thou dar'st wag thy tongue
> In noise so rude against me?

And again:

> Ay me, what act,
> That roars so loud, and thunders in the index?

But in the end he breaks down her defences, and she has to plead for mercy. Three times she interrupts him, begging him pitifully to "speak no more". Yet he only grows the more

[1] *Op. cit.* p. 138.

violent; and would apparently have proceeded to greater lengths, had he not been interrupted a fourth time—by the Ghost.

I emphasise this crescendo of excitement, not only because it is important to note it as we watch Hamlet, but also because if we miss it we miss part of the reason for the Ghost's entry, to which we must now give our attention. The apparition here, as earlier in the play, has been misunderstood, and is attended with its own problems. Why does the Ghost return at this point? How is it that, while he was visible enough to the sentries on the battlements, he is hid from Gertrude's eyes? What exactly takes place as he appears? Hamlet speaks of some "piteous action" on his part; what does he mean?

There is an obvious answer to the first question, which the Ghost himself provides:

> Do not forget! this visitation
> Is but to whet thy almost blunted purpose—

I am here, that is, to recall you to your duty, which is in danger of being altogether forgotten. The reprimand is also a reminder to the audience that Hamlet has no business to be with his mother at all at this critical moment: *he ought to be with the King.* Further, he is not only wasting precious seconds, but wasting them in shouting at his mother, in doing just what the Ghost had at the first enjoined him not to do:

> Nor let thy soul contrive
> Against thy mother aught—*leave her to heaven*,
> And to those thorns that in her bosom lodge
> To prick and sting her.[1]

[1] 1.5.85–8.

Yet here he is usurping Heaven's function and trying to reinforce the stings of conscience with his own dagger-words.[1] No wonder the Ghost appears with rebuke upon his lips. And that he should thus speak of Hamlet's "almost blunted purpose" annihilates the idea, seriously entertained in certain quarters,[2] that the procrastination is a modern invention and was not intended by Shakespeare at all.

But though the Ghost comes his "tardy son to chide", Shakespeare, we can be sure, wished us to see more in his advent than this. The scene is in the Queen's bedchamber; the spirit of King Hamlet appears in his dressing-gown;[3] it is the first and only meeting, since death and worse than death had separated them, of the royal family of Denmark; and the words that follow the rebuke show that the father's visitation is as much on the wife's behalf as on the son's. Hamlet's shending had reduced the Queen to a pitiable condition, which as he contemplates it drowns all other

[1] Cf. Bradley, *op. cit.* pp. 138–9.

[2] E. E. Stoll, *Art and Artifice in Shakespeare*, p. 99 n. The testimony of the Ghost is important because it makes certain that Hamlet's "blunted purpose" was part of Shakespeare's deliberate intention. In the Introduction to my *Hamlet* (p. lxi) I unnecessarily went beyond this and claimed that the Ghost, as a supernatural being, "sees Hamlet *sub specie eternitatis* and follows the secret motions of his heart". This is disputable, it being one of the moot points of scholastic theory whether "angels and separate souls have a natural power to understand thoughts". Cf. Donne, *The Dreame*:

> But when I saw thou sawest my heart
> And knew'st my thoughts, beyond an angel's art;

and H. J. C. Grierson's note (*Poems of John Donne*, II, 34–5).

[3] "in his habit as he lived", Hamlet informs us; and Q 1, which gives the stage-direction "Enter the ghost in his night gowne", tells us what the "habit" was. At that period, of course, "night gown" meant what we should now call "dressing-gown"; cf. *Macb.* 2.2.70; 5.1.5, 69.

thoughts in the Ghost's mind, so that at once he breaks off
with an appeal to Hamlet to give her spiritual aid:

> But look, amazement on thy mother sits,
> O step between her and her fighting soul,
> Conceit in weakest bodies strongest works,
> Speak to her, Hamlet.

His tender solicitude for the Queen who has so greatly
wronged him is already evident at his first interview with
Hamlet; and the pathetic line

> Conceit in weakest bodies strongest works,

is an epitome of all the excuses that blindly chivalrous
husbands have found for erring wives since the beginning of
time. Had the body or flesh of Gertrude been weaker, and
her conceit or imagination stronger, King Hamlet might still
have been alive and the "bed of Denmark" undefiled.

Unless I am much mistaken, however, the Ghost was
concerned to protect the "conceit" of Gertrude from more
than its present "amazement". He fears what Hamlet may
do next; and his appearance at this particular moment is, at
least in part, due to these fears, fears not of physical violence,
but spiritual. Hamlet does not know whether his mother is
an accomplice in the murder or not. He strongly suspects
her, as is evident from his sardonic comment—"That's
wormwood, wormwood"—upon the line,

> None wed the second, but who killed the first,

in the play scene. And one of his purposes in seeking, or
consenting to, this interview with her is to test these suspicions. He has already attempted to do so. But though her
perplexed repetition of his words "As kill a king!" clears her

character for us, it is not enough for Hamlet; and in his invective against Claudius, the last sentence of which begins "A murderer and a villain" and is cut short by the Ghost, he is, I think, working up towards a second and this time unmistakable disclosure of the assassination. If this be the correct interpretation, the Ghost appears just in time to stop Hamlet speaking of the murder and taxing her with knowledge of it. Hamlet may hint at her infidelity, may beseech her to abstain from the incestuous bed, may even publicly rail at her for her hasty second marriage; but the fact of the murder must be kept from her, and the Ghost intervenes to prevent a revelation which would lay too heavy a burden of shame and guilt upon her.

Some have imagined that Gertrude knew of the murder all the time. But this is impossible. Quite apart from her evident astonishment, just noted, there is other evidence in her favour. Before the play scene she and Claudius are only once together for a minute, during which the following conversation takes place:

King. He tells me, my dear Gertrude, he hath found
The head and source of all your son's distemper.
Queen. I doubt it is no other but the main,
His father's death and our o'erhasty marriage.

She would surely not have phrased the matter thus had she entertained any suspicion at all of the real facts. Moreover, in the play scene there is not a hint that she understands the reference to poison. Rather, she follows her second husband from the room with a solicitous enquiry after his health. She has a free soul; it touches her not. True, her innocence in this respect is far more patent in the First Quarto and the

Brudermord than in Shakespeare's own *Hamlet*. But that is only because Shakespeare is subtler than his perverters or his predecessors. Gertrude knew nothing, and the Ghost was determined, I believe, to shield her from the fatal knowledge.

Readers may perhaps think that it is to consider too curiously thus to consider the Ghost's tenderness for Gertrude. They can hardly withhold assent, however, from what follows therefrom. It is an aspect that deserves close attention, since it reveals a beautiful and, I think, hitherto unnoticed dramatic effect.

At his father's bidding Hamlet turns to his mother with the question "How is it with you, lady?" and her reply shows that she is entirely unconscious of the Ghost's presence. Dr Bradley explains this unconsciousness on the theory that "A ghost, in Shakespeare's day, was able for any sufficient reason to confine its manifestation to a single person in a company; and", he adds, "here the sufficient reason, that of sparing the Queen, is obvious". He supports his explanation by citing a parallel from Heywood's *Iron Age* (pt. II, act 5, sc. 1) in which the ghost of Agamemnon appears while Orestes and Clytemnestra are talking together, and yet remains invisible to the latter.[1] But he overlooks the point that Orestes takes Clytemnestra's blindness to her murdered husband's presence as evidence of her guilt. And that this is also the cause of Gertrude's insensibility is proved, I think, by the version of

[1] Bradley, *op. cit.* pp. 139–40 and footnote. Professor Stoll (*Shakespeare Studies*, pp. 211–13) insists that Elizabethan ghosts commonly appeared to one person only at a time. It may be so, but *this* Ghost certainly appears to three persons simultaneously in 1.1 and 1.4.

the bedroom scene in *Der bestrafte Brudermord*, which gives us the following illuminating dialogue:

> *Ghost passes across the stage. It lightens.*

Ham. Ah, noble shade of my father, stay! Alas! alas! what wouldst thou? Dost thou demand vengeance? I will fulfil it at the right time.

Queen. What are you about? and to whom are you talking?

Ham. See you not the ghost of your departed husband? See, he beckons as if he would speak to you.

Queen. How? I see nothing at all.

Ham. I can readily believe that you see nothing, for you are no longer worthy to look upon his form. Fie, for shame! Not another word will I speak to you. *Exit.*

All the poetry has evaporated from this travesty, the product of a century's degeneration from the original or the parent text; but it happens to have preserved two points in clearer, because cruder, form than they appear in Shakespeare.

First of all, Gertrude is unable to see the "gracious figure" of her husband because her eyes are held by the adultery she has committed.* The notion, as the parallel from Heywood suggests, was probably a common one at the period, and Shakespeare doubtless expected his audience to assume it without explicit statement on his part. He emphasises it, however, unmistakably enough—and this is the second point—not in words, but in the action of the Ghost himself. "See," says the Hamlet of *Der bestrafte Brudermord*, "he beckons as if he would speak to you." Here is the clue to the following as yet unexplained lines in Shakespeare's play:

Queen. ...Whereon do you look?

Ham. On him! on him! Look you, how pale he glares! His form and cause conjoined, preaching to stones,

Would make them capable. Do not look upon me,
Lest with this piteous action you convert
My stern effects, then what I have to do
Will want true colour, tears perchance for blood.

Hamlet's words indicate some strange agitation in the Ghost's face and actions, an agitation that wrings the son's heart with pity and forces tears to his eyes. What is it? The evidence of the *Brudermord* seems to leave no doubt of the answer. The Queen's words to Hamlet reveal to the Ghost that she is cut off from him, that she can neither hear nor see him; he holds out hands in supplication towards her; he turns a face full of anguish upon Hamlet; and, as the horror of the whole situation dawns upon him and he realises the reason of her insensibility, he "steals away" in shame, "out at the portal". It is the last glimpse we have of King Hamlet; he returns to his purgatory with the added torment that he is separated for all eternity from the being he loves best.

No wonder Hamlet is overcome by the pity of it. For he feels his father's grief not only as a son but as a lover. He too has held out hands in silent supplication; he too has stolen from the closet of a beloved one with pale and stricken face; he too has been met with a stony stare of fright and estrangement. The Ghost's farewell to Gertrude is a repetition of Hamlet's farewell to Ophelia at the beginning of act 2. Shakespeare does not do these things by accident.

Thus, Hamlet is "sobered", not by the death of Polonius, but by the apparition of the "gracious figure" of his father. The excited fit passes from him, and once more his pulse makes "healthful music", while the spiritual presence seems to leave a kind of holy peace in this room of bloodshed and shouting, between this exasperated mother and her infuriated son. Now indeed Hamlet exhibits "the peculiar beauty and nobility of his nature", here more than anywhere else in the play. After the Ghost's exit we get forty lines of exquisite tenderness from him, a tenderness that even embraces Polonius. He no longer exacerbates with dagger-words, but brings healing thoughts of confession, repentance and a new life. In short, he obeys the Ghost; he "steps between her and her fighting soul"; he turns her mind heavenwards and bids her examine her own conscience. And he does all this humbly and as a son should. "Forgive me this my virtue", he craves; and,

> Once more, good night,
> And when you are desirous to be blessed,
> I'll blessing beg of you;

and, yet again,

> I must be cruel only to be kind.

If only the mood had lasted, and he could have ended upon this note! He certainly intended to do so. Three times, in the speech we are considering, he bids the Queen good-night; and he concludes with a couplet, as if he is just about to leave. It would have made a perfect close. But as in the nunnery scene, he only goes to the door to turn back again; and the whole effect is destroyed by the hysterical violence and cynicism of what comes after. It is the old see-saw over again: frenzy followed by calm, calm followed by frenzy. And even the tender strain, lovely as it is, does not come of his own motion. It is music played by the Ghost upon the all too passive pipe.

What changes the tune so suddenly is the sight of the corpse of Polonius, and thoughts to which that gives rise. At first Hamlet, with his mind upon Heaven and repentance, treats the body with respect and expresses contrition for his deed; and if we compare his words here with those he employs earlier, and with

> I'll lug the guts into the neighbour room

and the scoffing phrases that follow at the end of the scene, we get a good measure of the difference between the three moods. But the pious resolution,

> I will bestow him and will answer well
> The death I gave him,

brings into consciousness for the first time the awkwardness of the deed, and its inevitable consequences for himself. He goes out, muttering

> This[1] bad begins, and worse remains behind;

and is back again almost immediately, a frenzied man once more, the Ghost and his charge forgotten, and his brain full of the fumes of disgust, together with schemes, not for killing, but for hoodwinking his uncle. Once again, a comparison between the two references to the royal couch, the first beginning at l. 159 with

> Good night, but go not to my uncle's bed,

and the second beginning at l. 182, with

> Let the bloat king tempt you again to bed,

---

[1] I.e. the death of Polonius makes a bad beginning. "This" is the reading of Q2; F1 and all editors read "Thus".

exhibits the striking contrast in mood. The return of hysteria destroys almost our last hopes that anything will be done. He has spared the King, knowing perfectly well that he will never have so good an opportunity again. He has since slain the wrong man, and by the rash deed has placed himself legally within the power of Claudius. And now his mind is running upon his journey to England and the great things he will be doing there! One can see "statists" like Robert Cecil or Francis Bacon at this point throwing up hands in despair.

Eclipse

Some critics have boggled at Hamlet's knowledge of the mission to England. But the King had decided upon it, for the sake of Hamlet's health, before the play scene; and, though we are not told so, it is natural to suppose that Hamlet would be informed of the royal pleasure in order that due preparations might be made. It was a political mission,

> For the demand of our neglected tribute,

as Claudius tells us. When such missions were undertaken by great personages, royal princes and the like, it was customary for the sealed commission in charge of some trusty gentleman or gentlemen to be sent on in advance. And Hamlet appears from the words,

> There's letters sealed, and my two school-fellows,
> Whom I will trust as I will adders fanged,
> They bear the mandate—they must sweep my way
> And marshal me to knavery,

to have heard that Rosencrantz and Guildenstern were to perform this duty.* What he did not know, because the King only decided it after the play scene, i.e. at the beginning of 3.3, was that the date of his own departure had been put forward and that the school-fellows were now to accompany him as his guards. No grass grows beneath the King's feet; he has a plan ready directly Hamlet (in the nunnery scene) gives him a hint of danger, a plan which can be easily adapted to meet the greater dangers that Lucianus and the killing of Polonius reveal.

Claudius tells Laertes later on that the reasons "why to a public count" he "might not go" in regard to Hamlet's

feats
So crimeful and so capital in nature,

were his popularity with the people and the love his mother bore him. But the main reason, of course, he could not tell, viz. that Hamlet knew too much and at any "public count" would be likely to accuse him of murder. Both protagonists were compelled to work in secret: Hamlet for the sake of the family honour and his mother's good name;[1] Claudius for his own sake. The only safe line for the King was to ship his nephew off to a foreign country and to have him suddenly done to death there. The murder of Polonius greatly eases the operation of this scheme; he could now brush Gertrude's objections aside, and take counsel with his "wisest friends", as we find him doing at the opening of 4.3, on the basis of known and indisputable fact. This consultation was an act of prudence on his part of which he reaped the fruits when it became necessary to explain the situation to Laertes. Hamlet's folly also makes *immediate* action possible; no sooner

[1] *Vide* above, pp. 46–9, 172.

does his uncle hear what has happened than he has him placed under arrest, and before nightfall he is out of the country.

Hamlet knew well enough that he had lost the game for the time being. "This man shall set me packing." But he spends some of his last moments in Denmark in sardonic sallies at the expense of his enemies, which coming from a man with his back against a wall endue him with something of epic greatness. His wit, however, is now macabre. The corpse, which has been his undoing and against which he seems to nourish a kind of grudge, has infected his imagination; and it amuses him to think of Claudius as a similar corpse fattening maggots. The strain recurs in the graveyard scene, though it has there become less ghoulish. That Shakespeare intended it to denote a morbid tendency seems to me unquestionable. On the other hand, those who find sexual repressions at the heart of Hamlet's mystery, should note that while "the royal bed of Denmark" may be responsible for making his "imaginations as foul as Vulcan's stithy" it is by no means the only cause of defilement. The nature Shakespeare depicts is the prey not of a single obsession but of any influence and suggestion which chance may bring his way. At times Fortune's finger will even happen to sound the stop of duty, as when he encounters the army of Fortinbras on his road to port. For, just as his mother's incest seems to turn the whole world into "an unweeded garden that grows to seed", as the dead body of Polonius fills the atmosphere with the odour of decomposition, so here he has only to be reminded of the unperformed task to exclaim

> How *all* occasions do inform against me,
> And spur my dull revenge!

Yet, though confessing to having "cause, and will, and strength, and means" for action, he allows himself to be led away to England, a prisoner, at the entire disposal of a deadly foe, and in the dark as to his intentions. The concluding words of the soliloquy are especially significant:

> O, from this time forth,
> My thoughts be bloody, or be nothing worth!

Having just declared

> I do not know
> Why yet I live to say "This thing's to do",

he is now looking forward apparently to a life-time of bloody *thoughts*. We remember that "Now could I drink hot blood" was followed by "Now *might* I do it".

Hamlet is lost to view for three scenes, or some 500 lines if we include the dialogue between the grave-diggers before he enters in 5.1. But we are never allowed to forget him for a moment. From the very beginning Shakespeare has been playing variations upon the Hamlet-theme through the mouths of other characters, and by diverse means, all the more effective because we are often unconscious of them, suggesting that sense of frustration, futility and human inadequacy which is the burden of the whole symphony. We have watched the hypnotist at work in act 1[1]; Hamlet plays obligato to his own melancholy throughout act 2; while the Player King heightens the tension of the play scene by expatiating on the subject of human instability in a speech of of nearly thirty lines, which concludes:

> But orderly to end where I begun,
> Our wills and fates do so contrary run,
> That our devices still are overthrown,
> Our thoughts are ours, their ends none of our own.

[1] *Vide* pp. 205–8.

Furthermore, as Dr Caroline Spurgeon has pointed out, constant references to hidden disease, rottenness, corruption, rankness, tumours, etc., supply the dominant imagery of *Hamlet*; a fact which in her view suggests that Shakespeare saw the problem he was dealing with "not as the problem of an individual at all, but as something greater and even more mysterious, as a condition for which the individual himself is apparently not responsible, any more than the sick man is to blame for the cancer which strikes and devours him, but which nevertheless, in its course and development, impartially and relentlessly, annihilates him and others, innocent and guilty alike".[1] This carries the doctrine of moral irresponsibility too far, to the shortening even of Hamlet's tragic stature. But though I believe Shakespeare wished us to the end to think of Hamlet as sinning as well as sinned against, there is no doubt that in contriving his "artful balance" he also suggests the other point of view.

With the departure of Hamlet to England Shakespeare gives greater place than ever to these contrapuntal devices; makes them indeed so conspicuous that they cease to be merely suggestive and are directly apprehended. The broadest effects of the kind are obtained through contrast of character; but everything that takes place in this section of the play is in the nature of a comment, an unfavourable comment, upon Hamlet. Ophelia goes mad and drowns herself, and for these disasters he is solely to blame. In his soliloquy on Fortinbras he compares himself to the

> delicate and tender prince,
> Whose spirit with divine ambition puffed

[1] *Leading Motives in the Imagery of Shakespeare's Tragedies* (Shakespearian Association Pamphlets), p. 13.

Makes mouths at the invisible event,
Exposing what is mortal and unsure
To all that fortune, death and danger dare,
Even for an egg-shell;

and points the moral. Taken as a whole the soliloquy is, indeed, a kind of backcloth which gives significance to all that happens in the next three scenes. There is, for example, the still more exact parallel with Laertes, a man of Hamlet's age, and with family troubles and a problem to solve almost identical with his own. Does he dally with the occasion or think "too precisely upon the event"? On the contrary, no sooner is he returned from Paris to find his father slain and his sister "driven into desperate terms", than he has organised a rebellion and forced his way into the palace. All that he says and does is a reflection upon Hamlet. "What would you undertake", asks Claudius of him,

To show yourself your father's son in deed
More than in words?

"To cut his throat i'th'church" comes the instant uncompromising reply; and we are at once reminded of the King upon his knees and Hamlet putting up his sword. Or take his first words to Claudius and Gertrude, as he breaks in upon them:

O thou vile king,
Give me my father.
Queen. Calmly, good Laertes.
Laertes. That drop of blood that's calm proclaims me bastard,
Cries cuckold to my father, brands the harlot,
Even here, between the chaste unsmirchéd brows
Of my true mother.

Is not Shakespeare deliberately echoing Hamlet's words a hundred and thirty lines earlier:

> How stand I then,
> That have a father killed, a mother stained,
> Excitements of my reason and my blood,
> And let all sleep?

Compare, too, Hamlet's "native hue of resolution... sicklied o'er with the pale cast of thought", or his "dread of something after death" which "puzzles the will", with the following outburst:

Laertes. How came he dead? I'll not be juggled with.
To hell allegiance, vows to the blackest devil,
Conscience and grace to the profoundest pit!
I dare damnation. To this point I stand,
That both the worlds I give to negligence,
Let come what comes, only I'll be revenged
Most thoroughly for my father.
  King. Who shall stay you?
  Laertes. My will, not all the world's:
And for my means, I'll husband them so well,
They shall go far with little.

Here the last lines echo, once again, the Fortinbras soliloquy:

> I do not know
> Why yet I live to say "This thing's to do,"
> Sith I have cause, and will, and strength, and means,
> To do't.

As for more oblique suggestion, Shakespeare at 4.7.110–22 gives the King a dozen lines of reflection upon Time and Resolution which express in different words exactly the same thought already enlarged upon, as we have seen, by the Player King. And it has been often remarked that we have the whole moral of *Hamlet* in the lines:

> That we would do
> We should do when we would: for this "would" changes,
> And hath abatements and delays as many
> As there are tongues, are hands, are accidents,
> And then this "should" is like a spendthrift sigh,
> That hurts by easing.

It is, moreover, significant that such procrastination is immediately afterwards described as an "ulcer".

Hamlet returns

If disease be the leading motive of *Hamlet* as a whole, that of its finale is death. It opens in a grave-yard where clowns, in whom custom has made interment a property of easiness, sing and jest amid the grim adjuncts of the charnel-house; and after an antimasque on the theme of the ancient profession of grave-maker, we are led to consider skulls of various kinds: a politician's, a courtier's, a lawyer's, a jester's, and lastly (in imagination) Alexander the Great's. There follows a funeral, the funeral of a suicide;[1] and men struggle horribly by the open grave.[2] The scene changes; and we are once more among the less enduring habitations of the living, only to be reminded that what the living live for is to compass the

---

[1] I am not suggesting that Ophelia *was* a suicide, only that the Grave-diggers' altercation, the maimed rites and the churlish priest's words make the funeral that of a suicide; it is the atmosphere not the fact that matters.

[2] *Vide* p. 300.

death of one another. The hero proudly relates how by his contrivance two men have been

> put to sudden death,
> Not shriving-time allowed.

And he in turn is then inveigled into a game of skill, in the which he is treacherously slain with a poisoned blade, after himself killing two other persons, while yet a fourth drinks death from a poisoned cup. The ground is strewn with corpses, like some forest glade at the end of a long day's chase. And the play closes with the invocation

> O proud death,
> What feast is toward in thine eternal cell,
> That thou so many princes at a shot
> So bloodily hast struck?—

with an inventory of its contents in the summary

> Of carnal, bloody and unnatural acts,
> Of accidental judgements, casual slaughters,
> Of deaths put on by cunning and forced cause,
> And, in this upshot, purposes mistook
> Fall'n on th'inventors' heads;

and with soldiers bearing off the bodies to the sound of a dead march and the peal of ordnance.

Yet this dance of death with its appalling catastrophe is less painful to contemplate than the hopeless frustration presented by the preceding movement of the drama. Our sense of relief is due in part to the purging of the emotions by the pity and terror of tragedy, in part to the excitement of the fencing-match before it suddenly becomes a shambles, but most of all to a renewal of our interest in and admiration for the hero himself. Hamlet returns from his voyage a changed man, with an air of self-possession greater than at any other time of the play. We are not told why; but we may fancy, if we like, that the seas have helped to expel the "something-settled matter in his heart", or that he has gained confidence from the hoisting of Rosencrantz and Guildenstern with their own petar, or that simply his "cause of distemper" is wearing off.[1] The real source of the change is, of course, a technical one. The requirements of tragic drama compel his creator to win back our respect for him before the end, to dissipate the clouds at sunset. Hamlet, we feel, is himself, or almost himself; and we begin to hope once again, though because he is the hero of a tragedy we know that our hope is vain.

Of this change, as with previous developments, we receive due forewarning. There is not a touch of despondency in his letters. That written to Horatio is business-like, shows its author master of the situation in which he finds himself, and fills us with anticipation for the future. The letter to the King is brief, not to say curt; but it contains one sentence which, we may guess, gave Hamlet great pleasure in the writing. "To-morrow shall I beg leave to see your kingly eyes." He had watched those smiling, furtive eyes as they blenched at the vision of one victim being done to death in mimic show; how will they look when confronted with a second intended victim safe and well? In any event, there will be no smile in them as they light upon the word "To-morrow".

---

[1] This is the explanation given by J. Q. Adams (*op. cit.* pp. 283, 288) who quotes Régis and Krafft-Ebing on the stages in melancholia. If only Shakespeare had read Krafft-Ebing!

When he appears in the grave-yard, Hamlet considers its human remains a little "too curiously" perhaps, but in very different mood from that of his jesting with the guts of Polonius. His mind is no longer infected; the nausea in "And smelt so? pah!" is sufficient indication of that. Further, though he meditates on death, and even seems to be resigned to it, there is no longing for it; thoughts of suicide have been put from him. As for the task, so far from worrying about it, or reproaching himself with neglect, he speaks of it calmly and with apparent assurance; telling Horatio that the King has filled the cup of his iniquity to the brim and that it is time an end was put to it. Lastly, the "antic disposition" has entirely disappeared; and though he makes fun of Osric he does so without bitterness, if with a good deal of contempt. Hamlet is, in short, except for one incident, the complete Prince; dignified, cool, reflective, very noble in his speech to Laertes before the fencing-match, and nobler still in death.

Yet beneath all this lurks the old Hamlet, the less excusable because his distemper has all but vanished. Shakespeare never lets us forget that he is a failure, or that he has failed through weakness of character. And as failures will, he has become a sentimentalist in his last phase. He stands by the newly made grave with the skull of Yorick in his hands, and the world, itself ever sentimental, loves to picture him thus. But the grave across which he casts his jests or utters his philosophy of vanity of vanities, that creed of sentimentalists, has been prepared for a woman whom he has brought to death. The corpse of Ophelia is real; the vanity, as Horatio hints, is Hamlet's over-curious imagination tracing "the noble dust of Alexander, till a' finds it stopping a bung-hole".

Moreover when the shrouded figure is borne in, and its identity is made plain, the man who has just been moralising almost tearfully upon the remains of a jester dead three-and-twenty years ago, can find nothing to utter but unconcerned surprise.[1] "What, the fair Ophelia!" It is very much what he says when he comes upon her first in the nunnery scene; and he could hardly have said less had he recognised the pretty daughter of his washerwoman being borne to her burial. Dr Bradley interprets the exclamation as the utterance of "one terrible pang";[2] but if Shakespeare had intended that, he must have phrased it otherwise.* The epithet "fair" makes it remote, almost callous. We are reminded of the bored Macbeth and his

> She should have died hereafter.

Such involuntary coldness produces its own reaction, as the speaker recollects what the dead has once been to him and is shamed by the recollection. Macbeth seeks to excuse his insensibility by generalising his loss in "Out, out, brief candle!" and the rest. Hamlet, being "most generous", will have the greater shame; it is moreover aroused by the Queen's

> I hoped thou shouldst have been my Hamlet's wife,

and is then immensely aggravated by the "bravery" of Laertes's grief. "O, it offends me to the soul, to hear a robustious periwig-pated fellow tear a passion to tatters, to very rags", Hamlet had declared to the First Player. The

[1] If we remember that when he last saw her he was thinking of her, and treating her, like a prostitute who had consented to tempt him to self-betrayal, the unconcern seems natural enough.

[2] *Shakespearean Tragedy*, p. 145.

indecent over-emphasis of Laertes likewise offends him to the
soul, a soul already offended by its own under-emphasis. The
result is explosion, the last exhibition of that uncontrolled
hysteria which we have seen at work throughout the play.
Hamlet explains it later to Horatio as a "towering passion"
of anger with Laertes; and there can be no doubt that the
rodomontade about "forty thousand brothers", drinking
eisel and eating crocodiles, which concludes

> nay, an thou'lt mouth,
> I'll rant as well as thou,

is in the main prompted by the desire to heap Ossa upon the
Pelion of Laertes. What more there is in it is not love for
Ophelia—that had been dead and buried long before she was
—but self-reproach that love is absent: he is careful to say,
"I *loved* Ophelia". The outburst makes a fine scene, however,
and the excitement of it no doubt brings him pleasure. And
if in retrospect he feels a little apologetic, that is only because
the similarity of their situations gives him a fellow-feeling
with Laertes; not on Ophelia's account. Indeed, he does not
mention her then, and at no time seems in the least conscious
that he is responsible for her death. He is outraged by the
staginess of Laertes; though he has himself come to prefer
dreams to reality and play-acting to deeds.

We do not, of course, realise all this at once as we sit and
watch the scene in the theatre. It is *there* ready to be seen as
we later ponder or talk over the sinuous, shimmering changes
in Hamlet's mood which flash in and out of sight like a lizard.
But Shakespeare, as so often, in this play above all others,
offers us a double plane of vision, the one for reflection and

the other for immediate apprehension. There can be no doubt that our first reaction to the funeral scene is intended to be in Hamlet's favour. The re-entry of Laertes in act 4 has given Claudius an ally, young, attractive, much wronged and, above all, most determined and energetic. His figure for a while overshadows that of Hamlet, and is meant to. But the time has come to redress the balance, and Shakespeare with his usual boldness brings the young men first face to face with each other by the open grave of her whose death gives the brother the strongest claim upon our sympathy, and is most likely to alienate us from the lover responsible for it. Hamlet's conduct is strange, even terrible. But when the attendants have parted them, and he stands away from the grave quivering with a passion that gradually subsides into a pathetic reminder of the old friendship between them, the ranting insincerity of Laertes has become commonplace and contemptible beside the agony of this great and tortured spirit. For we are left in no doubt about the agony, whatever be its cause. And as we note it and, prompted by the Queen, remember the mental distraction with which he is cursed, we acknowledge his essential nobility and pity his affliction. His affliction even leads us to condone his part in Ophelia's death. The unhappy girl is doubly buried; in the grave-yard and in the minds of the spectators. We forget her at any rate for the moment; and Hamlet's silence about his responsibility, noted above, helps us to forget. The showman does not wish our minds to be running upon that just yet.

It is the same story in the matter of Hamlet's revenge. Though he speaks of his duty and behaves as if he had returned fully intending to carry it out, he takes no effective

action to that end. Indeed, Shakespeare shows us that, but
for the discovery of the crowning treachery in the fence with
Laertes and his excitement thereat, he never would have
killed the King. He may demand passionately

> Is't not perfect conscience
> To quit him with this arm? and is't not to be damned,
> To let this canker of our nature come
> In further evil?

But it is only the old reflection: "now *might* I do it". And
Horatio, the clear-eyed, makes this striking rejoinder:

> It must be shortly known to him from England
> What is the issue of the business there.

In other words, if the deed is to be done at all, it must be at
once; for directly the news of the death of Rosencrantz and
Guildenstern reaches Claudius, all opportunity for action will
be gone. Hamlet brushes this aside impatiently:

> It will be short, the interim is mine,
> And a man's life's no more than to say "One";

a single pass, that is, will finish Claudius off. And he then, as
Dr Bradley notes, immediately changes the subject. But
neither Dr Bradley nor, I fancy, any other modern[1] has seen
that Shakespeare brings the English ambassadors in at the end
of the play in order to demonstrate how short the interim
actually is and to register the fact that though it had been at
Hamlet's disposal he fritters it away.

That these points generally escape notice shows how quietly
and unobtrusively they are made. For, once again, though
Hamlet is Hamlet to the end of the play, his creator wishes
now to emphasise the nobility of the man rather than his

---

[1] Contemporary "statists" would not have missed it.

weakness. Both nobility and weakness are exemplified in the business of the fencing-match which Hamlet ought never to have undertaken,* and by means of which the catastrophe is effected. We love him for the very carelessness with which he falls in with the designs of his enemies, culpable as that carelessness is; and our mingled feelings are well expressed for us in advance by the King's confident prophecy to Laertes that

> He being remiss,
> Most generous, and free from all contriving,
> Will not peruse the foils.

It is a comment Shakespeare gives Claudius on purpose to catch our sympathy with his victim. We love him, again, for the fatalism, reliance upon Providence, call it what you will, which he employs to justify this carelessness. He has been plucking the lapwing Osric, feather by feather; and hardly has the fop retired with his message than another lord enters with an enquiry from the King to know if his "pleasure hold to play with Laertes", or whether he "will take longer time". Mr Granville-Barker has taught me that this second, and at first blush entirely superfluous,[1] emissary was introduced by Shakespeare in order to interpose a brief interval between the raillery with Osric and the solemnity of the moment that follows the lord's exit. To expatiate upon such a moment is to suffocate it; a better way is direct quotation:

Horatio. You will lose this wager, my lord.

Hamlet. I do not think so. Since he went into France, I have been in continual practice. I shall win at the odds; but thou

---

[1] The F. text omits him; cf. *The Manuscript of Shakespeare's Hamlet*, I, 31–2.

wouldst not think how ill all's here about my heart—but it is no matter.

Horatio. Nay, good my lord—

Hamlet. It is but foolery, but it is such a kind of gain-giving as would perhaps trouble a woman.

Horatio. If your mind dislike any thing, obey it. I will forestall their repair hither, and say you are not fit.

Hamlet. Not a whit, we defy augury. There is special providence in the fall of a sparrow. If it be now, 'tis not to come—if it be not to come, it will be now—if it be not now, yet it will come—the readiness is all. Since no man, of aught he leaves, knows what is't to leave betimes, let be.

Hamlet is fey, as heroes have been since the dawn of literature; but was ever feydom so wonderfully set forth, or a doomed hero more adorable?

Finally, we love him for his attitude towards Laertes. His admiration for others, and his charming and easy bearing towards his inferiors in rank—the two traits are closely associated—have endeared him to us from the beginning of the play. Indeed, when the springs of the affectionate sympathy with which we follow his career are explored they will be found to consist, apart from the innate grandeur of his spirit, very largely in two things: first, the unreserved, almost boyish, delight with which he greets Horatio and Marcellus, Rosencrantz and Guildenstern, and the players, as they come in one after another; and secondly the affection he himself displays, especially in the confidential talk as the play scene opens, towards his friend Horatio. This impulsive magnanimity finds its last and most attractive expression in his behaviour to Laertes. "That is Laertes, *a very noble youth*", he exclaims to Horatio as he first catches sight of him in the funeral procession. And he captivates us completely by the "gentle entertainment" he uses before they fall to play; for to question the good faith of his request for pardon and of his plea of "a sore distraction", as most critics have done, is to murder a beautiful effect. Shakespeare intended the speech to win our hearts, and never for a moment expected us to take it at anything but its face value.[1] The proof of Hamlet's sincerity is that his later conduct is consistent with it and that Laertes is evidently shaken by his generosity. He calls Laertes "my brother"; he declares that he "will this brother's wager frankly play"; he compares his "ignorance" with Laertes's "skill"; and he asserts that the King "has laid the odds o'th'weaker side". He had told Horatio that, ashamed of his treatment of Laertes at the grave-side of Ophelia, he intends to "court his favours". He does so in simple-hearted and ingenuous honesty; for he admires Laertes, and his admiration at once redounds to his own honour and blackens that of the unworthy object of it.

"I'll be your foil, Laertes," he cries,

> in mine ignorance
> Your skill shall like a star i'th'darkest night
> Stick fiery off indeed.

The words, genuine enough on Hamlet's part, are dramatic irony on Shakespeare's. The rôles of the two men are now completely reversed. Hamlet's irresolution has shown drab in contrast with the brilliant impetuosity of his rival, fresh from Paris and burning with revenge for his father. In the sphere of action Laertes puts him utterly to shame. But

[1] Cf. above, pp. 216–17.

decision and determination do not make "character", though the world thinks so. There is also nobility and generosity, honour and integrity of soul, and in this sphere Hamlet shines "like a star i'th'darkest night" against the base iniquity of his opponents. The sword-play of the last act, in short, symbolises the conflict of two principles, the eternally recurrent, never concluded, battle between disinterested and material ends. From the time of Socrates, "who drank his poison and is dead", the champions of the spirit have paid the price; for the princes of this world are all-powerful. They are, moreover, unshackled by scruple; they have not to shrink at buying "an unction of a mountebank". That Hamlet dies fighting in this battle is his vindication. Called upon for deeds he fails, dismally and completely; he is immortal for what he is, for the "noble substance" which no failure can "dout", no death can annihilate.

The hero at bay

To the majority of Shakespeare's audience, however, the sword-play was what it pretended to be, and had no further significance. Nor would it occur to them to seek for any in a spectacle so fascinating in itself. Unhappily, few nowadays are interested in the ancient sport of fence; and so greatly have fashions in sword-play changed since the beginning of the seventeenth century, that editors have almost entirely neglected this scene, and it is very difficult even for the expert fencer of to-day to tell exactly how it should be played. I must ask the reader, therefore, to bear with me in one last essay in reconstruction, this time with the aid of books by the old fencing masters.[1] His patience will perhaps be rewarded, if I can recapture for him a little of the understanding with which the Elizabethan gallants followed this most thrilling climax to the most thrilling play of all time. For Burbadge, we may be sure, was an expert fencer and would have chosen a worthy opponent.

The scene is set and the plot laid, it will be remembered, by the King and Laertes in 4.7. The King tells Laertes that Hamlet is very anxious to meet him in fence, having recently heard great things of his skill from a French visitor to the Danish court. He proposes, therefore, to bring them together for a wager, when

> with ease,
> Or with a little shuffling, you may choose
> A sword unbated, and in a pass of practice
> Requite him for your father.

Laertes, not to be outdone in villainous suggestion, offers to anoint the point of the weapon with a poison in his possession, so mortal

> that if I gall him slightly,
> It may be death.

And Claudius caps this in turn with his project of the poisoned chalice, bidding Laertes attack furiously so as to make Hamlet thirsty for drink between the bouts. The next

---

[1] For a discussion of these and a justification of the account dogmatically set down in the following pages, *vide* my Introduction to George Silver's *Paradoxes of Defence*, 1599 (Shakespeare Association Facsimiles, no. 6, 1933). Since that was written, however, my views on the third bout and the exchange of rapiers have developed under the influence of a letter by Mr Evan John in *The Times Literary Supplement* (Jan. 25, 1934) and in subsequent conversation with him. Cf. notes on pp. 285, 286.

we hear of the scheme is from Osric, who accosts Hamlet at the beginning of the last scene and, having praised Laertes in his affected fashion with much precious talk of rapiers and poniards with their "liberal-conceited carriages", eventually comes to the point as follows:

The king, sir, hath laid, sir, that in a dozen passes between yourself and him he shall not exceed you three hits. He hath laid on twelve for nine. And it would come to immediate trial, if your lordship would vouchsafe the answer.

The speech has been universally misconstrued. "This wager", writes Dr Johnson, "I do not understand. In a dozen passes one must exceed the other more or less than three hits. Nor can I comprehend how, in a dozen, there can be twelve to nine. The passage is of no importance; it is sufficient that there was a wager." It is dangerous to contradict the Great Cham; but we can be certain that to the Elizabethans the passage *was* important, and that Shakespeare would be most careful to have the details of a sporting event both correct and intelligible. Had Samuel Johnson ever played James Boswell at golf, and been beaten by him "three up", he might have realised that it is seldom necessary to finish all the holes, or rounds, or bouts of an agreed match. The first part of Osric's statement I interpret as follows: the King wagers that Laertes will not win three up in the match. In the second, I think, the commentators have gone astray through failing to see that the "he" in "he hath laid on twelve for nine" is identical with the "he" in the preceding clause, viz. Laertes; and that "laid on" means "laid down conditions", not "wagered". In other words, Laertes on his side stipulates for a match of twelve bouts instead of the usual nine,[1] in order to give himself more elbow room to meet the heavy odds proposed by Claudius. Even so the odds were heavy enough. As we shall see, in the actual match Hamlet wins the first two bouts straight off and draws the third, which meant that he only had to win two more and draw another for all to be over, since Laertes could not possibly have finished three up with four points against him and six to play.

Having thus determined the character of the wager, let us next glance at the kind of fighting involved. "What's his weapon?" asks Hamlet; that is to say, what sort of fence does he propose? And Osric answers "Rapier and dagger". At the time when *Hamlet* was first staged by Shakespeare, three varieties of sword-play were possible: sword-and-buckler play, the old English fashion of fighting with the short broadsword in one hand and a light target in the other; single rapier-play, in which the combatants fought with long rapiers in their right hands, their left being covered with a gauntlet or glove of mail so that they could parry with it and, should the opportunity offer, seize their opponent's rapier and wrest it from him; and thirdly, rapier-and-dagger play, that is with a rapier in the right hand and a dagger in the left. At the end of the sixteenth century English methods had given place with persons of fashion to the rapier-play imported from abroad and the sword-and-buckler men were regarded as out of date, so much so that Hotspur can think

---

[1] I found difficulty in discovering from the old fencing-books the number of bouts usually played for a prize. George Silver, however, on p. 3 of his *Paradoxes of Defence*, 1599, issues a mock challenge to the foreign swordsmen he detested for a series of matches of nine bouts each, which he would hardly have done if nine bouts had not been customary.

of no epithet more contemptuous for Prince Hal than to call him "that same sword-and-buckler Prince of Wales". Single rapier, moreover, was less favoured at the moment than rapier-and-dagger, the popularity of which at the turn of the century is attested by an engraving of the City of London by John Norden in 1600, wherein duellists are depicted fighting in "George's Feeldes" with rapier in one hand and dagger in the other.[1] The vogue was a temporary one, and had passed away before the text of *Hamlet* was printed in 1623, so that it is not surprising to find no daggers mentioned in the Folio stage-direction for the setting of the match at 5.2.222. The corresponding direction in the Second Quarto, on the other hand, gives us "daggers" as well as "Foiles"; and there can be no reasonable doubt that both were used by Burbadge and his stage-opponent at the original performance.

By "foil", it should be added, we are not to understand the buttoned fleuret of modern fence, since buttons apparently did not come into general use until well past the middle of the seventeenth century,[2] but a weapon similar to that employed in serious fight but with edge bated and point blunted. Indeed, the treacherous scheme of Laertes would have been impossible had buttons been intended,[3] since it

[1] I owe this information to the courtesy of Dr Wieselgren of the Royal Library, Stockholm, which possesses a particularly fine copy of Norden's engraving.

[2] *Vide* Egerton Castle, *Schools and Masters of Defence*, pp. 191, 197. On the other hand, the *Oxford Dictionary* quotes Drummond of Hawthorndene (in a letter dated Aug. 6, 1606): "They would have most willingly taken the buttons off the foils." There is nothing, however, to show that Shakespeare knew anything of the fleuret.

[3] The buttons first used on foils were globular in shape and about the size of golf-balls; they would therefore have been easily seen from a considerable distance.

was just because a "foil" could only be distinguished from a "sharp" on close inspection that an "unbated sword" might "with ease or with a little shuffling" be introduced. But, though the introduction of the fatal weapon was easy, the actual choice of weapons required a little management, to which swordsmen in the original audience would no doubt be fully alive. Laertes must get possession of his sharp before Hamlet makes his selection, and the business must at the same time seem open and above board.

My own belief is that Osric was needed as an accomplice for this. He was one of the judges, and the judges were responsible for seeing that all was in order with the weapons, so that he would naturally enter with the foils on his arm, while his colleague perhaps bore the daggers, which of course were all bated. And if Osric does not bring in the unbated sword, then Laertes must do it himself, which will be less effective. Furthermore, Osric is suspect as the emissary who is "put on" by the King to praise the excellence of Laertes with his weapon and so lure Hamlet to the match, while it is to Osric that the falling Laertes whispers "I am justly killed with mine own treachery", which he would hardly do if there were not a secret understanding between them. That he was an accomplice might easily be conveyed to the audience by a significant glance on the part of Claudius, as he says "Give them the foils, young Osric".*

However this may be, a number of foils, with the unbated sword among them, are evidently first placed on some side table, and at the King's command Osric then brings forward a few for the combatants to take their choice. At this point the King distracts Hamlet's attention by discussing the wager with him, which enables Laertes to have first pick.[1] He takes a foil, makes a pass or two, declares it "too heavy", and forthwith goes himself to the table and fetches the sharp he finds there.* Meanwhile, Hamlet has made his choice from the foils Osric offers him and expressed himself satisfied. Mr Granville-Barker suggests that Laertes not only finds his unbated weapon on the side table but actually "anoints" it there and then with the poison, his back to the stage-audience but in full view of the spectators in the theatre. This seems a most attractive proposal, not only because of its theatrical effectiveness but also because it would leave no manner of doubt that he now had "the treacherous instrument" in his hand.

Next the combatants make ready and take their stations. Laertes probably enters already dressed. But Hamlet has to remove his doublet and put on a shirt of mail or breastplate, together with a kind of skull-cap and gloves of mail, which were commonly worn for protection in fencing at this time.[2] For a fight with heavy swords, although bated, was no child's play, and terrible blows might be given or received on unprotected parts.* Meanwhile, the servants bear in flagons of wine and cups, the latter at the King's command being set upon a table by his side.

The match now begins and Laertes, taking the offensive according to the King's suggestion,[3] at first presses Hamlet hard. But, after much thrusting and parrying on both sides,

---

[1] It may be that Laertes, as the fencer challenged, was entitled to this; I have no evidence on the point.

[2] *Vide* Vincentio Saviolo's *Practise* (1595) for these details.

[3] *Vide* 4.7.157.

Hamlet slips past his guard and scores "a very palpable hit" on his body. He has won the first bout for Claudius, and at once the kettle-drums sound, the trumpets blow and the cannon is fired, after which prelude his highness calls for wine in which to pledge his "son". An attendant fills one of the cups, and Claudius drinks from it. Then holding up a magnificent single pearl, a union

> Richer than that which four successive kings
> In Denmark's crown have worn,

he declares it to be Hamlet's by virtue of his prowess, seems to drop it into the cup and bids the servant hand the cup to the Prince. Whether the union is really a phial containing poison or the poison is otherwise conveyed into the cup we are not told. It suffices for us to know that the poison is now there, and that the drink is death. But though the first bout has been violent, Hamlet does not wish for drink. "I'll play this bout first," he says, "set it by awhile." And so the cup is put upon the side table behind him where the spare rapiers lie; and Claudius must bide his time.

The second bout is engaged; and Laertes redoubles his efforts. His chief object is, of course, to wound Hamlet with the poisoned point. But he has a second also, namely to keep him in such constant and vigorous motion as to make him "hot and dry", and so thirsty for the King's loving-cup. We must imagine, then, an exciting bout, lasting some minutes, at the end of which Hamlet again scores. He is now two up with ten to go, and in spite of the violent exertion is showing fine form. Laertes will be hard put to it, if he is to beat him three up. "Our son shall win", cries the King in well simulated glee at the success of his champion, though he is beginning to fear that the poisoned sharp may never touch its victim at all. The Queen too is delighted at the way her dear boy is holding his own against this Paris-trained scrimer. She comes up to him during the interval; and noticing that he is panting a little with the exercise and that the perspiration is beginning to trickle from his brow into his eyes [1]—a serious embarrassment for a fencer—she offers him her handkerchief. At the same time, finding herself close to the table upon which the cup stands, she hands it to him to quench his thirst, after first pledging him in it herself. But Hamlet is an experienced athlete, and knows that to drink while still exerting oneself is only to induce more perspiration and to make one thirstier still. "I dare not drink yet, madam", he declares; "by and by", i.e. when the match is over, or my victory is certain.

The King in helpless anguish of spirit watches Gertrude drink deep of the poison. His affection for her is genuine, and is the best thing about him. But more than her life is involved in the terrible accident. It will reveal the character of the drink, and perhaps before Hamlet is in any way touched. The "back or second" he had devised, in case the "venomed stuck" should fail,

And that our drift look through our bad performance,

---

[1] This, I am convinced, is the meaning intended by "He's fat, and scant of breath". The offer of the napkin shows that Hamlet is perspiring, and his reluctance to drink points to it too. Cf. 1 *Hen. IV*, 2.4.1: "Come out of that fat (=sweaty, or stuffy) room." The notion that "fat" refers to the hypothetical corpulence of Burbadge is absurd on the face of it; for, if the player was actually growing over-stout for the part of "young Hamlet" in 1601, the last thing Shakespeare would do would be to draw attention to the fact.

threatens itself to expose the whole plot. The situation looks black indeed for the conspirators, and they snatch the opportunity of Hamlet's being engaged with the Queen, as she wipes his face, for a brief word together. "My lord, I'll hit him now", says Laertes. To wound Hamlet at once is his only hope, for the Queen may drop at any moment. But Claudius doubts his capacity to pass Hamlet's guard. "I do not think't", he rejoins gloomily.

His doubts are justified by the third bout which ends in a draw. Hamlet, having taken the measure of his opponent and now confident that he can hold his own, rallies him upon his vehement tactics:

> You do but dally,
> I pray you pass with your best violence.
> I am afeard you make a wanton of me.

Laertes needs no such provocation. He attacks with a better violence than ever. Quick as he is, however, Hamlet is quicker still, and parries every thrust. And, as often happens when too much force is used in rapier-play, a lock ensues. The point of Laertes's weapon, as Hamlet wards off a particularly furious stroke, becomes jammed in the projecting hooks on the hilt of his dagger,[1] and the judges are obliged to intervene and part them, while the announcement "Nothing neither way" means that the bout is at an end. Laertes is desperate. The Queen is beginning visibly to droop in her chair of state; Hamlet shows no sign of wishing to drink from the cup; and three bouts have passed without his being even touched with the anointed sharp. The only resource remaining is open foul play; and so, the bout over and

[1] I owe the suggestion to Mr Evan John (*vide* p. 286, n. 2).

Hamlet off his guard, Laertes suddenly lunges, and shouting "Have at you now!"—wounds him at last in the arm.[1] But he has reckoned without his host. The dastardly foul with the unexpected sting of the wound infuriates Hamlet, and Hamlet infuriated is a very dangerous person. His bleeding (made visible to the audience) shows him that Laertes holds a sharp, and he determines to get possession of it. Accordingly, he closes with him, beats aside his dagger with the dagger in his own left hand, and suddenly dropping to the ground the foil in his right, seizes with the empty hand the hilt of the sword he covets and wrests it from his enemy's grasp.[2] The feat, we may be sure, is greeted with thunders of applause from the spectators in the theatre, as he pauses in ironical courtesy to allow Laertes to pick up the discarded foil. Claudius, who has seen all, now makes one last attempt to save his accomplice. "Part them, they are incensed", he cries to the judges.[3] But Hamlet is not to be tricked thus. He counters the King with a grim "Nay, come again", and before Osric can intervene, he has run his man through with the point that had already wounded himself. Laertes staggers back into the arms of Osric, dying; and the "brother's wager" is at an end. Hamlet has won "at the odds"—and spite of them!

Details here and there may be wrong in the foregoing

[1] This, I am told by fencers who remember it, is how the scene was played by Irving at the Lyceum in 1878 under the direction of Alfred Hutton, the well-known and learned swordsman.

[2] This explanation of the exchange, at once technically satisfactory and highly dramatic, I once again owe to Mr Evan John; see his letter published in *The Times Literary Supplement* on Jan. 25, 1934.

[3] *Vide* Bradley, *Shakespearean Tragedy*, pp. 422–3.

account; but this was, in general, I believe, the way the fatal match was played out on the Globe stage in 1601. It was a fence fought by expert swordsmen before an understanding audience, many of them expert swordsmen themselves and all of them trained from boyhood to use eye, hand, wrist and arm in self-defence. Thus, every motion of the combatants, every turn of the fight, was followed with concentrated attention and the keenest appreciation. To such watchers, the exchange of swords must have seemed the most thrilling moment of the play. How different an atmosphere from that of the modern theatre! With us the rapiers are exchanged by accident, as the result of a vulgar scrum in which both weapons clatter to the stage. And the match as a whole, fought by two

> vile and ragged foils,
> Right ill-disposed in brawl ridiculous,

before spectators none of whom has ever handled a sword in his life, is only saved from tedium by the knowledge that treachery is at work.

What we lose is far more than interest in an exciting game of skill. Elizabethans would see Hamlet, for the first time in the play, fighting his enemies, instead of talking. Since the Ghost delivered his charge all their thoughts have been centred upon that right arm and the deed required of it. And here it is at last in action, sword in hand and giving an excellent account of itself. The opponent is the agent of Claudius, not Claudius himself; but they know that Claudius's turn will come. Hamlet is at first unconscious of the situation; but they can see that he must presently realise. Meanwhile he holds his foes at bay, as he wins bout after bout, as he puts the cup from him, as he keeps out of reach of Laertes's weapon. All the forces of evil against which he has been pitted from the beginning seem to find consummation in the triple treachery of naked point, envenomed steel, and poisoned chalice. He is "be-netted round with villanies" as never before. He is the epical hero fighting overwhelming odds with his back against the wall. And the hope steals into the hearts of the spectators that he may even yet win through; until the dastardly lunge and the bleeding arm remind them that he is doomed, that this is tragedy, of which the end must be his death. Yet they still hope that he may fulfil his task and satisfy the demands of justice, lest "this canker of our nature" should "come in further evil". It is time the earth were rid of the crowned monster smiling upon his throne. Thus, when Hamlet discards the bated rapier and seizes the sharp from his opponent, the exploit excites not only ardent admiration but the keenest anticipations. His enemies are now at his mercy, the instrument of vengeance is the engine of their own treachery, and he has added a cubit to his stature!

For, if the occasion be auspicious, still more is the bearing of the Prince. There is no procrastination or hesitation here. We have noted the return of his sanity; we have already forgotten his weakness in our delight at his large-hearted and careless generosity; we are now to see him rise to the height of his whole greatness. The dying Hamlet leaves upon us a sense of power, of terrific force, which we have caught sight of in his fierce threat to those who would prevent him following the Ghost, in his struggle with Laertes by the grave, in his treatment of Rosencrantz and Guildenstern, but which we have never before seen at full. The pitiless way he spits

Laertes with his own point shows us what to expect. The Queen falls, overcome with her husband's poison; and though Claudius, inexhaustible as ever in resource, explains it as a fainting-fit at the sight of blood, she is able with her last breath to warn her son of the cup. It is a titanic figure who at this calls out in a terrible voice of mingled anguish and fury

> O villainy! ho! let the door be locked—
> Treachery! seek it out.

He knows where the treachery is; there is to be no escape for King Paddock this time. But all has not yet been told; for Laertes, repenting in death of the sorry part he has played, now confesses the venomed stuck, and cries "The King, the King's to blame". And so, at length, Hamlet faces his uncle, a naked poisoned sword in his hand. His "interim" has narrowed down to less than "half an hour of life", and he can already feel the poison at work in his veins. The end, so long delayed, comes with a dreadful suddenness. First the envenomed point and then the "potion" are turned against the "incestuous, murderous, damnéd Dane"; and as he forces the cup between his teeth, Hamlet dispatches him with one last bitter quibble:

> Is thy union here?
> Follow my mother.

It is a repetition of a former farewell: "father and mother is man and wife, man and wife is one flesh". John-a-dreams tarried long, but this Hercules "sweeps" to his revenge.

The task accomplished, Hamlet has a moment to exchange a noble forgiveness with Laertes, when he too falls; and his remaining thoughts are occupied with the future of the

kingdom he cannot inherit, and with his own good name.
This last is the only thing left him amid the ruin of his life and
family, and now the unhappy Queen is dead, it can do no
harm that the truth should be told. How much it means to
him is shown by the ferocity with which he foils Horatio's
attempt to drink the poisoned dregs, one more outbreak of
the tremendous self that death has recovered for him, an
outbreak which renders the final appeal to his friend all the
more lovely and pathetic:

> If thou didst ever hold me in thy heart,
> Absent thee from felicity awhile,
> And in this harsh world draw thy breath in pain,
> To tell my story.

Shakespeare is justly famous for the words he sets "upon the
lips of dying men"; but he never betters these, which tell us
Hamlet's story as Horatio cannot tell it, and tell us too that,
duty now performed, he no longer fears what dreams may
come

> When we have shuffled off this mortal coil.

And so, to Horatio's leave-taking of the passing soul—

> Now cracks a noble heart. Good night, sweet prince,
> And flights of angels sing thee to thy rest—

we may add Hamlet's own words to one already dead:
"Rest, rest, perturbéd spirit!"

APPENDICES

APPENDIX A

The Adultery of Gertrude

There are those who deny the fact of adultery before the murder of King Hamlet, on the ground that the word "adulterate" is only once used in the play, and that it is possible to take this as a reference to the marriage, which would of course be regarded as no marriage at all by the Church whether Protestant or Catholic.[1] But such a view runs directly counter to the Belleforest story, the source of all other versions, which, speaking of the murderer of Hamlet's father, declares "that before he had any violent or bloody hands, or once committed parricide upon his brother, he had incestuously abused his wife". This does not of course prove that Shakespeare's Claudius was an adulterer, but it provides the clue to the following somewhat cryptic speech of the Ghost's, which will, as Dr Bradley contends, admit of no other interpretation:

> Ay, that incestuous, that *adulterate* beast,
> With witchcraft of his wit, with traitorous gifts,
> O wicked wit and gifts, that have the power
> So to *seduce*; won to his shameful lust
> The will of *my most seeming-virtuous queen*;
> O Hamlet, what a falling-off was there!
> From me whose love was of that dignity,
> That it went hand in hand *even with the vow*
> *I made to her in marriage*, and to decline
> Upon a wretch whose natural gifts were poor
> To those of mine;
> But virtue, as it never will be moved,
> Though lewdness court it in a shape of heaven,
> So lust, though to a radiant angel linked,
> *Will sate itself in a celestial bed*
> *And prey on garbage.*

[1] *Vide* Wolfgang Keller, *Shakespeare Jahrbuch*, 1919, p. 152; van Dam, *The Text of Shakespeare's Hamlet*, pp. 55–6.

Is the Ghost speaking here of the o'er-hasty marriage of Claudius and Gertrude? Assuredly not. His "certain term" is drawing rapidly to an end, and he is already beginning to "scent the morning air". Hamlet knew of the marriage, and his whole soul was filled with nausea at the thought of the speedy hasting to "incestuous sheets". Why then should the Ghost waste precious moments in telling Hamlet what he was fully cognisant of before? He had come from his "prison-house" to incite his son to revenge by bringing him *news*, news which only he could communicate to him. Moreover, though the word "incestuous" was applicable to the marriage, the rest of the passage is entirely inapplicable to it. Expressions like "witchcraft", "traitorous gifts", "seduce", "shameful lust", and "seeming-virtuous" may be noted in passing. But the rest of the quotation leaves no doubt upon the matter. The comparison of the "natural gifts" of King Hamlet with those of his brother, taken in conjunction with the reference to the "marriage-vow", "celestial bed", and "preying on garbage", can have but one meaning. The Ghost is speaking of Gertrude's infidelity before his death. He breathes not a hint of her possible complicity in the murder; on the contrary, his special charge to Hamlet concerning her seems to imply that he acquitted her of any knowledge of it. Consequently Hamlet's fierce cry "O most pernicious woman!" uttered shortly after his father's disappearance can refer to nothing else than the new fact he has just gleaned as to her unfaithfulness during her husband's lifetime.

Again, the scene in act 3 between mother and son is inexplicable unless Hamlet has something more against her than her hasty marriage. He does not accuse her of adultery in so many words, yet the speech beginning

> Such an act
> That blurs the grace and blush of modesty,
> Calls virtue hypocrite, takes off the rose
> From the fair forehead of an innocent love
> And sets a blister there, *makes marriage vow*
> *As false as dicers' oaths*, O such a deed

> *As from the body of contraction plucks*
> *The very soul*, and sweet religion makes
> A rhapsody of words,

is a clear enough indication of what he has in his mind, and is altogether extravagant if taken as referring only to her marriage. The Queen sees that he knows all, and, in her mood of facile repentance, implicitly admits her guilt. Moreover, the word Hamlet shrinks from uttering to her he makes no bones about with Horatio later, when he declares that Claudius had "whored" his mother,[1] while Horatio himself in the summary of the events of the play which he gives to the astonished Fortinbras comprises the history of Claudius in one line:[2]

> Of carnal, bloody and unnatural acts,

in which murder significantly stands between adultery and incest. The adultery, like many other things in *Hamlet*, is not perhaps as explicit as it might be; but there can be no doubt that it was intended.

[1] 5.2.64.   [2] 5.2.379.

APPENDIX B

The Funeral of Ophelia

I contend above (pp. 68–70) that the funeral in 5.1 was intended by Shakespeare to be conducted by an Anglican, or at any rate a Protestant, Doctor of Divinity. As the service has long been considered a Roman Catholic one, it is well to insist that none of Shakespeare's references to it are incompatible with Anglican usage in the reign of Elizabeth. In compiling these notes I have received much help from Dr Percy Dearmer, who allows me to quote his authority as a liturgiologist in support of my interpretation.

(i) *maiméd rites*. I have little doubt that the real origin of these "maiméd rites" was theatrical convenience. Shakespeare needed a funeral, but elaborate ceremonial, such as was customary at Elizabethan court burials, would have involved singing men and boys and have taken time. He therefore informs us through the mouths of the gravediggers and the priest that a conflict of opinion had arisen over the death of Ophelia, and that while the "crowner" had brought in a verdict of "Christian burial", i.e. had refused to find her guilty of *felo-de-se*, the officiant himself had taken the opposite view, according to which

> She should in ground unsanctified have lodged
> Till the last trumpet: for charitable prayers,
> Shards, flints and pebbles should be thrown on her;

in other words, she should have been buried in the manner after which all suicides were buried in this country up to 1823, when the practice was abolished by law. The gravediggers are clearly persuaded that the coroner has been influenced unduly by the rank of the deceased. "Will you ha' the truth an't? if this had not been a gentlewoman, she should have been buried out a Christian burial." And the priest corroborates this by declaring that "great command", i.e. royal injunctions, had "o'erswayed" the law of the Church. In this way Shakespeare provided a perfectly reasonable explanation of the simple stage-procession without ceremony of any kind, which was what he wanted. We glean the impression that, as a reluctant concession to pressure from the King, the Church had allowed some kind of shortened burial service in the royal chapel,[1] the tolling of the bell, and interment in sanctified ground, but nothing else. And Hamlet's comment as the procession enters:

> But soft, but soft, awhile—here comes the king,
> The queen, the courtiers. Who is this they follow?
> And with such maiméd rites? This doth betoken
> The corse they follow did with desp'rate hand
> Fordo it own life. 'Twas of some estate—

is clearly put into his mouth for the enlightenment of the audience. He grasps the situation with uncanny comprehension because it was necessary for the spectators to grasp it.

But the situation itself accords both with probability and with the procedure of the Church of England at that date. The old Canon Law, apart from such ordinances as be "contrariant or repugnant to the laws, statutes and customs of this realm", had become the ecclesiastical law of England by 1 Eliz. ch. 1, § 2, and is still in force. An early canon, cited on pp. 182–3 of the standard *Book of Church Law* by Blunt and G. Edwardes Jones (1899) from which I have taken these facts, lays it down:

Concerning those who *by any fault* inflict death on themselves, let there be no commemoration of them in the Oblation....Let it be enjoined that those who kill themselves by sword, poison, precipice, or halter, or by any other means bring violent death upon themselves, shall not have a memorial made of them in the Oblation, nor shall their bodies be carried with psalms to burial.

These words come close to those of Shakespeare's "churlish priest", when he says:

---

[1] I.e. as a preliminary to the interment. But there is nothing in the text about it and perhaps Shakespeare does not mean to imply it.

> We should profane the service of the dead
> To sing sage requiem and such rest to her
> As to peace-parted souls;

and the canon, which "expresses the general principle of the canon law on the subject", may well have been invoked in cases like Ophelia's, whose "death was doubtful" and on whose behalf powerful parties were pressing for special consideration. For the ordinary suicide ecclesiastical burial, as the priest asserts, was forbidden, and a rubric to this effect is to be found before the Burial Office in the Book of Common Prayer. The rubric was not actually inserted until 1662, but it merely regularised the traditional practice.

On the difference of opinion between Church and coroner, the following passage from *The Book of Church Law* (pp. 183–4) is illuminating. Discussing the canon quoted above, the authors continue:

This principle certainly indicates that a distinction should be made between those who "by any fault" cause their own death, and those who do so when they are so far deprived of reason as not to be responsible in the sense of doing it by "any fault", wilfully and consciously. And the rubric being thus to be interpreted by a law of charity, the responsibility of deciding in what cases exceptions shall be made...is thrown upon the clergyman who has cure of souls in the parish where the suicide is to be buried.

In coming to this decision, the verdict of the coroner's jury should have respectful attention, though it is not to be considered as an invariable law for the clergyman. He will of course remember that, however unsatisfactory such a tribunal may be, it is the only tribunal before which the question is tried at all....If, however, after giving full weight to all these circumstances, the clergyman should feel convinced beyond doubt that there was no such insanity as to deprive the suicide of ordinary moral responsibility, then he is to remember that he is a "steward of the mysteries of God", who has no right to misapply the blessings given him to dispense etc. etc.

Laertes's indignation with the "churlish priest" and the whole tenor of the text go to show that the difficulties had been caused by the officiant himself, who could not "feel convinced beyond doubt that there was" insanity sufficient "to deprive the suicide of ordinary moral responsibility".

(ii) *bell and burial*. "The bringing home of bell and burial" means the laying to rest with the passing-bell, and a grave in consecrated ground. There is nothing here incompatible with Anglican usage, despite the dislike of puritans for the ceremonial use of bells. As a writer in *Shakespeare's England* (II, 148) puts it, "Funerals during Elizabeth's reign were...conducted with many of the traditional ceremonies and rites of pre-Reformation times, the passing bell being one of these"; while reference to Archbishop Grindal's Articles for York, quoted in vol. III of *Visitation articles and injunctions of the period of the Reformation* (ed. by W. H. Frere for the Alcuin Club) shows even that extremist ordering the use of the "passing bell", i.e. "one short peal before the burial and another short peal after the burial, without any other superfluous and superstitious ringing".[1] The truth is that no ceremonial customs alter so slowly or are so difficult to change as those connected with interment.

(iii) *sage requiem*. The foregoing observation is well illustrated by this reference. It might be supposed that after the Reformation the requiem mass would cease to be possible as part of the burial service in the English Church. Yet, such a mass is simply a celebration of the office of Communion in connection with a funeral or in memory of a departed person, and that requiem masses continued in use, at least occasionally, during the reign of Elizabeth is certain. They might even be celebrated in Latin; and Dr Dearmer draws my attention to an edition of the Latin Prayer Book, printed in 1560, which contains a requiem mass of this kind. The title of the book runs:

Liber Precum Publicarum, seu ministerii Ecclesiasticæ administrationis Sacramentorum, aliorumque rituum & cæremoniarum in Ecclesia Anglicana.

Cum priuilegio Regiae Majestatis.

[1] *Vide* also index to vol. I of same under "bells", including nine references to "passing bells", and cf. *Sidneiana*, ed. by S. Butler for the Roxburgh Club, 1837, p. 30: "My passing bell and knell with care did ring" (from verses describing Sir Philip Sidney's funeral).

It contains a service entitled "Celebratio cœnæ Domini, in fune-bribus, si amici & vicini defuncti communicare velint", which gives a Collect, Epistle and alternative Gospels, and though omitting the Introit (thus avoiding the words "requiem Aeternam") is undoubtedly the Communion Service, "commonly called the Mass" as the First Prayer Book of Edward VI describes it.[1]

I doubt, however, whether Shakespeare had such a service in mind in *Hamlet*. For the name "requiem" was also generally used for the choral singing which appears to have been the normal accompaniment of well-to-do funerals. *Shakespeare's England* (II, 150) quotes a writer of 1598, as follows:

> It is a custome still in use with Christians to attend the funerall of their deceased friendes, with whole chantries of choyce quire-men singing solemnly before them.

The *Oxford Dictionary*, again, after giving the ordinary meaning of "requiem", glosses it as "any dirge or solemn chant for the repose of the dead (Chiefly *poet.*)" and quotes from Beaumont and Fletcher's *Philaster* (v. iii):

> I'll provide
> A masque shall make your Hymen turn his saffron
> Into a sullen coat, and sing sad requiems
> To your departing souls.

But the best illustration, as Dr Dearmer suggests, comes from Shakespeare himself, who in *The Phoenix and the Turtle* gives us the lines

> Let the priest in surplice white,
> That defunctive music can
> Be the death-divining swan,
> Lest the requiem lack his rite.

Here the words "surplice white" prove that the "priest" is not intended to be a Roman one, seeing that the Roman requiem mass would be celebrated in mass vestments, without surplice.

---

[1] This Latin Prayer Book is reprinted in *Liturgies and Occasional Forms of Prayer set forth in the Reign of Queen Elizabeth*, ed. by the Rev. W. K. Clay, Cambridge University Press, 1847 (Parker Society Publications).

(iv) *the churlish priest*. The speech-heading for his two speeches in Q 2, as stated on p. 69, are "*Doct.*", which I interpret as "Doctor of Divinity", and which, as Dr Dearmer agrees, would mean a clergyman of the Church of England. "He would wear", he writes, "a gown and a tippet over his cassock, and a square cap, as ordered in the canon of 1604, the tippet being what we call a black scarf." It has been suggested that the heading "*Doct.*" might equally well denote "Doctor of Canon Law" and so refer to a Roman Catholic priest. Logically, indeed, it might. But *Hamlet* is a stage-play, not a novel, and the only conceivable purpose of such a heading in a playhouse manuscript is to indicate costume. Is it in the least likely that a character would appear on the Elizabethan stage dressed as a doctor of canon law, unless his title were carefully noted before his entry and had some important dramatic point? Here things are very different: there is no reference to "doctor" in the text, and the costume must therefore have been intended to represent some quite ordinary type of priest. It is surely reasonable to suppose that normally only two such types were seen upon the stage in Shakespeare's day: the "friar", who would wear the frock and hood, and the "parson" or "doctor" (Anglican), who would wear a black gown. All that Shakespeare meant to imply by "*Doct.*", I think, was "gown".

Postscript: The struggle at the grave. As I go to press I rejoice to learn that Mr Granville-Barker will in his forthcoming book (*vide* pp. 21-2 above) be able to show that Shakespeare intended the struggle between Hamlet and Laertes to take place at the graveside of Ophelia, instead of—horribly and grotesquely—*in* her grave where for over three hundred years theatrical tradition has usually staged it. The stage-direction in Q 1 from which the tradition derives seems difficult to set aside, but I think Mr Granville-Barker's reasons for so doing will be found amply sufficient. Yet, Professor Parrott reminds us, Burbage began the tradition, as a line in his elegy proves (*vide The Library*, 5th series, June 1948, p. 64).

APPENDIX C

The Identity of the Gonzago troupe[1]

I suggest in the notes to my edition of *Hamlet* that the First Player was intended to be a caricature of Edward Alleyn, the leading tragic actor of the Lord Admiral's Men, who were the principal competitors with Shakespeare's company, the Lord Chamberlain's Men, for the suffrages of the London public.[2] There are not a few clues pointing in this direction. Most commentators take the players who visit Elsinore to represent Shakespeare and his fellows. The notion is based, apparently, upon a reference to "Hercules and his load"[3] at the end of the passage relating to the War of the Theatres, in which the Children of the Chapel had, Rosencrantz says, seriously affected the fortunes of the "common players". But the Globe is mentioned some twenty-five lines later than the talk of the Gonzago company, and is expressly distinguished from it by Rosencrantz. "Do the boys carry it away?" asks Hamlet. And Rosencrantz answers: "Ay, that they do my lord, Hercules and his load *too*"; which, as I read it, means that the Children have not merely forced the Gonzago company to go on tour but have actually injured the takings at the doors of the great Globe itself.

In any case, quite apart from my theory of the burlesquing of the players in the play-scene, points are made against them which

[1] *Vide* above p. 163.

[2] I am glad to find that my suspicions, first entertained though not expressed when I was working at the original draft of chapter V for publication in *The Athenaeum* in 1918, are shared by Dr G. B. Harrison. *Vide* his essay on Shakespeare's Actors (pp. 81–5, *Shakespeare and the Theatre*, Shakespeare Association, 1927) and *Shakespeare at Work*, pp. 273–6.

[3] The sign outside the Globe Theatre.

render incredible any identification with the company for which *Hamlet* was written:

> *Ham.* Do they hold the same estimation they did when I was in the city; are they so followed?
> *Ros.* No, indeed, are they not.

It is surely absurd to suppose that Shakespeare's company would thus bluntly proclaim their own unpopularity; the respectful glance at the Globe later is in very different tone. Or take Hamlet's long denunciation in 3.2, already quoted in part, of the staginess of the players. Is it to be imagined for a moment that this criticism is directed against the very actors who utter it? Yet, that it was aimed at the Gonzago cast is proved by the First Player's haughty admission "I hope we have reformed that indifferently with us, sir", together with Hamlet's brusque reply "O reform it altogether", and by the personal attack upon a clown unnamed which appears in the First Quarto but not in the later *Hamlet* texts and has no relevance to the players in *Hamlet* at all. Moreover, Rosencrantz's description of these players as "tragedians of the city" would be quite inappropriate to a company like Shakespeare's, which during the decade preceding the appearance of *Hamlet* had specialised in comedy, though it would well suit the Admiral's men, with their famous tragedian Edward Alleyn, and their repertory which included *The Spanish Tragedy* and Marlowe's plays.

More pointed clues occur when the players make their first entry. As Polonius comes bustling in to announce their advent, a day behind the fair, Hamlet forestalls him with "When Roscius was an actor in Rome". The interruption need mean no more than "Queen Anne is dead", as we should put it; but when it is remembered that "Roscius" was the title almost universally conferred at that time upon Alleyn,[1] another interpretation is credible. Or again, when a few lines later Hamlet, interrupting

---

[1] *Vide* Chambers, *Elizabethan Stage*, II, 297, citing Nashe, Weever, B. Jonson and Fuller. Cf. also Dekker, *Satiromastix*, 1.633.

Polonius for the second time, ejaculates, "O Jephthah, judge of Israel, what a treasure hadst thou!", the hit at the Fishmonger Secretary of State takes on further point when we recall that a play called *Jephthah*, written by Dekker and Munday for the Lord Admiral's men, was being acted in July, 1601, a few months probably before *Hamlet* was first given in its final form. Then there is the Pyrrhus speech from some play upon Dido and Aeneas the identification of which has perplexed the critics sorely. In my edition of *Hamlet* in "The New Shakespeare" I have attempted a solution of this problem, and I need not repeat it. The only point which concerns us here is that, whatever the origin or meaning of the First Player's recital, there can be little doubt that the speech he quotes had some connection with the lost *Dido and Aeneas*, of which we know nothing except that it was performed on Jan. 8, 1598, by the Admiral's company. Finally, it is at least possible that the old *True Tragedy of Richard III*, a quotation from which Hamlet hurls at the head of the mouthing Lucianus, may have belonged to the repertory of the Admiral's men, seeing that on June 27, 1602, Henslowe, their financial director, is found advancing money to Ben Jonson in earnest of a play book called *Richard Crookback* which suggests a revision of the earlier text.

Taking everything together, therefore, I find it difficult to avoid the conviction that the Gonzago troupe represented the Lord Admiral's men and that in the First Player Shakespeare's audience, with the help perhaps of costume, wig and gestures resembling his, were meant to see a caricature of Edward Alleyn. Flashy contrivances like the dumb-show would be in keeping with what we know of the dramatists who wrote for this company, while Hamlet's description of the "robustious periwig-pated fellow" who tears "a passion to tatters, to very rags, to split the ears of the groundlings", to say nothing of the other criticisms, might very well express Shakespeare's own opinion of the founder of Dulwich College. All this adds little or nothing to *our* enjoyment of the comic under-plot in the play scene which continually threatens to interfere with the operation of Hamlet's main purpose; but it must have immensely increased the fun for the Elizabethans. One has only to think of Lucianus mimicking the "damnable faces" of the great tragedian to see what such fun involved. To some of my readers it may seem desecration to intrude these supposed topicalities into the solemn moments of the King's unmasking. I do not think it appeared so to Shakespeare.

Mr T. S. Eliot's Theory of Hamlet

Of the modern psycho-analytic solutions of the Hamlet problem I have perhaps already said enough elsewhere.[1] But a special application of them suggested by a well-known living English critic must here be glanced at. Premising that "so far from being Shakespeare's masterpiece, the play is most certainly an artistic failure", and basing this judgment upon the highly disputable thesis of the "historical" school, "that Shakespeare's *Hamlet*, so far as it is Shakespeare's, is a play dealing with the effect of a mother's guilt upon her son, and that Shakespeare was unable to impose this motive successfully upon the 'intractable' material of the old play", Mr T. S. Eliot continues:

This, however, is by no means the whole story. It is not merely the "guilt of a mother" that cannot be handled as Shakespeare handled the suspicion of Othello, the infatuation of Antony, or the pride of Coriolanus. The subject might conceivably have expanded into a tragedy like these, intelligible, self-complete, in the sunlight. *Hamlet*, like the sonnets, is full of some stuff that the writer could not drag to light, contemplate, or manipulate into art....Hamlet (the man) is dominated by an emotion which is inexpressible, because it is in *excess* of the facts as they appear. And the supposed identity of Hamlet with his author is genuine to this point: that Hamlet's bafflement at the absence of objective equivalent to his feelings is a prolongation of the bafflement of his creator in the face of his artistic problem. Hamlet is up against the difficulty that his disgust is occasioned by his mother, but that his mother is not an adequate equivalent for it; his disgust envelops and exceeds her. It is thus a feeling which he cannot understand; he cannot objectify it, and it therefore remains to poison life and obstruct action. None of the possible actions can satisfy it; and nothing Shakespeare can do with the plot can express Hamlet for him....

We must simply admit that here Shakespeare tackled a problem which proved too much for him. Why he attempted it at all is an insoluble

[1] *Vide Hamlet* ("The New Shakespeare"), Introduction, pp. xliv–xlvi.

puzzle; under compulsion of what experience he attempted to express the inexpressibly horrible, we cannot ever know. We need a great many facts in his biography....[1]

These sentences give, I think, the gist of the argument. Mr Eliot has his eye on both "historical" and "psychological" worlds, and would compromise between them, though he never indicates exactly how the compromise is to be effected. What he does is to suggest vaguely that, in addition to the difficulties of his inherited plot, Shakespeare had difficulties in himself to contend with, that Hamlet's attitude towards his mother and still more (though Mr Eliot does not mention this) his conduct towards Ophelia reveal a hidden conflict in the nature of his creator. He would not perhaps go the length of the psycho-analyst Dr Ernest Jones, who declares that Hamlet suffers from an Œdipus complex, because Shakespeare did also;[2] but he seems to hint at such a solution.

I have some sympathy with this point of view. A "strain of sex-nausea", I pointed out in *The Essential Shakespeare*, "runs through almost everything Shakespeare wrote after 1600." The strain, however, I associate, not with any mysterious complex, but with the more common-place derangement known as jealousy, jealousy of the same kind as, if not identical with, that described so savagely in the *Sonnets*. If I may be allowed to quote:

Jealousy is the mainspring of no less than four plays: *Troilus and Cressida, Othello, Winter's Tale*, and *Cymbeline*, while there are traces of it in *Antony and Cleopatra*, and one may suspect that it furnished material for the scene between Hamlet and his mother. That "couch for luxury and damned incest", which, unseen, is ever present to the mind of Hamlet and of the audience, is, I think, symbolic. Far more than the murder, it is this which transforms the Prince's imagination into something "as foul as Vulcan's stithy". The imagination of Othello is as foul and more explicit. Even Lear...broods "over the nasty sty" and begs "an ounce of civet to sweeten his imagination", while to Posthumus and Leontes is given utterance scarcely less outspoken than Othello's. Above all in *Timon of Athens*, which breathes a hatred of mankind that rivals Swift's,

---

[1] *The Sacred Wood* (2nd ed.), pp. 98–101.
[2] *Essays in Applied Psycho-analysis*, 1923.

nearly a whole act is devoted to the unsavoury topic. Collect these passages together, face them as they should be faced, and the conclusion is inescapable that the defiled imagination of which Shakespeare writes so often, and depicts in metaphor so nakedly material, must be his own.[1]

But to say that Shakespeare, as all poets and dramatists must, worked some of his own emotional experience into the stuff of his art does not necessarily imply that the art suffered thereby. In only one of the plays just mentioned, *King Lear*, might the sex-nausea be criticised as out of character; and inasmuch as the expression of it forms part of the ravings of a madman, that is of one traditionally privileged to utter his mind freely upon such matters, even there the charge must be disallowed. As for Hamlet, he too has the excuse of mental instability for his obscene language to Ophelia and his shending of Gertrude, and that goes for something—it went for a good deal more with the Elizabethans than it does with us. "The 'madness' of Hamlet lay to Shakespeare's hand" writes Mr Eliot; but J. M. Robertson hath him in thrall and he only thinks of the "madness" as a legacy of which Shakespeare makes use to let out a little of his own pent-up distemper. He forgets too, when he asserts that Hamlet's emotion "is in excess of the facts" of the play, one very big fact, though once again a fact bigger in the seventeenth than in the twentieth century; I mean the fact of incest. The hideous thought of incest, as we have seen, is the monster present in Hamlet's mind throughout the First Soliloquy. It is that, far more than the indecent haste of the wedding, which makes "all the uses of this world" seem "weary, stale, flat, and unprofitable", sullies his very flesh, causes him to long for death and prompts the bitter cry "Frailty, thy name is woman!" Is the passion of that speech in excess of the facts? This is the test question by which Mr Eliot's thesis stands or falls; for if the First Soliloquy be accepted as dramatically appropriate all the rest follows. It is a question of personal opinion and critical judgment. Speaking for myself, I can find nothing wrong with the soliloquy; and I do not believe that the Elizabethans, who

[1] *The Essential Shakespeare*, pp. 118–19.

were less interested in Shakespeare's private life than we are, saw anything wrong either. Given Hamlet's youth and the nobility of spirit which the soliloquy reveals, given the imagination of a great poet, which no one will deny him, given the fact of incest and the revelation of the Ghost, and given the "sore distraction" which disgust and horror bring in their train, what facts external to the play do we need to explain his behaviour to Ophelia and his mother, or to account for his inaction? Whether they are sufficient to *excuse* him raises another and different problem.

APPENDIX E

Shakespeare's Knowledge of A Treatise of Melancholie *by Timothy Bright*

A Treatise of Melancholie, first printed in 1586 by T. Vautrollier, is an 8vo of 286 pages in small type and entirely without paragraphing, so that it is not an easy book to read. Its author, Timothy Bright, a protégé of Walsingham's, was in 1585 appointed resident physician at St Bartholomew's Hospital, but later took orders and died as "public preacher" and vicar of St Mary's, Shrewsbury. He was a man of many parts, and has several books to his credit, three of which were of considerable importance in his own day: the *Treatise of Melancholie* (1586), *Characterie; an arte of shorte, swifte and secrete writing by character* (1588), and *An abridgement of the booke of Acts and Monumentes of John Foxe* (1589): a remarkable harvest in four years. The second-named has earned him the title of "the father of modern short-hand"; his "charactery" was much used at the time, especially for the reporting of sermons by popular preachers, and many have supposed that the pirates or pirate, responsible for the "stolne and surreptitious" Shakespearian quartos, made notes at performances by means of it.

The earliest writer to suggest that Shakespeare had read Bright's *Treatise of Melancholie* was apparently an anonymous contributor to *Notes and Queries*,[1] who in June 1853 pointed out that Hamlet's expression "discourse of reason" (1.2.150) is to be found in the Epistle Dedicatorie to the *Treatise*.[2] Nineteen years later William Blades, advancing the theory, in his *Shakspere and Typography* (1872), that the poet started life in London as a press-reader or

---

[1] 1st series, vol. VII, p. 546.
[2] *Vide* below, p. 314.

shop-assistant to Vautrollier, to whom he had been introduced by his fellow-townsman, Vautrollier's apprentice and successor, Richard Field, observed: "It would be an interesting task to compare the Mad Folk of Shakespeare, most of whom have the melancholy fit, with *A Treatise of Melancholie*, which was probably read carefully for press by the youthful poet." This was probably little more than a lucky shot. But when Richard Loening, whose *Die Hamlet-Tragödie Shakespeares* (1893) is perhaps the most elaborate attempt ever made to solve the problem of Hamlet on psychological lines, pointed in the *Shakespeare Jahrbuch* of 1895 to Bright as the source of Shakespeare's psychology both in *Hamlet* and other plays, his testimony deserves every consideration. Even more striking are the words of the cautious Dowden in his edition of the play published in 1899: "I can hardly doubt that Shakespeare was acquainted with Bright's *Treatise*."[1] It is therefore no new thesis I am here advancing.

The strength of the case rests, however, upon the parallels not merely of thought but also of phrase. I am not aware that anyone has yet observed how many and close these parallels are, and I have never seen any attempt to set them out after an orderly fashion. Had Shakespeare showed acquaintance with Bright's psychological notions only, it would be arguable that he might have found them elsewhere. But the remarkable feature of the parallels to me is that they often seem to show borrowing by the poet of chance words and ideas which have no necessary connection with psychology at all, still less with Hamlet's character. To some slight extent Bright's book appears to have influenced the mind of Shakespeare after the fashion of those travel-books which, as Professor Livingston Lowes has so beautifully demonstrated, suffered a sea-change in the subconscious

---

[1] Note on 2.2.310. Cf. also his "Elizabethan Psychology" in *Essays: modern and Elizabethan* and J. Q. Adams, *Hamlet*, pp. 196–7. For many of the facts in the foregoing couple of paragraphs I am indebted to a memoir by W. J. Carlton entitled *Timothe Bright, Doctor of Phisicke*, 1911.

depths of Coleridge's imagination and so became transformed into the rich strangeness of *The Ancient Mariner* and *Kubla Khan*.[1]

My quotations include only specially striking parallels with *Hamlet*. I am not trying to demonstrate the nature and extent of Bright's influence upon Shakespeare but merely to prove that Shakespeare had read his book.

2.2.382–3. I am but mad north-north-west; when the wind is southerly, I know a hawk from a handsaw.

Treatise, p. 257. The ayre meet for melancholicke folke, ought to be thinne, pure and subtile, open and patent to all winds: in respect of their temper, especially to the South, and Southeast.

1.4.28.   Oft breaking down the pales and forts of reason.

Treatise, p. 250. There keepe the straightest hand, where the lists of reason are most like to be broken through.

2.2.301–7. It goes so heavily with my disposition, that this goodly frame the earth, seems to me a sterile promontory, this most excellent canopy the air, look you, this brave o'erhanging firmament, this majestical roof fretted with golden fire, why it appeareth nothing to me but a foul and pestilent congregation of vapours.

Treatise, p. 106. The body thus possessed with the vnchearefull, and discomfortable darknes of melancholie, obscureth the Sonne and Moone, and all the comfortable planetts of our natures, in such sort, that if they appeare, they appeare all darke, and more then halfe eclipsed of this mist of blackenes, rising from that hidious lake.

5.1.65–70.
Ham. Has this fellow no feeling of his business that a' sings in grave-making?
Hor. Custom hath made it in him a property of easiness.
Ham. 'Tis e'en so, the hand of little employment hath the daintier sense.

Bright more than once stresses the effect of occupation upon the character and manners of those who engage in them, e.g.

[1] *Vide The Road to Xanadu*, by J. Livingstone Lowes.

Treatise, p. 51. We may obserue the nature of mariners, occupied in the sea surges, who haue their maners not much vnlike framed, tempestuous and stormie: likewise the villager, who busieth him selfe about his plow and cattell only, hath his wits of no higher conceit: butchers acquainted with slaughter, are accompted therby to be of a more cruell disposition: and therefore amongst vs are discharged from iuries of life & death.

p. 78. The objection rising from custome of life in saylers, butchers, and plowmen, receiueth the same answere. For their instruments of action through continuall practise of such artes, maketh them in common sense, imagination, and affection, to deliuer thinges vnto the minde after an impure sort, alwayes sauouring of their ordinary trade of life.

1.4.73–4.

> Which might deprive your sovereignty of reason,
> And draw you into madness.

3.1.160.   ...that noble and most sovereign reason.

Treatise, p. 61. It followeth to proue the spirite[1] and body to be wholly organicall: by organicall I meane a disposition & aptnes only, without any free worke or action, otherwise then at the mindes commandement: else should there be mo beginninges & causes of action then one, in one nature: which popularity of administration nature will none of, nor yet with any holygarcicall or mixt: but commandeth only by one soueerainty: the rest being vassals at the beck of the soueraigne commander.

1.5.68–9.

> And with a sudden vigour it doth posset
> And curd, like eager droppings into milk.

Treatise, p. 13. The braine as tender as a posset curd.

[1] By "spirite" Bright does not mean the soul but the "vital spirit" or "spirits", a psycho-physiological conception. Cf. Burton, *Anatomy of Melancholy* (1638), p. 15, quoted by H. J. C. Grierson, *Poems of John Donne*, II, 45.

3.1.161.

Like sweet bells jangled, out of tune and harsh.

1.4.65-7.

I do not set my life at a pin's fee,
And for my soul, what can it do to that
Being a thing immortal as itself.

Treatise, p. 38. This affecting of the minde [by the body], I vnderstand not to be any empairing of the nature thereof; or decay of any facultie therein; or shortning of immortality; or any such infirmitie inflicted vpon the soule from the bodie (for it is farre exempt from all such alteration): but such a disposition, and such discontentment, as a false stringed lute, giueth to the musician...which with better instruments would...satisfie the eare with most pleasant and delectable harmonie. Otherwise the soule receaueth no hurt from the bodie, it being spirituall, and voyde of all passion of corporall ʳhinges, and the other grosse, earthie, and farre vnable to annoy a nature of such excellencie.

p. 250. This effect as it is wrought by that kinde of disorder, in like manner, a perturbation whereon reason sitteth not and holdeth not the raine, is of the same aptnes to disturbe the goodly order disposed by iust proportion in our bodies: & putting the parts of that most consonant and pleasant harmony out of tune deliuer a note, to the great discontentment of reason and much against the mindes will, which intendeth far other, then the corporall instrument effecteth.

1.5.70.   The thin and wholesome blood.

Treatise, p. 270. Melancholy blood is thicke and grosse, & therfore easily floweth not though the vaine be opened.

2.2.299-300. I have of late...lost all my mirth, forgone all custom of exercises.

Treatise, p. 130. custome of exercise. (Here Bright is not speaking, like Hamlet, of physical exercise, but of keeping the wits sharp by exercise; yet the similarity of phrasing is the more striking on that account, since the expression occurs in a long passage which possesses many affinities with *Hamlet*, *vide* below.)

p. 31. exercises...wholy intermitted...causing the blood to be thicke through setling.

1.2.150. ...discourse of reason.

Treatise (Epistle Dedicatorie). I haue enterlaced my treatise besides with disputes of Philosophie that the learned sort of them, and such as are of quicke conceit, and delited in discourse of reason in naturall things, may find to passe their time with.

The expression occurs several times in Florio's *Montaigne*, and is found elsewhere, e.g. in Philemon Holland's trans. of Plutarch's *Morals* (1603), as is pointed out in *Notes and Queries*, 1st series, vol. VII, p. 497.

2.2.123–4. whilst this machine is to him.

Bright never actually calls the body a "machine"; but as Dowden notes, he has a lengthy argument explaining the nature of the body as that of a kind of living instrument, tool or engine of the soul. On p. 61 he distinguishes between three sorts of instruments: (i) "dead in itselfe, and destitute of all motion: as a saw before it be moued of the workman, and a ship before it be stirred with winde and hoised of saile"; (ii) with "power in it selfe" and requiring "direction only, as the beast and fowle"; (iii) requiring "not only direction, but impulsion also from an inward vertue and forcible power: as the motion of the hand and the variety of the hand actions do most euidently declare. Of these three kinds of instruments, I place the spirit and bodie both to the mind, as the saw or axe in the workmans hand, or the lute touched of the Musician (according to the sundry qualities & conditions of the instruments of the body) in the thirde sort; but so, as the spirit, in comparison of the bodie, fareth as the hand to the dead instrumentes".

Again on pp. 63–4: "Then seeing neither body, nor spirit are admitted in the first, or second sort of instruments, they fall to the third kinde, which being liuely, or at the least apt for life, require direction, and also foreine impulsion: foraine, in respect of them selues, destitute of facultie, otherwise then disposition: but inward and domesticall, in that it proceedeth from a naturall power (resident in these corporall members) which we call the soule: not working as ingens by a force voide of skill and cunning in it selfe, & by a motion giuen by deuise of the Mechenist: but farre otherwise indued with science, & possessed of the mouer: as if Architas had bin him selfe within his flying doues, & Vulcanne within his walking stooles, and the mouing engine as it were animated with the minde of the worker, therein excelling farre all industrie of art."

On pp. 67–9 Bright compares the "many and diuerse actions" of the body under the direction of the soul's "one single facultie" with the complicated mechanism of "automaticall instrumentes, as clockes, watches, and larums".

5.1.270. Woo't drink up eisel?

Treatise, p. 30. Bright notes vinegar among "sauces" which "are chieflie to be auoided of melancholicke persons".

Hamlet is, of course, suggesting to Laertes means of inducing melancholy.

1.5.172. antic disposition.
2.2.210–12. How pregnant sometimes his replies are! a happiness that often madness hits on.

Treatise, p. 102. The perturbations of melancholy are for the most parte, sadde and fearefull, and such as rise of them: as distrust, doubt, diffidence, or dispaire, sometimes furious, and sometimes merry in apparaunce, through a kinde of Sardonian, and false laughter. [While Bright's diagnosis of melancholy in general seems hardly to tally with Shakespeare's conception of Hamlet's "sore distraction", the passage just quoted summarises most of Hamlet's moods.]

p. 130. Sometime it falleth out that melancholie men are found verie wittie, and quickly discerne: either because the humour of melancholie with some heate is so made subtile, that as from the driest woode riseth the clearest flame...in like sort their spirits...receauing a purenesse, are instrumentes of such sharpnesse....To this, other reasons may be added: as exercise of their wittes, wherein they be indefatigable.

2.2.259.   I have bad dreams.

Treatise, p. 124.   Giuen to fearefull and terrible dreames.

2.1.75–81.

> Lord Hamlet with his doublet all unbraced...
> Pale as his shirt, his knees knocking each other,
> And with a look so piteous in purport
> As if he had been looséd out of hell
> To speak of horrors.

Treatise, p. 102. That melancholick humour...counterfetteth terrible obiects to the fantasie, and polluting both the substance, and spirits of the brayne, causeth it without externall occasion to forge monstrous fictions, and terrible to the conceite.

pp. 103–4. This taking hold of the brayne by processe of time giueth it an habite of depraued conceite, whereby it fancieth not according to truth: but as the nature of that humour leadeth it, altogether gastely and fearefull. This causeth not only phantasticall apparitions wrought by apprehension only of common sense, but fantasie, an other parte of internall sense compoundeth, and forgeth disguised shapes, which giue great terror vnto the heart, and cause it with the liuely spirit to hide it selfe as well as it can, by contraction in all partes, from those counterfet goblins, which the brayne, dispossessed of right discerning, fayneth vnto the heart. Neither only is common sense, and fantasie thus ouertaken with delusion....

1.5.97–104.

> Remember thee?
> Yea, from the table of my memory
> I'll wipe away all trivial fond records...

> And thy commandment all alone shall live
> Within the book and volume of my brain,
> Unmixed with baser matter.

3.4.110–11.

> Do not forget! this visitation
> Is but to whet thy almost blunted purpose.

4.4.40.   Bestial oblivion.

Treatise, p. 104. Neither only is common sense, and fantasie ouertaken with delusion, but memory also receiueth a wound therewith: which disableth it both to keepe in memory, and to record those thinges, whereof it tooke some custody before this passion, and after, therewith are defaced. For as the common sense and fantasie, which doe offer vnto the memory to lay vp, deliuer but fables in stead of true report, and those tragicall that dismay all the sensible frame of our bodies, so eyther is the memory wholly distract by importunity of those doubtes and feares, that it neglecteth the custody of other store: or else it recordeth and apprehendeth only such as by this importunity is thrust therupon nothing but darkenes, perill, doubt, frightes, and whatsoeuer the harte of man most doth abhor.

4.4.40–1.

>   some craven scruple
> Of thinking too precisely on th'event.

5.1.200. 'Twere to consider too curiously, to consider so.

Treatise, p. 130. Melancholy breedeth a ielousie of doubt in that they take in deliberation, and causeth them to be the more exact and curious in pondering the very moments of things.

3.2.52–72.

> Horatio, thou art e'en as just a man
> As e'er my conversation coped withal
> . . . . for thou hast been
> As one in suff'ring all that suffers nothing,
> A man that Fortune's buffets and rewards

> Hast ta'en with equal thanks; and blest are those
> Whose blood and judgement are so well co-medled,
> That they are not a pipe for Fortune's finger
> To sound what stop she please: give me that man
> That is not passion's slave, and I will wear him
> In my heart's core, ay in my heart of heart,
> As I do thee.

Treatise, p. 97. A bodie of sanguine complexion...the spirits being in their iust temper in respect of qualitie, and of such plenty as nature requireth, not mixed or defiled, by any straunge spirit or vapor, the humours in quantity & qualitie rated in geometricall and iust proportion, the substance also of the bodie, and all the members so qualified by mixture of the elementes, as all conspire together in due proportion, breedeth an indifferencie to all passions.

2.2.246. Denmark's a prison.

2.2.257–9. O God! I could be bounded in a nut-shell, and count myself a king of infinite space; were it not that I have bad dreams.

Treatise, p. 100. Melancholie...of fewe comfortable spirits; and plentifully replenished with such as darken all the clernesse of those sanguineous, and ingrosse their subtilnesse, defile their purenesse with the fogge of that slime, and fennie substance, and shut vp the hart as it were in a dungeon of obscurity, causeth manie fearefull fancies, by abusing the braine with vglie illusions, and locketh vp the gates of the hart, whereout the spirits should breake forth vpon iust occasion, to the comfort of all the family of their fellowe members.

p. 263. The house, except it be cheerefull and lightsome, trimme and neat, seemeth vnto the melancholicke a prison or dungeon, rather then a place of assured repose and rest.

4.4.36–9.

> Sure he that made us with such large discourse,
> Looking before and after, gave us not
> That capability and god-like reason
> To fust in us unused.

Treatise, p. 70. Moreouer, if a man were double fronted (as the Poets have fained Ianus)...the same facultie of sight would addresse it selfe to see both before and behind at one instant, which now it doth by turning.... So the mind, in action wonderful, and next vnto the supreme maiestie of God, and by a peculiar maner proceeding from him selfe,...varieth not by nature, but by vse only, or diuersity of those thinges whereto it applieth it selfe: as the same facultie applied to different thinges, discerneth: to thinges past, remembreth: to thinges future foreseeth: of present things determineth: and that which the eye doth by turning of the head, beholding before, behind, and on ech side, that doth the mind freely at once.

Since compiling the above list I have had my attention drawn to an article entitled "*Hamlet* and Dr Timothy Bright" by Miss M. I. O'Sullivan in *Publications of the Modern Language Association of America* (vol. xli, no. 3, pp. 667–79). The writer has noted a number of my parallels, but not I think the most striking. Some of the rest of her coincidences with *Hamlet* and other plays or poems appear to me explicable as commonplaces of the period. But I quote a couple of the more significant:

Sonnet 129.   The expense of spirit in a waste of shame.

Treatise, p. 63. expence of spirit.

p. 250. You haue had declared how the excessiue trauaile of animall actions, or such as springe from the braine, waist and spende that spirite which as it is in the world the only cheerer of all thinges....

p. 251. by lauish waste and prodigall expence of the spirite in one passion.

Sonnet 27.

> Weary with toil, I haste me to my bed,
> The dear repose for limbs with travel tired;
> But then begins a journey in my head,
> To work my mind, when body's work's expired.

Treatise, p. 79. Euen as a man that hath trauelled all the day on horsebacke, or sailed on the Sea, though he be laid on his bed, yet keepeth an imagination of trauell still, his body fairing after a sort, as though it were on horsebacke or yet embarked, iudgeth not so lightly of rest: by reason of former inured trauell.

Miss O'Sullivan's summary of Bright's references to the connection between melancholy and procrastination is also worth quoting:

"Unnatural melancholy 'destroyeth the braine with all his faculties and disposition of action' (p. 110): the melancholy man is 'doubtfull before, and long in deliberation: suspicious, painefull in studie, and circumspect' (p. 124): his 'resolution riseth of long deliberation, because of doubt and distrust' (p. 131): the 'sorrowful humour' of the melancholy men 'breedeth in them...a negligence in their affairs, and dissolutenesse, where should be diligence' (p. 135): 'contemplations are more familiar with melancholicke persons then with other, by reason they be not so apt for action' (p. 200). Moreover, although 'melancholy breedeth a ielousie of doubt...and causeth them to be the more exact and curious in pondering the very moments of things', 'while their passions be not yet vehement', yet 'the vehemencie of theyr affection once raysed...carieth them...into the deapth of that they take pleasure to intermeddle in' (p. 130). The melancholy man, in other words, ponders and debates long, and does not act until his blood is up: then acts vigorously. Thus again, does he explain Hamlet's combination of delay in revenge with 'zeal and promptitude' in other business."

APPENDIX F

Hamlet as Cesare Borgia

(being a review of *On Hamlet* by Salvador de Madariaga, 1948, reprinted from *The Modern Language Review*, XLIV, pp. 390–7)

The name of Don Salvador de Madariaga, publicist, literary critic, and historian; ambassador, professor and delegate to the League of Nations; a master of forceful and graceful English, a leading authority upon our national life and institutions, and at the same time the most eminent of living Spaniards, needs no introduction to readers. Many of them will already have seen the book before us. Those who have not are no doubt preparing to turn with a very special interest, even excitement, not unmixed with astonishment at the author's versatility, to see what he has to say on the ever discussed never-to-be exhausted topic of *Hamlet*, perhaps the greatest of English literary masterpieces, certainly one might suppose the most English of all Shakespeare's plays. Well, the first thing he has to say is to deny that supposition. You English, he tells us, think of Hamlet as a modern Englishman, and so have completely misapprehended his character. "The era of Shakespeare is the era of Spain" (p. ix). "Spaniards should be particularly apt to appreciate the spirit of the sixteenth century; for in that century what came to the surface in any one nation was that which in that nation was most in harmony with Spain" (p. x). The modern actor, he continues, who has plucked off Hamlet's beard and robbed him of feathers and sombrero, only gives outward expression to that inner transformation by which the modern Englishman, compact of inhibitions derived from post-Shakespearian Puritanism, has converted "the Elizabethan, the volcano of manly energies, ever in spontaneous eruption... into a grassy hill"; has forced "Hamlet, the man born in an era of no gentleness whatever", to "become a gentleman" (p. 2). Thus Don Salvador plays himself in, and all modern critics out.

Yet he would not have written and published his book in English had he not desired to convince us, and he will no doubt be ready to listen to some of the difficulties it raises in our minds. The foregoing conclusions, for example, rest upon a number of broad historical and political generalizations which, coming from so eminent a publicist, are not for me a mere commentator to question, but which an Englishman, who has read a little in the literature of Shakespeare's time, finds somewhat perplexing. To begin with, his phrase, "an era of no gentleness whatever", invokes the shade of "gentle Sir Philip Sidney", godson it is true of Philip of Spain, yet English of the English, who, if ever man did, embodied the best ideals of his time, whose refusal of the cup of cold water at Zutphen was its most admired action, and at whose unprecedented funeral all classes in the nation united to pay homage to its noblest and finest representative. It reminds me too—dare I mention it?—that "gentle" was the epithet his contemporaries most often used in praising Shakespeare himself. I hasten to add that such "gentleness" was not of course identical with the quality implied in Dr Thomas Arnold's ideal of a Liberal Christian Gentleman, since "liberalism" at any rate stands for a complex of ideas, mainly political, unknown to the sixteenth century. But it was certainly Christian; and was not without a strain of what I think Don Salvador would call Puritanism. Or does he deny that label to Milton's master, "our sage and serious Spenser", the Elizabethan poet *par excellence*, who wrote *The Faerie Queene* expressly "to fashion a gentleman or noble person in vertuous and gentle discipline"?

And the recollection of Spenser brings up a further if related perplexity. Señor de Madariaga writes that Shakespeare, "we may be sure, lived in holy horror of all teaching" (p. 1), and suggests that the moral function of poetry was first proclaimed by Wordsworth. It is true that Dr Johnson remarked of Shakespeare "he is so much more careful to please than to instruct, that he seems to write without any moral purpose". But this, while it appears to lend colour to the Señor's first statement, conflicts with his second, since it proves the doctrine of didacticism to be at least as old as Johnson. But in truth was there ever a time before the aesthetic movement of the nineteenth century when the doctrine was not generally accepted in this country? And was it ever more often affirmed and acted upon than by writers in the sixteenth? Apart from the moral enthusiasm which inspired Spenser, no less than Milton, to compose his epic, there is Sidney again, whose *Arcadia*, the most popular prose reading of the age, was written, his friend Greville tells us,

to limn out such exact pictures of every posture in the mind, that any man being forced, in the strains of this life, to pass through any straits or latitudes of good or ill fortune, might (as in a glass) see how to set a good countenance upon all the discountenances of adversity, and a stay upon the exorbitant smilings of chance.[1]

As for drama, listen to Chapman:

material [i.e. pregnant] instruction, elegant and sententious excitation to virtue, and deflection from her contrary, [are] the soul, limbs and limits of an authentical tragedy.[2]

In all this their tutor was primarily, not Puritanism, but Horace, and the Elizabethans were never weary of quoting from his *Ars Poetica* the tag:

> omne tulit punctum qui miscuit utile dulci,
> lectorem delectando pariterque monendo,

though they generally gave a more moral twist to "utile" than the Roman poet intended. Is Don Salvador really "sure" that Shakespeare's aim was so utterly different from that of his contemporaries? It is Hamlet himself who declares that "the purpose of playing [which of course includes play-making]...both at the first [i.e. in the time of Horace and Seneca] and now is, to hold as 'twere the mirror up to nature"; which last may be translated into modern English "to enlighten our human nature by setting examples before it". In other words, Hamlet's "mirror"

---

[1] *Life of Sir Philip Sidney*, ed. Nowell Smith (1907), p. 16.
[2] Dedication, *The Revenge of Bussy d'Ambois*.

is the same as Sidney's "glass", and what he calls "the purpose of playing" is identical with what Chapman calls "the soul, limbs and limits of an authentical tragedy". Did Shakespeare then give his Prince of Denmark a conception of drama other than his own? "He *seems*", as Johnson says, "to write without any moral purpose." But he was the subtlest of all dramatists in the Elizabethan field; and it is at least possible that the aim of his greatest plays was not altogether unlike what Greville states was the aim of *Arcadia*.

But let us leave these "outward flourishes" and come to the matter of the book before us, which is *Hamlet*, or rather Hamlet; for it is concerned more with the character of the Prince than with the dramatic composition in which he is but one, if the central, figure. In this Don Salvador, apparently without realizing it, follows the lead of the "romantic" critics he so roundly contemns. "No [previous] attempt", he claims, "seems to have been made to endow the explorer of that labyrinth which is his [Hamlet's] soul with an Ariadne's thread—or in other words, his character with a psychological spine" (p. 4). Yet his attempt is, of course, only the latest of a long series, which goes back to Goethe if not before; Goethe, whose formula, "a beautiful, pure, noble and most moral nature, without the strength of nerve which makes the hero, sinking beneath a burden which it can neither bear nor throw off",[1] is the earliest and most extreme statement I know of that "sentimental falsification" which Madariaga attributes to the "prim and respectable" British. When *they* began spinning thread for Ariadne it was much more "psychological" in texture; for there is no break in the genealogy which links Coleridge's "overbalance in the contemplative faculty" with Bradley's "morbid melancholia" induced by severe moral shock, or that with Dr Ernest Jones's "Œdipus complex"—divergent as these findings are. *Quot critici, tot Hamletes*, in fact; while from among the various "psychological spines" offered by the critics, each age selects the one which

[1] *Wilhelm Meister*, bk. i, ch. xiii.

corresponds best with the human type most in the popular eye. Thus it was left to the period of Hitler to reveal Hamlet as a ruthless paranoiac. Such in effect is Señor de Madariaga's solution; for though he speaks of the Spaniard Cesare Borgia, not the Austrian Adolf Hitler, the two men belong to the same type; and I hazard the guess that but for the paperhanger of Vienna the eminent publicist from Spain would never have taken to redecorating Hamlet's soul. If I may summarize an extended argument, the New Look he designs for it is something like this: a nature at once barbarous, volcanic, and supersubtle, impelled by a sheer and unconditioned egotism; completely indifferent to any other human being, and reacting savagely and without pity against anything or anybody that touches it on the raw, offends its *amour propre*, or threatens its life; in short the soul of a Renaissance aristocrat, who lives by the "Borgian philosophy, the philosophy of success, expressed not as a thought consciously held, but as a belief taken for granted" (p. 22). Let the reader compare this with Goethe's solution quoted above, and ask himself whether there may not after all be something in a suggestion made fourteen years ago that in Hamlet's character Shakespeare deliberately set himself to create a mystery which readers and spectators would never tire of discussing but never be able to solve, and which would allow to the actor impersonating it almost any interpretation he chose.[1]

Almost, but not quite; for there are limits, of course; conceivable interpretations that Shakespeare could never have conceived or if he had would have ruled out as unlikely to make a good play. And these limits are, quite simply, those of human sympathy, the sympathy the average member of a theatre audience, whether in Greek, Elizabethan or modern times, feels for a tragic hero. Don Salvador laughs at critics who stipulate for this sympathy, and writes them off as sentimental Englishmen. But Aristotle stipulated for it as a test of tragedy nearly twenty-three centuries ago, and would certainly have written off the

[1] See chapter VI above.

Madariagian Hamlet as a repulsive monster, at once too unlike the ordinary man for him to be able to feel for him in his sufferings, and too much deserving of these sufferings for the ordinary man to have any pity for him.[1] To this the Señor will, no doubt, reply that Shakespeare knew nothing of Aristotle, and that anyway the ordinary Elizabethan was sufficiently Borgian to sympathize with a Borgian hero. I will therefore get off that high horse and meet him on his own ground. Did time and space allow I should rejoice to dispute every inch of it. For I have read him carefully, and believe I could show that not a single one of the ingenious interpretations he offers of the various incidents and speeches in this excellently varied play will hold water when brought to the test of its textual context. But I must leave this sport to students in our British University honours classes, to whom I recommend his brilliantly wrong-headed book as a whetstone for their wits, and its author a worthy foe upon which to show the mettle of their pasture. Enough for my present purpose to demonstrate that his Spanish Hamlet cannot be Shakespeare's, inasmuch as it derives from (i) a misreading of Elizabethan English, and (ii) a complete misunderstanding of Elizabethan dramatic art.

One, if not the main, corner-stone of the theory of a Borgian Hamlet is Ophelia's description

> The expectancy and rose of the fair state,
> The glass of fashion and the mould of form,
> The observed of all observers.

[1] See S. H. Butcher, *Aristotle's Theory of Poetry and the Fine Arts*, pp. 258–60, and note especially the following passage on p. 226: "Aristotle does not indeed demand of the poet that he shall set before himself a didactic aim, nor does he test the merit of his performance by the moral truths that are conveyed. His test of excellence is pleasure; but the aesthetic pleasure produced by any ideal imitation must be a sane and wholesome pleasure, which would approve itself to the better portion of the community. The pleasure he contemplates could not conceivably be derived from a poem which offers low ideals of life and conduct and misinterprets human destiny."

"Poor, unfortunate prince", comments Don Salvador in what is I think the only sympathetic reference to him in the book, "he must satisfy all observers, fulfil all expectations, passively reflect all fashions and take into his soul any paste or dough in search of form! And we wonder he was unhappy!" (p. 8). Ophelia neither says nor implies anything of the kind. She is contrasting the former splendour and brilliance of "that noble and most sovereign reason" with its present ruin, and the line

The observed of all observers,

so far from suggesting an unhappy loneliness or a circle of exacting onlookers narrowly watching his every step, simply means "one whom all had respected and looked up to".[1] Yet it is from this that Don Salvador deduces an "exceptional susceptibility to social pressure" which he claims as "the chief feature in the character" (p. 12) of Hamlet, the marrow as it were of the "spine" which is Hamlet's egotism. Scarcely less unfortunate is his misunderstanding of "I took thee for thy better" which Hamlet mutters over the dead Polonius as he discovers him behind the arras. "Note", runs Madariaga's comment, "that for Hamlet, the King, that is his own father's murderer, is the 'better' of Polonius, the father of Ophelia: i.e. that Hamlet's scale of value is not one of merit, virtue; but of power, *virtu*" (p. 22). In a word, Hamlet's philosophy is of "the Renaissance Borgian" school. Yet had the Señor known the English Church Catechism or troubled to look up the substantive "better" in Schmidt or any other Shakespeare lexicon he would have found that it commonly means "a superior in rank", as it assuredly does here, and therefore carries no moral implications whatsoever. At the outset of his book he tells us that he has translated *Hamlet* into Spanish verse, and claims the experience as his credential for assuming the role of critic. If the

[1] Cf. "For he is gracious, if he be observed" (2 *Hen. IV*, 4. 4. 30), and "Princes are the glass, the school, the book | Where subjects' eyes do learn, do read, do look." (*Lucr.* l. 615.)

translation exhibits throughout the same ignorance of Elizabethan English as do these two comments, and others I could mention, I am afraid his Spanish readers will acquire some strange ideas of Shakespeare's intentions.

I turn from verbal interpretation to critical method. It is characteristic of this that Ophelia's lamentation just alluded to is the first passage he quotes from the text as evidence upon Hamlet's character, lines which do not occur until the play is almost half-way through; that he then proceeds to appraise Hamlet's moral standpoint in a lengthy analysis of his relations with Rosencrantz and Guildenstern, which do not commence until well on in Act 2; and lastly that he turns for confirmation of conclusions thus reached to a consideration of Hamlet's attitude towards Polonius in Acts 3 and 4, and towards Laertes in Acts 4 and 5. This is to read *Hamlet* like a book, a historical monograph or a personal record such as the *Autobiography* of Benvenuto Cellini, instead of being, as it was and is, an elaborate work of dramatic art, written for an acting company in London at the beginning of the seventeenth century. The purveyor of kaleidoscopic illusions designed to lay a powerful spell of two or more hours' duration upon the audience that watched them, Shakespeare produced his effects by means of an uninterrupted series of impressions, not unlike those we experience as we listen to a great symphony. And the only criticism relevant to such an art is one that follows these impressions in the order in which the dramatist released them, and then considers the total impression left behind upon the audience after the play is finished. The right perspective is everything; and to begin in the middle and then jump forwards and backwards as Señor Madariaga does is like looking down at St Paul's from an aeroplane instead of from the ground, which was the only perspective Wren had in view.[1] How misleading the wrong angle of vision can be is evident from Señor Madariaga's attitude towards the minor characters of the play.

If Hamlet, as he has persuaded himself, is a Borgia, those we

[1] Cf. pp. 94, 229–31 above.

have hitherto been accustomed to think of as his real or suspected foes must become more or less innocent victims of his savagery. Rosencrantz and Guildenstern are represented therefore as a couple of pleasant and perfectly innocuous young gentlemen, whom he rejoices to send to their death, "no shriving time allowed". Polonius he kills by accident, it is true, but treats the corpse as so much offal immediately after, and the living man before that as a mere butt, without showing the least regard for his feelings; Polonius, the father of the woman he is supposed to be in love with! As for Ophelia, she is the vessel of his lust; a willing whore, it seems, since the bawdy passages in the play-scene are not, as had been hitherto assumed, outrageous sallies by Hamlet which she parries as best she can, but "dialogue" in which she gives as indecently as she gets (p. 67). For her brother the Prince shows more respect, but only out of Machiavellian policy because he needs his help, whence it follows that the seemingly noble appeal, before the duel, to let bygones be bygones, as between brothers, is "heavy flattery", the "stuffing with unmeant words" of a man he despises (p. 30). Even Claudius, though admittedly a murderer, "is a better Christian than Hamlet, who indeed is hardly a Christian at all" (p. 83). All this, and a good deal more, is argued as I say with the force, subtlety, and brilliance that one expects from one of the leading thinkers of Europe. Yet it is all utterly unconvincing because it is based upon a highly selected group of the dramatic facts, taken out of their dramatic sequence, and rearranged according to the critic's fancy. In particular, apart from a single passage which he misinterprets, Señor Madariaga ignores Act I altogether, until he has completed his abuse of Hamlet to damn him. The interview with the Ghost, it may be noted, is only dealt with at the very end of the book under the heading of "Shakespeare's Comic Sense" and Shakespeare is represented as being overpowered by "flippant mirth" as he composes the speeches for "the majesty of buried Denmark"! Suppose, however, that all but the first act of *Hamlet* had been lost in the fire which destroyed the Globe Theatre in 1613, what sort of person should we, including Señor Madariaga, have then taken its hero to be? Certainly not a brutal egotist. On the contrary, in Act 1 he appears as a young prince without a touch of arrogance in his disposition; engagingly friendly with acquaintances, ardently so with a fellow-student, witness the delightful greetings and farewells to Horatio, Marcellus and Bernardo at the beginning and end of their talk in 1. 2; a devoted son who adores his father's memory and mourns his loss with profound and passionate grief; a loyal, generous and affectionate nature, as yet inexperienced in life, upon whom the incestuous and indecently speedy remarriage of his mother comes as an overwhelming moral shock, that seems to rob existence of all meaning but lust and to defile his very being. What is there of Cesare Borgia in all this? The only scrap of text Señor Madariaga can find in Act 1 to support his case is the outburst,

> Unhand me, gentlemen,
> By heaven I'll make a ghost of him that lets me!

uttered as Horatio and the soldiers try to stop him following his father's spirit. "It is one of the key points in the drawing of his character" runs the comment: "when it comes to doing what he is determined to do, he will not hesitate to kill even his closest friend.... Hamlet's spontaneous tendencies are therefore essentially individualistic" (p. 14). What pedantry! A being has returned from the next world with a message to be imparted to him alone, a being whom Hamlet can only call "King, father, royal Dane". He already "doubts some foul play". Duty, filial piety, his mother's honour, the health of the state of Denmark, all require him to learn what the portentous message may be. His very "fate cries out". And these well-meaning fellows would forcibly hold him back! What would the critic have him do? Tamely submit? Or reason it out while the supernatural visitor patiently attended the upshot of the argument? What would "gentle Sir Philip Sidney" have done?

Now an Elizabethan audience, unsophisticated by the "study"

of *Hamlet* in secondary schools, knowing nothing of what is to come except that the play is a tragedy (i.e. must end in the death of the hero), would at the end of Act 1 be in exactly the same position as we should be had we lost the last four acts. In other words, words which I borrow from the Señor, they would be "of Hamlet's party". In their eyes Claudius would be a villain of the type they most detested, a "bloody, bawdy villain", a "treacherous, lecherous, kindless villain" (for though that is Hamlet's description at the end of Act 2, it only summarizes everything we learn of Claudius in Act 1); an Italianate monster, who works by Machiavellian policy and Borgian tricks of poisoning, and wins his to-be-murdered brother's wife to his incestuous lust in order to thrust the rightful heir from the throne with a show of legality. And his chief agent in this usurpation, as the address to the Council (sc. 2) shows, was Polonius, the Burghley of the court of Elsinore. Is it egotism on the young heir's part to hate and distrust this old man, or to use his "antic disposition" (whether real or feigned) to vent his bitterness upon him? After following that heir throughout Act 1 and entering fully into the appalling situation in which he finds himself, no audience, Elizabethan or modern, could think so. And Ophelia is Polonius's daughter! For that and not the other way on is how the relationship looks in their perspective. Hamlet may well wonder, they feel, whether she is an accomplice like her father, or at least his pawn. Had he been genuinely in love with her, declares the Señor, he could not have so wondered. But those who have heard him revealing his mind in the First Soliloquy, which culminates in that bitter cry "Frailty, thy name is woman!" know that his mother has taught him how little a woman's vows, her tenders of affection, are to be trusted. And it is thoughts and doubts of this kind, coupled with the "antic disposition", which, they will realize, account for the silent yet passionate scrutiny of her face which she reports to Polonius at the beginning of Act 2. His chance overhearing of the eavesdropping plot, and the unlucky words, "I'll loose my daughter to him", confirm his fears that she is at least her father's pawn, while the nunnery scene seems to furnish proof of her being an actual accomplice, a willing decoy; after which his conduct to her in the play-scene is to Elizabethans explicable enough.

As for Rosencrantz and Guildenstern, to a man who knows all that Hamlet knows they must seem just spies. On their arrival he welcomes them as old schoolfellows with all his accustomed frankness and unassuming friendship. But once they begin harping on his ambition, his suspicions are naturally aroused; and after they admit to having been sent for by "the good king and queen", he has done with them: he knows his uncle; and the audience, who know him also, perfectly understands. Of course his language to Ophelia in the play-scene, and his anxiety to send his enemies straight to hell without giving them a moment in which to make their peace with God, are both very shocking to our modern notions of decency and Christianity. For Señor Madariaga is perfectly right to insist upon the barbarism of the Elizabethans in certain directions, more particularly in manners and religion. Where he is wrong is in supposing this barbarism to have been Spanish or that it included their notions of dramatic art. Anyhow, it is certain that Shakespeare's audience found nothing especially shocking in Hamlet's conduct, even when it was most outrageous; otherwise the play could not have ended as it does.

In the tragedy of character-development, which is Shakespeare's, our impressions of the protagonist in the first act are all-important, because everything we learn about him later is built upon and into these, and without them may be altogether misapprehended, as we have seen our critic misapprehending. No less important in another way are the impressions conveyed by the last scene or scenes, since they give us the dramatist's final judgement, the thoughts about his hero which he wishes his auditors to carry home with them. Think of *Julius Caesar* without Antony's *laudatio* over the dead Brutus, of *Othello* without the Moor's last words before plunging the knife into his own heart, or of *King Lear* without the entry of the old man with Cordelia dead in his arms, and it becomes at once obvious how much the heroes of these plays would lose in stature and beauty did they lack their creator's final benediction. It is the same with *Hamlet*. Yet the Señor, silent upon Act 1, is equally silent upon the death scene. In particular, beyond a single sneering reference to "sweet" Hamlet, which once again exposes his ignorance of Elizabethan English,[1] he altogether suppresses Horatio's farewell,

> Now cracks a noble heart. Good night, sweet prince,
> And flights of angels sing thee to thy rest!

And no wonder, for it would have made hay of his whole argument, since even a Spanish Shakespeare could hardly have invited his audience to picture angels heralding with anthems the entry into heaven of a Cesare Borgia!

All this will not, I fear, persuade Don Salvador that William Shakespeare, if a little barbarous in some of his ideas, was a true-born Englishman. But it may disincline one or two Englishmen, who have been fascinated by this brilliant book, to allow the Spaniards altogether to appropriate him.

[1] The epithet is equivalent to the colloquial "dear" (e.g. "dear fellow") in modern speech.

NOTES

(to second edition, 1937)

p. 16. W. W. Greg replies (*M.L.R.* XXXI, 146) "I don't think I ever assumed even tacitly that Shakespeare could no more believe in ghosts than I did; I merely *doubted* whether he believed, or rather whether he actually based his play on the necessity of such a belief". What I had in mind was (i) his conclusion, from a survey of ghosts in Shakespeare apart from *Hamlet*, that "Shakespeare's attitude towards ghosts may be described as *frankly sceptical*" (*ibid.* XII, 395), and (ii) his summing up that, while "Shakespeare, it must be supposed, expected his ghost and its story to be generally taken on the stage at their face value...may we not believe that for himself, as for other humaner minds among his contemporaries, such crude machinery would appear as a blot upon a noble piece of work?" (*ibid.* XII, 419–20).

p. 37. Cf. also 1.2.108–9. Claudius' declaration (referred to again at 3.2.90–2 and 342–4) indicates clearly in what sense Shakespeare regarded the throne as "elective".

p. 38. This section of the book has been subjected to interesting criticism by J. P. Malleson and others in letters in *The Times Lit. Sup.* (*vide* issues for Jan. 4, 11, 18, 25, Sept. 26, Oct. 3, 10, 17, 1936) which limitations of space forbid me to discuss here.

p. 39. W. F. Trench (pp. 257–60, *Hamlet, a new commentary*, 1913) well notes that, "the case of Gertrude, being precisely parallel with that of Catherine of Aragon", the subjects of Anne Boleyn's daughter would be peculiarly susceptible to suggestions on this head.

p. 43. Even Granville-Barker (*Preface to Hamlet*) speaks of Hamlet's "weakness" on p. 44 and again on p. 72, and quotes in support

> no more like my father
> Than I to Hercules.

But in this comparison Hamlet is thinking of Hercules, not as the strong man but as the purifier of the world, as Travers shows, citing from Marston's *Antonio's Revenge*, 5.6:

> Thou art another Hercules to us
> In ridding huge pollution from our State.

p. 49. Cf. J. Q. Adams, *Hamlet*, pp. 226–7.

p. 65. More pertinent to *Hamlet* is the following (*Religio Medici*, I, xxxvii, Golden Treasury ed. p. 61): "I believe...that the Souls of the faithful, as they leave Earth, take possession of Heaven: that those apparitions and ghosts of departed persons are not the wandring souls of men, but the unquiet walks of Devils, prompting and suggesting us unto mischief, blood, and villany; instilling and stealing into our hearts that the blessed Spirits are not at rest in their graves, but wander sollicitous of the affairs of the World. But that those phantasms appear often, and do frequent Cœmeteries, Charnel-houses, and Churches, it is because those are the dormitories of the dead, where the Devil, like an insolent Champion, beholds with pride the spoils and Trophies of his Victory over Adam."

p. 80. (1) The fact that the "cellarage" (i.e. the space under the stage) was commonly called the "hell" in Elizabethan theatres adds much point to the stage-situation here; cf. add. note 1.5.151 in my *Hamlet* (ed. ii).

(2) n. 1. [add] and Shane Leslie, *St Patrick's Purgatory: a record from history and literature*, 1932.

p. 82. (1) Perhaps rather too definite: Cf. Granville-Barker, p. 60.

(2) *Vide* p. 76 above and note 1.5.156 in my *Hamlet*.

p. 94, n. Cf. Granville-Barker, p. 16.

p. 98. Travers (at 2.1.79, *Hamlet*, Librairie Hachette, 1929) notes that in Rowe's edition (1709) Hamlet is represented with one stocking half down in the bedroom scene, 3.4. The cut, which forms a frontispiece to *Hamlet*, illustrates the entry of the Ghost.

p. 107. Granville-Barker (pp. 200–1 n.) is "strongly tempted to accept" this solution, but rejects it mainly on the ground that it means surrendering the traditional sentimental (I use the word in no bad sense) playing of the Nunnery scene. I note, however, that the "Fishmonger" episode troubles him and he attempts to explain it (1) by assuming "clairvoyance" on Hamlet's part (pp. 68–9, 79, cf. p. 47), and (2) by suggesting that it actually followed the Nunnery scene in an earlier draft of the play, a draft reflected, he assumes, in Q 1, which gives us this order of the scenes, and that Shakespeare in revision changed the order and left Fishmonger Polonius and his carrion daughter in mid-air (pp. 194–202)!

p. 111, n. 2. Granville-Barker (p. 64) puts it less absolutely and perhaps more persuasively:

Here is surely something more than "antic"; and "affrighted" as the girl has been, she is evidently telling the truth. As to Hamlet, then, we shall be left puzzled. Is he still as frenzied as we have ourselves seen him to be, or only pretending to be so, partly pretending to be so and partly—? But what Shakespeare wants is just to this extent to puzzle us, to make us curious to see Hamlet for ourselves again, and to prepare us to put the same questions when we do see him; when, however, we shall still be left almost as puzzled. He could hardly do better, surely, than use Ophelia for this purpose. Hearsay is necessary: if we saw the scene for ourselves, Hamlet's conduct could not be left quite inexplicable.

This is admirable and would fit in with what I write below, pp. 220–4, 229. Yet Granville-Barker himself seems to come down definitely on the "mad" side of the fence when he speaks of Hamlet's "undoubted suffering" on p. 65.

p. 115, n. 2. F. S. Boas, *Shakespeare and his Predecessors* (p. 392) writes "a criminal never feels secure save when he can keep his eye on all whom he mistrusts". Travers, on the other hand, quotes Q. 1:

> We hold it most unmeet and unconvenient,
> Being the joy and half heart of your mother.

p. 117. The relation between Shakespeare's art and the knowledge of his time is admirably put, in a passage unhappily too long to quote here, by Professor Hardin Craig (*The Enchanted Glass*, 1936, pp. 234–5).

p. 118. Cf. Granville-Barker (*op. cit.* p. 70), "Claudius did not need to tell two supple young courtiers whereabouts to seek for the disinherited Hamlet's secret".

p. 119. Cf. Adams, *op. cit.* p. 240.

p. 120. I note that Adams, *op. cit.* pp. 240–1, and W. F. Trench, *op. cit.* pp. 96–7, have both observed it.

p. 123. Greg suggests (privately) that "puts on his confusion" indicates that Claudius regards the "antic disposition" as "put on".

p. 126. Granville-Barker (p. 78 n.) would keep her invisible during the soliloquy (so as not to distract our attention) and let her enter on the inner stage and kneel at her faldstool at the cue "...lose the name of action".

p. 128. "The phrase itself is too smooth for the utterance of a man in 'the pangs of despised love'; and Hamlet is speaking to himself, not *acting* indifference. 'Nymph', on the other hand, in affected gallantry, will be said as if he did not know her" (Travers, *op. cit.* note on 3.1.89). Travers suggests that Hamlet goes on pretending not to recognise her down to l. 114 ("I did love you once"). Cf. W. F. Trench, *op. cit.* p. 142 and Granville-Barker, pp. 78, 304 n., who refuses to see irony: we must agree to differ.

p. 132. i.e. "We are both 'honest' lovers, so where's the harm?" —said a little coyly.

p. 133. The idea of the nunnery is first, no doubt, suggested to Hamlet by Ophelia's "prayer-book" and "orisons". Cf. review by W. Keller, *Shakespeare Jahrbuch*, 1936, p. 146.

p. 135. Trench (p. 148, n. 2) suggests that Hamlet turns the tables here and eavesdrops on the King and Polonius. This would explain his knowledge in 3.4.200 of the mission to England; cf. also 4.3.47. On the other hand, it would make him aware beforehand that Polonius was to be hiding in his mother's bedroom, which is incredible.

p. 142 n. In the theatre there is no perplexity. As Granville-Barker (p. 75) writes: "We are given the one arresting hint of ' *The Murder of Gonzago* . . . a speech of some dozen or sixteen lines. . . .' That is enough to hold us expectant through the self-reproachings of the soliloquy; until, towards its end, the hint is given substance, the plan revealed, our roused curiosity satisfied, and the offensive against the King is started again."

p. 144. The debate continues! *Vide* Granville-Barker (pp. 82–97) for a different interpretation and his p. 97 n. for a reply to mine. See also *Preface to the Second Edition* and Mr Child's *Letter*, above, p. xiv, for recent performances of the play scene in the theatre.

p. 147. Cf. *Review of English Studies*, XI, 385 (Oct. 1935), B. R. Pearn, "Dumb-show in Elizabethan Drama".

p. 149. Greg points out (privately) that the "bank" had to be provided for the Gonzago play anyhow.

p. 158. For a different interpretation v. "'Miching Malicho' and the play scene in 'Hamlet'", by Alice Walker (*M.L.R.* XXXI, 513 ff.).

p. 164. But W. F. Trench (*op. cit.* p. 160, n. 2) does so and comes very near to my conclusion. Granville-Barker ignores the "Nephew to the King" point altogether—as beneath contempt?

p. 191. But there is a hint, as Greg (*M.L.R.* XXXI, 150) teaches me. He paraphrases "Let the galled jade wince", etc. "Your majesty will observe that the outrageous knavery of the play is directed not at you but at the Queen. Why bother? Let your jade of a wife show her galled withers, it has nothing to do with us." This interpretation, which seems to me most convincing, confirms my suggestion of "a start or flinching on her part" (p. 189).

p. 207. Granville-Barker agrees (p. 51) and adds: "The actor can show this well enough."

p. 210. I now think this too absolutely expressed: cf. note on p. 111 above.

p. 217. Greg (*M.L.R.* XXXI, 153) makes the interesting suggestion "that Hamlet, at last fully sane and calm, is really himself in doubt how far his distraction went, and is seeking to convince himself quite as much as Laertes of his innocence".

p. 222. Cf. Constance in *K. John*, 3.4.48–60:

> I am not mad, I would to heaven I were,
> For then 'tis like I should forget myself:
> O, if I could, what grief should I forget!
> For being not mad, but sensible of grief,
> My reasonable part produces reason
> How I may be delivered of these woes,
> And teaches me to kill or hang myself:
> If I were mad I should forget my son,
> Or madly think a babe of clouts were he:
> I am not mad; too well, too well I feel
> The different plague of each calamity.

p. 243. Cf. Granville-Barker (*op. cit.* p. 101): "this 'mother... mother...mother' beating like a pulse."

p. 245. (1) The reader should, however, consider A. J. A. Waldock's criticism of Bradley here (*vide Hamlet, a Study in Critical Method*, pp. 39–40).

(2) Travers aptly cites "Would I had met my dearest foe in heaven, Or ever", etc. (1.2.152).

p. 247. Travers quotes the account of Hamlet's action given by the Queen to the King in Q. 1, an account which probably reproduces what the pirate saw upon the stage:

> Whenas he came, I first bespake him fair,
> But then he throws and tosses me about
> As one forgetting that I was his mother.

p. 254. I find that W. J. Lawrence (*Pre-Restoration Stage Studies*, 1927, p. 117) has noted this and cites *Brudermord*.

p. 258. Greg (*M.L.R.* XXXI, 150) argues that here I am weaving "a little drama of diplomatic etiquette" out of my own imagination. But Hamlet's "sweep my way" is surely intended to convey that he has heard of the King's original suggestion, and I am interested to see that Granville-Barker (*op. cit.* p. 82) appears to make the same point independently.

p. 269. Granville-Barker (*op. cit.* p. 161) calls it a "soft cry", wrung from him by Laertes' revelation of the identity of the corpse.

p. 273. But he had more excuse for so doing than I have allowed. Cf. Adams (*op. cit.* pp. 321–3) who points out that it all follows on from his contrition for the ranting scene with Laertes and the resolve "I'll count his favours" (5.2.75–80), uttered just before Osric delivers the challenge.

p. 281. For further support *vide* "Der bestrafte 'Brudermord'' and 'Hamlet', act v", by A. H. J. Knight (*M.L.R.* xxxi, 385 ff.).

p. 282. (1) Laertes needs first pick in order to make certain he will get to the table before Hamlet, should Hamlet wish to try another foil.

(2) After reading "The Fencing-match in 'Hamlet'" (*R.E.S.* xiii, 326 ff.) by A. A. Gay, I was at first inclined to think I was wrong about the shirt of mail, skull cap and gloves, a point I took from Egerton Castle's *Schools and Masters of Fence* (p. 346, n. 1) and not from Saviolo as my footnote states in error. As Gay remarks, it would be difficult for Hamlet to run Laertes through the body if he wore a coat of mail. And yet, in view of the violence of the bouts, which Burbadge and his opponent had to make the most of, would they not, to insure against accident, avail themselves of any protection for face and body that the custom of the day countenanced?

INDEX OF PASSAGES FROM *HAMLET* QUOTED OR DISCUSSED

GENERAL INDEX